Wonderful Ontario Wine

The Odyssey of Ontario Winemaking after the Concord Grape Era

Jim Warren

tellwell

Tellwell Talent
www.tellwell.ca

ISBN
978-0-2288-8543-6 (Paperback)

This book is dedicated to my wife Charlotte who long ago motivated my interest in wine and winemaking, then provided the encouragement to follow my dream…

PREFACE

"SO, YOU WANT TO START A WINERY, EH?"

"Owning a winery in Ontario is all about learning how to make a small fortune out of a much larger one!" Don Ziraldo, co-founder of Inniskillin Wines and industry icon

"There is every reason to believe that our wine industry can challenge countries like New Zealand and Australia, and areas such as Oregon and Washington." John Peller, CEO, Peller Estates/Andres Wines

In 1985, Jack Couillard, an executive with the LCBO, was THE man responsible for new winery development in Ontario: and appropriately so, after serving with the Canadian Wine Institute for several years. When we met him in his office in Toronto to discuss our proposed winery, he loomed as a somewhat stern and serious figure, older and wiser than ourselves, and very direct. His first words to us were... "So, you want to start a winery, eh?" He carefully outlined the 'rules' at that time including the need to make at least 3,000 gallons of Ontario wine "for the Liquor Board to evaluate and give its approval". If the wine did not meet expectations, we would be obligated to dump it. If it passed, then the winery licence fee would be $500, the same as for any other winery at that time.

We were intending to establish the winery on partner Bryce Weylie's farm on the escarpment in Vinemount above Stoney Creek – hardly a great location for tourist traffic! But Bryce and his wife Jennifer were growing French Hybrid grapes there and owned a small barn and shed where we could make the wine. Unfortunately, there was no city water on the property and no sewers. Along with our third partner, fellow amateur winemaker Brian Alexander, we outlined our intentions to make only 500 gallons of wine the first year as we all had other 'day jobs' and this was to be a part-time endeavor. I don't think that Mr. Couillard was at all impressed with our concept or with our chances, but our enthusiasm must have won the day for he gave us the green light to proceed! And so, the dream became reality as Stoney Ridge Cellars opened as Ontario's 19th winery that year, outfitted with a screw press and dejuicer, one 450 gallon tank, and a collection of related winemaking necessities. As complete neophytes in the wine business, we had a lot to learn!

Our timing seems amazing after the fact, but then many of my friends thought I was just crazy to leave the security of the teaching profession to become a businessman/winemaker in an industry which was just beginning to emerge from its much-maligned past. Looking back, I would have to say perhaps I was, just a little! After all, we did not have 'deep pockets' and, as a rather conservative individual, I certainly did not fit the mould of an entrepreneur.

I had enjoyed a lot of success as an amateur winemaker in the annual Amateur Winemakers' of Ontario competitions (3 times Ontario and Canadian Champion Winemaker!) and I was editor of the A.W.O. Association newsletter, writing articles and organizing seminars on various aspects of winemaking for the membership and self-educating myself in the process. But I had never actually intended to start a winery. It was only after Bryce and myself had bought a press to process his grapes into juice to sell to home winemakers that the thought struck us, why not take the next step? Such was our apparent motivation with little thought to what we were really getting into. I do have to admit that the idea of actually owning a winery did seem appealing to me after we had visited several cottage wineries in New York State and Niagara and my observations left me feeling we could do the same. What we did know was that members of A.W.O. were making wines every bit as good as the commercial wineries from the 'new' French Hybrid and Vinifera grapes, if they could find them, and I did feel there was a real opportunity to create even better wines, to put my winemaking talent to work on a limited scale with two like-minded friends… and be successful.

In short, we moved forward with tremendous enthusiasm and passion, but lacking any form of business plan – an absolute necessity for starting a winery to-day. I didn't for one moment consider the risks I was taking that might affect my livelihood, my wife Charlotte and son Marshall, and how this might change our lives. By 1985 it was simply full speed ahead with no time to look back for we had many people who thought it could not be done – and part of the satisfaction for me would be in proving the sceptics wrong. I had many acquaintances who were still cynical about Ontario wines to whom I would love to be able to say "I told you so"! Dan Kislenko, wine writer for the Hamilton Spectator, heralded our arrival as being on the cusp of significant change: the beginning of another wave of new 'boutique' wineries opening across the province. And he was right!

To-day we are blessed with what has become a wonderful grape and wine industry in Ontario, acclaimed not only for its various icewines but also for the outstanding overall quality of its fine table and sparkling wines. This represents a 180 degree shift from our original native wine industry which made primarily inexpensive port and sherry style wines and almost no table wines at all, an industry which came to suffer ridicule for questionable vinous concoctions during the infamous Prohibition era and through the five decades that followed.

Inspiring this transformation has been an amazing renewal of our vineyards where 'vinifera' vines, which many thought for a long time could never grow in Eastern North America, have almost completely replaced our older 'labrusca' vines and are now producing the raw material making our new wines possible. Growers, who used to follow the philosophy of "plant and pick" (and usually as many tons to the acre as possible!) are now quick to assert that "wine is made in the vineyard", stressing quality over quantity, and to-day rely on the latest technological advances to support this.

For consumers, the most visible and remarkable change in the industry is the emergence over the last forty years of some 200 new wineries, with many of these winners of numerous awards in international competitions. Wineries have developed from Ottawa to Windsor and north to Lake Huron and Georgian Bay, making classic vinifera wines, exciting experimental hybrid wines, stunning ciders and delicious fruit wines to enhance the notion that all of Ontario has become a wine region.

How this industry has transformed, achieving credibility and respect for our Ontario wines at last, is a dramatic story that features individuals who decided to start a winery knowing that an opportunity existed for them to lead our winemaking in a new direction while also aware of the significant risks they would be taking (sometimes not as much as they should have been!). As a group, these are people who have shown the courage to invest their time and resources and endure some very difficult moments when many feared the industry would simply cease to exist. And it would be wrong to believe that the rewards for such individuals are based on immediate financial returns, for the costs of establishing a winery are immense and achieving profitability is a long-term endeavour.

Starting a winery is "no easy art" as many involved in the industry to-day will attest. Indeed, few consumers are aware of the sheer hard work, and the intriguing interplay of government, growers, and winery owners that lurks behind the romantic façade of the industry. Imagine a business whose operations depend almost entirely on the state of the weather to ripen their sensitive grapes in what is considered a 'cold climate', with growers and winemakers both dreading any dramatic changes like sudden freezes in spring or rain for days on end at harvest. While a poor vintage can impact negatively on production and sales, to achieve success at any time in what has become a very competitive business in Ontario with so many smaller players is even more challenging. All wineries must deal with the Liquor Control Board and its mandate to provide wines from everywhere in the world, leaving precious little shelf space for local products. In this highly regulated and demanding environment, the 'profits' on wine are truly slim, with punitive government mark-ups and annually increasing taxation on wine posing ongoing financial challenges. All of this makes running a winery a very vulnerable vocation!

Still, every year, new 'recruits' to the industry, committed to a cause in which they strongly believe, continue to open wineries, both in established viticultural areas and in new 'terroirs' with an increasing list of new grape varieties, preparing to amaze the world! Their zeal merits consideration, whether they think their wine will be the 'best', or they will make a fortune, or enjoy a fascinating lifestyle, or be a part of history, or leave Ontario better off than when they started.

As a former winemaker, winemaking consultant, and educator over the last half-century, I am proud to present this review of the changes in Ontario winemaking, recalling the people who became the pillars of the modern industry, those who played such a major role in redefining the industry while helping to initiate a true wine culture in our province. It is the sequel to my book on the origins of a native wine industry in the province, "When Concord was King!", which reviewed the early years of our winemaking. As the wine industry has achieved so many milestones in recent years, it is only fitting to examine what has been a fascinating evolution from Concord to Cabernet!

Jim Warren, M.A. - October 2020

Milestones and stepping-stones in the search for greatness...

Odyssey: a journey of considerable length, fraught with perils and obstacles but achieving a happy ending!

Ontario's Wine Odyssey

-1860's: The first commercial wineries open in Grimsby and Cooksville. Clair House Vineyards wins the first ever medal for an Ontario wine at the Paris Exhibition, 1867.

-1891: The Census of Canada reports that there are 35 wineries in Ontario, confirming the 'birth' and health of a wine industry.

-1918: As Prohibition begins, Ontario wine is declared the only alcohol that can be purchased legally, and this stimulates winery development.

-1927: Poor quality wine produced during Prohibition damages the reputation of the wine industry. The LCBO is created to 'control' the alcohol business.

-1933: With the 'Depression' underway, Harry Hatch buys Bright's Wines and introduces changes which represent the first steps in the renaissance of Ontario winemaking.

-1946: Bright's winemaker, Adhemar de Chaunac, brings in a shipment from France of new French Hybrid vines, along with a few Chardonnay and Pinot Noir vines that mark the innocent beginning of Vinifera viticultural in Ontario.

-1947: An association of grape growers is established called "The Grape Growers of Ontario Marketing Board". The GGO will lobby on behalf of growers and protect their interests in newly established price negotiations with wineries while promoting the future of the Grape and Wine Industry overall.

-1955: De Chaunac makes the first Vinifera grape wine in Canada, Bright's 'Pinot Chardonnay' following the successful introduction of the first 100% French Hybrid wine called Manor St. David's Claret.

-1960: The wine industry enters its second century with continuing corporate consolidation of wineries.

-1970: Andrew Peller buys the Beau Chatel Winery in Winona and changes the name to Andres Wines. In no time, a new product called 'Baby Duck' will be up and quacking, a fizzy, sweet concoction that becomes Canada's top-selling wine. Ontario wines reach sales of 8.4 million gallons!

-1972: After a record harvest of 84,000 tons of grapes in 1971, the following vintage produces a short crop of only 52,000 tons, giving the wineries an opportunity to request government permission to use imported material in making their wines. A second short crop in 1976 would lead to additional 'blending', helping the remaining half dozen corporate wineries to improve their 'table' wines…and their bottom line! But is this 'Ontario' wine?

-1973: For the first time ever, sales of imported wine surpass those of all Ontario products, continuing a trend that also saw the sales of traditional Ontario ports and sherries falling to less than 40% of the market they once dominated. It is now becoming obvious that it would take more than a Baby Duck to save this industry.

-1975: On July 5, Donald Ziraldo and Karl Kaiser receive a licence to operate an Ontario winery, the first new grape winery to open its doors in 45 years in the province. You could argue that the arrival of Inniskillin House Wines marks the 'rebirth' of the Ontario Wine Industry, establishing the template for a 'cottage' or 'boutique' style winery that would handcraft small lots of premium wine from the new French Hybrid and Vinifera grapes, grown mainly by the winery itself.

-1979: The French Hybrids represent 17% of vineyard plantings and the Viniferas a scant 2.5% (compared to 80% for American hybrids) but both are increasing yearly, with over 50 different varieties of grapes now available in Ontario for winemaking.

-1983: The first commercial icewines are made in Ontario by Reif, Hillebrand, and Pelee Island wineries and before long Icewine will become the new flagship of the Ontario Wine Industry and a game-changer for the reputation of the entire industry.

-1988: In a year of monumental industry change, the government introduces a revised Wine Content Act that banishes all labrusca grapes for use in Ontario table wine and increases the use of import material in blended wines to 70%. Free Trade discussions with the United States result in the loss of the preferential mark-up on Ontario wines, a pricing advantage that the industry had long enjoyed, and which a GATT ruling declares to be an unfair trade practice.

As a result of the new 'level playing field', Ontario wine sales will decrease to a historic low point by 1990 with some predicting the end of the industry.

-1990: A government Grape and Wine Adjustment Program funds the removal of almost 9,000 acres of grape varieties considered surplus to industry needs while encouraging the planting of preferred Vinifera varieties which are now producing five times as many tons as ten years before.

While many of these changes were being implemented, Donald Ziraldo was leading the planning for the creation of an Ontario Appellation system for 100% Ontario grown grapes with a group of like-minded industry individuals. A Board of Directors met for the first time in December 1989 to establish the "Vintners' Quality Alliance" (VQA). In June 1990, the regulations are approved with Peter Gamble becoming the first Executive Director. This is a monumental achievement for Ontario winemaking even though complying with the rules at this point was still voluntary, as it would serve as the stepping-stone to the recognition of Ontario as a respected, world-class wine region.

-1994: On January 1, a new government viticultural policy takes effect that will make every new winery a 'farm' winery, obligated to grow and use a percentage of its own grapes. The rules will be 'massaged' over the next few years so that by 2000 a grape or fruit winery with an on-site retail store could be established anywhere in Ontario. This policy inspires the opening of forty more wineries in the province while creating a heightened interest in the industry and marking the beginning of 'agri-tourism', a policy to encourage wineries to become tourist destinations and entice consumers to visit wine country.

-1996: Donald Ziraldo and John Howard co-chair a fund-raising campaign to raise $4 million to establish the Cool Climate Oenology and Viticulture Institute (CCOVI) at Brock University. The building is called "Inniskillin Hall" in recognition of a significant donation by Vincor International.

-1999: After persistent efforts by the Wine Council of Ontario, the Conservative government agrees to allow "Direct Delivery" of wine to restaurants with the normal LCBO mark-up now directed to the supplier. This concession is for VQA wines only, not blended wines, and will stimulate sales of Ontario wine to restaurants while providing much-needed additional revenue to wineries.

-2000: Niagara College opens a 'Winery and Viticulture Technician Program' to supply trained individuals for the expanding industry.

At the same time, the government agrees to an industry proposal to change the status of the VQA and on June 1, Minister David Tsubouchi signs the law that makes VQA a provincially regulated body. On January 15, 2000, Laurie Macdonald is hired as the first Executive Director of the VQAO, Ontario's new independent wine authority. This change in status brings added credibility to the wine industry and will serve as a magnet to attract dozens of new wineries in the next two decades while improving sales for VQA wines.

-2001: For the first time in history, Vinifera grapes outproduce all Hybrids in the province, a fundamental necessity for establishing a world-class wine industry.

Unfortunately, much of the production from this vintage is ruined by an invasion of Asian lady bugs that taint the wines and force wineries to react to the problem for the future. Sorting tables are invented and eventually technology will produce optical grape scanning equipment that provides a significant step-up in overall processing quality.

All industry stakeholders collaborate on a new strategic plan for the industry in a combined effort to increase sales. The vision for the future is called “Poised for Greatness”.

Frog Pond Winery opens the wine industry’s first “Organic” winery, providing the inspiration for additional organic as well as biodynamic grape growing and winemaking.

-2002: The industry hits the million case mark in VQA production and that will double within 10 years. VQA wines represent 22% of all wine sold in Ontario. One year later, VQA wines gain free access to European markets as Canada agrees to forsake terms like Champagne, Sauternes, and Port in return.

-2003: A short crop of 26,000 tonnes forces a change in the Wine Content Act, with blended wines obligated to have only 10% Ontario content. Just 2 years later, another short crop causes this to change to just 1%.

And for the first time ever, screwcaps are allowed as a closure for VQA wines.

-2005: To expand on the three Designated Viticultural Areas (DVAs), an additional ten ‘sub-appellations’ are created to better inform consumers.

-2006: The Conservative Government agrees to provide an Excise tax exemption for 100% Canadian wines. At the same time, the Ontario Government decides to provide support for VQA wines sold in the LCBO system, providing a rebate to wineries on the first 13,000 litres of wine sold. These concessions represent significant tax relief, particularly for the smaller wineries, and will stimulate further growth and development.

-2007: Ontario welcomes Prince Edward County as a new VQAO appellation.

-2008: VQAO membership will hit the century mark as wineries continue to proliferate. In another 10 years, there will be 99 members in Niagara alone, making the choice of wine for Sunday dinner extremely challenging.

-2010: The Wine Support Program for VQA wines sold in the LCBO is renewed for 5 years although the government decides to impose a 'surtax' on blended Cellared in Canada wines sold in winery stores to fund the $57 million cost. This move inspires the larger wineries and growers to create the Winery and Growers' Association of Ontario (WGAO) to promote the interests of the CIC wine category.

Ontario's vineyard revolution is confirmed as the harvest will generate 32,000 tonnes of fine vinifera grapes while 'labruscas' fall to less than 3,000 tonnes.

-2015: The Liberal Wynne government surprises the industry by allowing the sale of wine at Farmers' Markets. This will at first apply only to VQA wines, although the Fruit Wineries had been advocating for the privilege in vain for 15 years!

The VQAO designates a new sub-appellation called South Islands within the Lake Erie North Shore (LENS) appellation.

-2016: Orange wine arrives in Ontario and soon becomes eligible for VQA status, joining the appassimento wine category. More and more wineries are certified to produce Organic and Biodynamic wine. And in 3 years, there will be over 100 wineries producing sparkling wine. Ontario's talented winemakers are proving to be just as creative as their peers in any world wine region.

-2019: Although defining 'greatness' may be challenging, there is absolutely no doubt that the Ontario Grape and Wine Industry has achieved success over the first two decades of the new millennium. From 2009-2019, VQA sales have grown by 63% and ICB wines by 48%, as consumers show increasing confidence in buying local wine. Over the same time, sales of imports have increased just 26.2%. And most impressive, exports of VQA wines have shot up 90% during the same period, a stunning indicator of progress in a category that was once limited virtually to icewines.

-2020: The Grape and Wine industry contributes more than $4 billion in annual economic impact within Ontario while supporting 18,000 jobs. Agri-tourism continues to soar as the industry attracts over 2 million visitors to Ontario wine country.

As one indicator of 'greatness', VQA sales reach $460,000,000!

CHAPTER ONE

Grapes and Wine in early north-eastern America

"I have been informed by such as have bin in Virginia, that there grow infinite number of wilde Vines there, and of several sorts...some bring forth great quantities of small blacke Grapes...another sort maketh deepe red Wine, which they call a fox-grape." "His Majesties Gracious Letter to the Earle of South Hampton commanding the present setting up of Silke works, and planting of Vines in Virginia", 1622. John Bonoeil

"It will be well to push the culture of the Alexander grape without losing time and efforts in the search of foreign vines which it will take centuries to adapt to our soil and climate." Thomas Jefferson, 1809

"It is almost impossible to get any definite idea of the early days of the grape in the Niagara District...In 1858 Mr. W. Kitchen and Mr. J.R. Pettit planted some grapes at Grimsby." Revett, "Ontario Department of Agriculture Bulletin #202, from the Annual Report of the Fruit Branch, 1909

"Being native to eastern North America, Phyloxera found European grape vines an easy target because they lacked the resistance that native American vines had developed." M. Laube, "Wine Spectator", 2017

What wine drinker is not familiar with names like Chardonnay, Riesling, Pinot Noir, or Cabernet Sauvignon, grapes that make highly esteemed wines that are consumed everywhere in the world to-day, and which now play such an important role in Ontario winemaking? These grapes and many more are descendants of grapes that date back to the time that civilized man first began to make wine in the 'Old World'. There are numerous varieties, and sometimes one grape will have different names, but they all belong to just one grape species, vitis vinifera, a Latin descriptor that suggests what they do best – 'wine bringing'.

With the help of our ancestors, vitis vinifera migrated over time successfully throughout Europe, setting down roots as native vines in many places and becoming the source of a treasured beverage over several thousands of years…wine. Without this one grape species, the world would be a much less happy place indeed!

Just over 400 years ago, the first British colonists arrived in North America and discovered to their delight wild grape vines growing everywhere. This abundance of grapes must have led them to believe they had found the Garden of Eden, with the promise of a wonderful source of wine. They would have needed this as an inexpensive and healthy beverage for everyday consumption, often safer to drink than available water, with the potential to become a lucrative, future export product as well.

They would be disappointed on all counts.

The wines they made did not turn out as expected. In fact, they were virtually unpalatable, thin and tart, short-lived, and with unusual musky aromas and flavours that were quite different from wines they had enjoyed in the past. This unfamiliar character in both the grapes and the wines soon came to be called 'foxy', and it was not a compliment (i.e. akin to the spray of a fox). The colonists could not have known that the vines they found were not vitis vinifera or that this species was not even indigenous to North America but were in fact some of the twenty-five other species that had developed naturally in the 'New World'. Later in time, the native vines would be classified with scientific names like vitis labrusca, or vitis riparia, or vitis rotundifolia, all truly 'wild' grapes! How ironic it was that grapes which grew so well and so abundantly proved virtually useless for enjoyable wine, unless sweetened or 'brandied', and it was no wonder that the early Americans turned to growing tobacco!

Needing to make wine that people could drink and enjoy, colonial governments as early as 1619 arranged for the importation of vines from Europe which they knew made good wine and believed would certainly prosper in their new home, especially with rules put in place to obligate all the colonists to plant them. To ensure success from the beginning, several vignerons were brought over from France to supervise plantings, much to the indignation of the English colonists, and punishments were announced for anyone caught stealing grapes!

However, virtually every effort to grow these vines failed as they met up with insects and vine diseases which were not understood at that time and for which they had no natural resistance. As well, soils were different than in Europe and the damp, cold climate much less suitable for the species. This made it almost impossible for them to survive no matter where they were planted, in Virginia and in other colonies, notwithstanding government incentives. Yet, amazingly, many people would continue to try growing 'European stems' throughout the developing Eastern States over the following 300 years only to meet with disappointment and even ridicule for wasting their time and money. The sad reality was, if good wine were to be made in this part of America, it would not be with either foxy indigenous grapes or the much desired 'vinifera' from Europe, and the hope for acceptable local wine at this time simply died on the vine.

If the numerous vinifera plantings had succeeded, making American viticulture an early happening, the course of winemaking in this part of the world would have been much different. Good wine would have played a much more important role in American life, and rum and whiskey, 'hard liquor', might never have soared to popularity as they did. It is possible that some of the 'history' which followed might have changed as well, for with a more acceptable drink of moderation available, the Temperance movement that fought against the social ills that the misuse of 'booze' inspired, and the Prohibition era that followed, might never have seen the light of day. However, that was not what happened, and it would not be until the mid 20th century that vinifera vines would finally and happily take root in eastern North America – as we shall see!

Just when it seemed that Mother Nature had played a cruel joke on would-be grape growers, the unexpected discovery of a 'new' grape near Philadelphia in the 1740's would rekindle enthusiasm for the fruit of the vine. In 1682, William Penn brought French vines to Pennsylvania and planted them at his home near the Schuylkill river outside Philadelphia. The vineyard did not grow well but after his death in 1716, it was passed on to his son Thomas. Sometime around 1740, the gardener for Thomas, a man named James Alexander, discovered an unusual vine near the river and he propagated it successfully. The original vine was an "accidental creation" which had developed spontaneously from a wild labrusca parent and one of Penn's imported vinifera vines, a cross between two different species described by scientists as a chance inter-specific hybrid. Such a vine would display contributions from each 'parent', offering a wild vine's ability to survive American winters better than a vinifera vine and with improved resistance to native diseases, while providing much better wine quality than a wild grape.

In 1759, he made a wine from the grapes, now called "Alexander", that was said to be of the claret type, dark red in colour, and with a musky character. Indeed, when Alexander wine was served to Maryland Governor Sharpe in early 1760, it was "much admired by all" although its quality faded soon after and the vines barely survived the following very cold winter. Yet, further propagation of the vine would ensue with even President Jefferson commenting some 50 years later that wine made from the Alexander grape was "worthy of the best vineyards of France" and that it would be preferable to plant this grape instead of 'foreign vines' which still could not be adapted to American soil.

Before the end of the century, with the vines being sold by a nursery near Philadelphia, this 'accident of nature', an amazing consequence of William Penn's importation of vinifera vines, would be planted around

Northeastern America. Historically, the Alexander vine is acknowledged to be the first of several other similar hybrids that would be found 'by chance' over the following half century, opening a new era for American viticulture and stimulating a true American winemaking industry.

Although no one knows for certain, it is reasonable to believe that the Alexander was the first American hybrid grape to cross the border to the Niagara area where at least two vineyards were planted before the war of 1812-1814. It was virtually the sole American hybrid available and might have been brought north along with several fruit trees that came to Niagara-on-the-Lake in the 1790's from a nursery on Long Island. We are left wanting to know more about the beginning of grape growing in Upper Canada, but unfortunately the actual origins are still somewhat of a mystery to us.

Important as the Alexander was in changing the prospects of American winemaking, it would be overshadowed in the early 1800's by the discovery of two other 'chance American hybrids', called the Isabella and the Catawba, with plantings of both vines expanding significantly after 1820. And over the next 30 years, they would be joined by other hybrid vines discovered in different States including the Clinton, the Delaware, the Diana, and the Concord which was destined to become the most popular of them all. Together, they would transform American viticulture. In short order, American hybrids would be responsible for a transformation in European vineyards as well, but of a different, and most unwelcome kind!

With the arrival of so many spontaneous hybrids in such a short time, a true 'grape mania' spread throughout Northeastern America inspiring the science of hybridization and the man-made creation of many hundreds more inter-specific vines. The hope was to improve on Mother Nature and develop grapes that would be more resistant to disease, or show less 'foxiness', or simply make better wine. The Roger's creations of the 1850's were well received and a few others including the Elvira and the Niagara would become important in time. But many of the man-made grapes were disease prone or ripened too late and failed to catch on for either wine or table use, proving to be less successful than the 'natural' hybrids.

In Upper Canada, the Isabella became available as early as 1827 when it was listed in the nursery catalogue of William Custead of Toronto Township and it would be highly recommended by another nurseryman, Dr. Chauncey Beadle of the St. Catharines Nursery, in the 1840's. Catawba became very popular in Ohio and made its way to Pelee Island as early as 1854 where it would become the leading grape variety for the next four decades.

It is surprising how quickly most of the new varieties made their way north to be planted in various locations in Upper Canada by the 1850's. Initially, grapes were considered a novelty fruit but once they became available at nurseries, they took root in private gardens and small farm plots with people growing them as a hobby, entering their grapes in local fairs and competitions for prizes as early as the 1840's. John Kilborn, who owned a 17 acre property in Beamsville, admitted to growing an amazing 30 varieties of grapes as a 'hobby' and began to create his own wine for sale in the late 1850's declaring that it was "far superior to the miserable stuff sold by our merchants".

However, there was at the same time a general belief that the cold, unfavourable climate was simply not suitable in Upper Canada for grape growing and that the available new hybrids, which continued to show traces of 'foxiness' in varying degrees, made wines which were not of the same quality as those which were imported – a stigma that prejudiced these grapes during their entire history.

All things considered, it is nothing short of remarkable that a wine industry would develop in the mid-19th century in what would become 'Ontario' where wine, if available, was imported, expensive, and little consumed other than by the wealthy elite, and grapes for winemaking, until only very recently, had never been available. Thus, there was really no demand for a product like local wine that had never made any significant impact on daily life.

Other forms of alcohol, including both locally made beer and whiskey, were inexpensive and readily available and would play a pre-eminent role in most people's life as they engaged with 'booze' in all aspects of socializing and family matters. 'Drinking' came to be a way of life, important for many not only to produce or enhance pleasure or as a solace for pain and depression, but to strengthen their bodies and ward off illness. Breweries and distilleries abounded in Upper Canada/Canada West, but wine made from the wild grapes was certainly not fit to sway people away from the more potent stuff whose consumption quickly became engrained in society. Indeed, the use of alcohol had become such a divisive issue that already a strong temperance movement was casting a foreboding shadow over the use of all alcohol!

In such an environment, and with the 'new' hybrids still a rarity, who in his right mind would want to become a winemaker? Fortunately, there are always people willing to take a chance, to play the role of the underdog, who are willing to gamble for an appropriate reward, or who simply have a passion for something that is beyond comprehension.

For anyone contemplating planting a commercial-size vineyard these were important considerations yet, beginning in the late 1840's a number of individuals decided to take the risk and planted a variety of the American Hybrids. Extensive plantings of the Clinton grape, a hybrid of two American wild species that was discovered around 1830, were made by the Parker family in Cooksville by 1850, and a 13 acre vineyard was established just outside Hamilton by William Haskins (Chief Engineer for the City of Hamilton) and Henry Bauer. In Grimsby, William Whitney Kitchen and J.R. Pettit planted a variety of grapes in 1858 while numerous other 'growers' began planting considerable acreage throughout Niagara by the early 1860's.

Already some 60 Agricultural Societies had developed in the province including a Fruit Growers' Association as well as the County of Lincoln Grape Growers' Association and at these meetings both the growing and selling of fruit were discussed, as well as the challenges and the potential of the various grapes in making wine. And optimism was in the air!

When would a winery breakthrough take place and who would attempt the first commercial production of native wine?

Almost overnight, and certainly by the end of the 1850's, grape growing had become an important undertaking, with prominent plantings of an impressive number of American hybrid grapes established around the horseshoe from Niagara to Toronto. Noticeably absent were 'foreign sets': varieties of vitis vinifera which continued to prove challenging to grow successfully in eastern North America. Efforts were made to grow some in an experimental greenhouse environment ("under glass") but this was not a practical consideration for a vineyard.

The emergence of a native wine industry, then, would have to depend entirely on the availability of vines that were unique to this region: the American hybrids, created by chance or by human effort. Although they were not invulnerable to severe winter weather or some grapevine diseases, they were proving winter-hardy and they tended to produce abundant crops, and many people found the grapes intriguing themselves. Considerable interest had developed in these vines, not only locally but also from horticulturalists outside of North America who were eager to see them for themselves. To satisfy this interest, shipments of vines headed to England and France at mid-century for botanic use and perhaps experimental winemaking. After all, these were totally 'new' Hybrid vines involving species not indigenous to Europe, and they had only recently been discovered. Thus, there was a certain amount of mystery about them from a scientific point of view.

Europe was in for a very unpleasant surprise!

Arriving in an environment where they had previously been unknown, without anyone realizing it at that time, the vine cuttings brought along with them a trio of invisible invaders: powdery mildew, downy mildew, and a microscopic mite that would not be identified in America until 1854. All three were able to survive the ocean crossing which now took less than two weeks by steamship. These three 'invaders' would quickly wreak havoc on vulnerable vinifera vineyards, causing the near collapse of European winemaking over the next quarter century, and eventually spreading world-wide. How ironic it was that the American hybrids, which were responsible for the new-found success of viticulture in eastern North America, were now the reason for the devastation of the very species which, in part, had given them birth!

Finding remedies to eradicate the problems began immediately and would continue through the remainder of the nineteenth century, showcasing the innovative genius of man. Although perfect solutions were not found for all the issues, the efforts would inspire amazing changes in viticulture by the end of the 1800's.

A treatment for powdery mildew, which cracks berries and leads to rot, of powdered sulphur dusted on vines was devised by the early 1860's. But then a new form known as 'downy' mildew began to reduce crops, requiring additional science to deal with it. In 1885, a scientist named Millardet working in Bordeaux, created a spray of copper-sulphate and lime, known as the 'Bordeaux mixture': a fungicide that helped prevent the problem. For farmers, using these tools meant extra work and expense with regular spraying when the weather was very humid. But they helped control the invasive mildews.

An even more serious problem was noted in France in the early 1860's that, within twenty years, would devastate hundreds of thousands of acres of vines in French and European vineyards. Vines would first lose their leaves, grapes would not ripen, and the plant would die from a loss of their root system within three years. With the damage spreading around France, a pharmacy professor at Montpellier University named Jules-Emile Planchon led the charge to find out the source of the problem. He discovered an almost invisible insect in hordes on the roots of vines in distress. He named the aphid-like insect 'Phylloxera vastatrix' for the galls it formed on roots, akin to Phylloxera galls on oaks. It took him a few more years to conclude that Phylloxera, which was causing vines to shut down their roots in defence, was a native of America whence it had come to Europe. American vines showed various levels of resistance to the insect, and this had made possible the successful growing of the hybrids on American soil without anyone knowing about the insects.

The first step in replacing vines was to plant millions of cuttings of phylloxera-tolerant American varieties like Isabella, Clinton, Othello, and Noah in France. But they did not grow well and made wine unacceptable to most French drinkers who found the foxy labrusca character objectionable.

Then it was suggested that grafting French vines to resistant American rootstalks might solve the problem, although achieving success would require huge quantities of vines from America. As well, European alkaline soils, which were different than American acidic soils, might be a problem for the roots and there could also be a negative impact on the resulting wine quality. In the monumental struggle to find a cure, other remedies were suggested as an alternative to 'grafting', including fumigating soils with chemicals, which was successful to a degree, and flooding vineyards, and many others which proved to be a complete waste of time. By using Phylloxera-resistant American varieties to cross with lime tolerant Vinifera, research institutes and universities created new tolerant vines whose rootstalks could then be used for grafting with the classic Vinifera varieties.

Another group of individuals in the private sector believed this was a less than ideal solution to the crisis and suggested that it would be better to create new hybrid vines by crossing less foxy American species that were phylloxera resistant with Vinifera vines, then reconfigure vineyards with these. Before long, a number of dedicated hybridizers including Albert Seibel, Francois Baco, Georges Couderc, Eugene Kuhlmann, Bertille Seyve, and several others, succeeded in developing thousands of new vines. They came to be called 'French Hybrids' or 'French-American Hybrids': vines that grew on their own roots with no need of grafting. Some of those with winemaking potential were widely planted in less favourable regions of France - nearly half a million acres by 1929 - proving popular because they produced good crops on vines that were less susceptible to mildew and other diseases, and at much less expense than grafted vines which French wineries believed still had to be used in the most famous wine producing areas.

In time, the combination of efforts would save the French grape and wine industry, although there was considerable concern that the quality of the wine had changed, and not for the better. As well, these efforts would generate beneficial consequences for viticulture around the world, significant learning about grape vines, rootstalks, and grafting, sprays to remedy grape vine diseases, and new French Hybrid vines. It would not take long for 'the world' to sit up and take note!

While all of this was happening, a wine industry had started in Ontario without any vinifera vines to prove worrisome, and it had continued to grow rapidly, not without problems of its own but certainly of a different nature than in Europe. The industry must have been aware of the crisis in and the 'cures', but, pre-occupied with the First World War and then Prohibition, it seems to have taken little interest. Some French Hybrids had already made their way to America early in the new century, but it was not until 1927 that the first vines from half a dozen French hybridizers came to the Geneva Research Station in New York State, with a small shipment of Seibel 1000 making its way to Ontario.

The world had seen shipments of hybrids across the Atlantic from America with disastrous results several years before. Hopefully, the outcome would be different this time with vines coming to North America. But no one at this time could have predicted a complete transformation of the Ontario wine industry!

Note: for a more detailed history of the birth and development of Ontario's native Grape and Wine Industry, see my text "When Concord was King", 2018.

CHAPTER TWO

The "birth" of a wine industry with the birth of a nation!

"A new kind of wine always has to make its way against settled prejudices and in the present case, where the supposition has been general that this was not a wine-producing country, the difficulty was increased. The use of the light wine by the people is increasing every year. Probably there are now a hundred gallons of claret drunk in Toronto where one was drunk ten years ago..." Toronto Leader, July, 1867.

"The view from the Stephenson House (in St. Catharines) is extremely beautiful, extending for miles over a very fertile country...Cherries, currants, apples, pears and peaches grow in profusion. Grapes also, of the usual varieties, grow most luxuriantly, and I find that winemaking is becoming an important manufacture." Unidentified writer in the St. Catharines Journal, July 17, 1869.

"Prohibition more than anything else turned Canadians into a nation of wine drinkers." Tony Aspler, "Vintage Canada".

By 1860, life in what was now Canada West was changing and improving rapidly, although four out of every five workers were still involved in farming. With the increasing interest in growing grapes spreading from the Peninsula through Hamilton and further east around the north shore of Lake Ontario, it seemed that the time was ripe for someone to take amateur winemaking to the next level and introduce what could be called a commercial winery.

In fact, the first two larger-scale wine making endeavours happened virtually at the same time shortly before Confederation: the one established in Cooksville by Sir Henry Parker, an Englishman, as the Clair House Vineyards, and the second in Grimsby operated by a cattle breeder named William Whitney Kitchen who later attempted to incorporate his operation under the name Grimsby Union Wine Company. Both men planted several acres of a variety of American hybrid grapes for winemaking. There are abundant records, newspaper ads, letters, maps, and documents that provide considerable insight into the nature of each business and allow us to obtain a good idea of the kinds of wine that were made at each winery. Parker planted a significant amount of the Clinton grape as the best suiting his conditions, although he thought the Catawba and the Isabella would grow for him as well. Kitchen planted several different varieties, which he also propagated and sold to the public, including Concord, Delaware, Diana, and Hartford Prolific.

Kitchen advertised his award-winning wines as being ideal for use by churches as communion wine and for medicinal purposes since they were sweet and tended to be high in alcohol. There was general agreement that his wine was "invaluable for Diarrhea and Dysentery…and not hard to take". He made a port wine from Concord and a sherry from Delaware declaring that his wine was sent everywhere to private homes and hotels. He appears to have been successful, selling wine in volume lots at a significant discount and offering coupons which he called 'Commission Scrip' to increase sales (think of Canadian Tire money!). Doctors and ministers were quick to offer their praise when he asked for their support in trying to sell stock in his venture.

In Cooksville, Henry Parker became involved with a man named Justin de Courtenay in the early 1860's and before long their relationship evolved into the Canada Vinegrowers' Association (CVGA). De Courtenay was an Englishman with grape and wine experience in Europe who came to Canada East in the 1850's and planted grapes hoping to convince the government there that good wine could be made in Canada. After some frustration with government officials, he became friends with Parker and journeyed to Cooksville to pursue his passion heading up the CVGA. Plans were initially to make a dry red and a dry white wine, a sherry, and a champagne, in total as much as 50,000 gallons of native wine which was pre-sold to people in Canada East. The company was incorporated with government blessing and De Courtenay continued to make the wines with considerable success, even producing the first icewine which he called'congealed wine' (vin congele)! In 1867 he sent wines to the Exposition in Paris and won the first ever medal for a Canadian wine in international competition with his red wine that was judged to be "of excellent quality".

The 'Toronto Leader' followed up on de Courtenay's achievement with an amazing prophecy in July 1867: "The time will come, we hope and verily believe, when grape growing and wine making will be one of the principal employments of our population. And when it does come, the cause of temperance will be advanced to a degree that could be reached by no other process." Amen!

The success of these first two commercial operations, in spite of the many challenges facing a winery at that time, would quickly inspire several others to plant grapes and make local wine from Pelee Island in the south-west, to Hamilton and Toronto and as far east as Prince Edward County.

On Pelee Island, a grape grower and winemaker from Kentucky, D.J. Williams, with his brother Thomas and a relative named Thaddeus Smith bought a 40 acre property in 1865 and began to plant 25 acres of Catawba, Delaware, and other grapes the following year. They built a wine cellar and a house above that would become the location of the Vin Villa winery, coinciding with the arrival of Confederation and the 'brand-new' country of Canada. At the same time Williams invited two fellow Englishmen, brothers named Edward and John Wardroper, who had been living in the U.S., to visit Pelee and in 1866 they purchased 15 acres with the intention of planting grapes for a winery. In addition to Niagara and Cooksville the new province of Ontario now had its third wine region, Pelee Island, where expansion would continue over the next twenty years to some 225 acres of grapes and six wineries!

The planting of grape vines had happened so rapidly in the province that by 1870 they represented the third most significant fruit crop and other entrepreneurs were being attracted to the wine business. An Irishman named William Haskins had emigrated to Canada in 1852 becoming City Engineer in Hamilton 4 years later. By 1859 he established a 13 acre vineyard with a partner, Henri Bauer, just to the east of the city with several different American hybrids headed by the Clinton grape. In 1880, when he spoke to the Ontario Agricultural Commission, he mentioned his winery which had been active for some time, talking about the wines he had been making which included ports and sherries, clarets and sauternes, and how he produced them. This would be the first of several wineries to evolve in the Hamilton area over the following half century.

In the late 1850's an American named Sylvanus Joy, who took his medical training at Queen's in Kingston, settled in Tillsonburg in Oxford County where he served as coroner as well as running his own practice. Here he is reported to have developed the "largest apple orchard and general fruit farm in Ontario", planting 20 acres of grapes in 1865 and building extensive vaults where he would produce 10,000 gallons of wine. The "Brantford Expositor" at the time tells us that the Doctor sent wine to the World's Fair in Paris and was awarded a diploma for excellence of quality. In addition, the wine was "favourably known throughout the province of Ontario"!

In Prince Edward County to the east of Toronto, amateur winemakers had been making their own wine and entering competitions at various fairs. One man, J.H. Morden of Rednersville, was making wine from his own grapes and he advertised this for sale in the "North American Newspaper" of December 1865. He proudly proclaimed that his wine was "superior for medicinal purposes, especially invalids, to the adulterated and drugged mixtures daily exposed for sale" and that it was highly recommended by the 'best judges in Canada West and suitable for sacramental purposes". Unfortunately, Prince Edward County would go 'dry' in the following decades ending this kind of artisanal winemaking and a full century would pass before there would be a resurgence of grape growing and winemaking in "the County" in the 1990's.

Two additional wineries that developed in the early 1870's would blossom into the province's largest commercial operations by the end of the century. The first was started in St. Catharines by George Barnes, an Irishman who had come to Hamilton in 1833 to open a bookstore. At some point he became excited about grapes, planting some in Hamilton, and proceeded to sell his very successful business. In July 1873, with his brother Thomas and six other partners he received a charter to operate the Ontario Grape Growing and Wine Manufacturing Company on 52 acres of grapes near the winery in an area that came to be called Barnesdale, alongside the Welland Canal. Within 20 years it would have 25 employees and be producing over 15% of the province's wine. In 1934, long after George's passing in 1877, the winery was renamed Barnes' Wines in his honour.

One year after the opening of the OGG&WM Co., two businessmen, F.A. Shirriff and Thomas G. Bright, opened their winery, The Niagara Falls Wine Company, strangely not in Niagara Falls but in Toronto where there was a ready market. Sixteen years later they did move the business to Niagara Falls, much closer to vineyards, where they expanded rapidly to become Ontario's largest winery and a leader in the wine industry. After 1911 the winery changed its name to T.G. Bright and Co. (Bright's Wines) when the son of the founder purchased the shares held by Shirriff who went on to marmalade making fame!

By the end of 1874, with wineries of various size having set down roots from one end of the province to the other, one could legitimately say that the new country of Canada and specifically Ontario had given birth to a grape and wine industry. This might have been humble and quite unsophisticated at the start, but these wine pioneers were serious about their work, and although there was no established wine culture yet to speak of, their winemaking was a very personal and artisanal undertaking that had become "an important manufacture". The quality of the wines being produced was affirmed by awards won in provincial and international competitions and by the recommendations of many leading citizens.

At this point the business of the wineries was still considered agricultural in nature and not industrial and thus they had avoided involvement by the provincial government either in encouraging or impeding their activities. Although the consumption of alcohol remained a controversial issue in society, local wine, with its emphasis on health and sacramental use, was not really on the radar of temperance activists who had become particularly enamoured of the alcohol-free potential of Concord grape juice developed by an American dentist named Welch.

All things considered, the growing of grapes and the making of local wine had enjoyed an auspicious and exciting beginning with the number of new vineyards and wineries both increasing dramatically in the first decade of what could now be called an 'industry'.

This foundation would serve as a prelude for the industry's roller-coaster ride over the next half century. After 1880 more wineries opened from the Windsor area and Pelee Island to Niagara and Toronto with 23 wineries located in Essex County alone out of the total of 35 according to the 1891 Census of Canada. Many were tiny, even part-time operations, selling to a local clientele with the smaller number of wineries in Niagara still producing 50% of the province's wine. The Census boasted some 5,000 acres of grapes in total, a number that would soar to 11,000 acres by the end of the century.

The irony of all this was the increasing success of an industry that depended on vines that many people were still not convinced would grow in our cold climate, some of which were prone to native vine diseases. Yet, it continued to find success in spite of the lengthening shadow of a temperance movement that was beginning to have a negative impact on the alcohol business in general. But the wines were highly recommended by doctors for medicinal purposes and by the clergy for use in churches and proved to be a worthy substitute for other alcoholic beverages once tried! These unique American hybrids producing the wines were certainly not in the same league as vinifera vines for making fine table wine, although several wineries by now had received awards in competitions with them.

Unfortunately, this impressive growth was followed by a sudden downturn at the beginning of the new century when many vineyards in southwestern Ontario were torn out and replaced by a more lucrative crop – tobacco. This resulted in the closure of several wineries in Essex County before World War One due to a shortage of grapes.

In combination with activism by advocates of 'patriotic temperance', World War One brought Prohibition to Ontario and one might have thought that this would be the end of the entire alcohol industry. However, responding to a lobby from the grape growers who would have no home for their grapes, the Government exempted Ontario produced wine from the restricted sales list making it the only form of alcohol that could legally be purchased in the province. Indeed, it could be argued that without this opportunity, the wineries still producing but with no market for their wines, would have had to close their cellar doors.

Almost overnight, numerous 'entrepreneurs' applied for a winery licence to take advantage of the loophole in the law, and this caused the winery roller coaster to ascend again, reaching a high point with over 50 licences in existence by the end of the Prohibition era. Not surprisingly, the consumption of legal, native wine soared from some 222,000 gallons in all of Canada at the beginning of the 1920's to over 2,200,000 gallons in Ontario alone just ten years later, and, for a short while, the Government allowed the wineries to source grapes from American growers.

The Ontario Grape and Wine Industry was indeed 'on a roll', but unfortunately, much of the wine manufactured during this period by less than "satisfactory hands" was of a scandalous quality, with many wines so high in acetic acid that they were barely palatable while others refermented in bottles. Although some wineries did make a good product, the overall result was an indelible stain on the reputation of our native wine industry.

After 1927, with the creation of the Liquor Control Board of Ontario, the Government focused considerable attention on the wine industry in an attempt to improve the health and quality of all Ontario wine which would now be more accessible to the public in an expanding LCBO retail store system. As fast as new wineries had risen with the coming of Prohibition, just as fast would they begin to disappear, with many unable to cope with the new and demanding regulations and improve their winemaking. That left them locked out of the new system.

As the Depression of the 1930's followed on the heels of Prohibition, sales of Ontario wine faced further challenges including a sharp decrease in the sales of wine. This left many wineries with substantial inventories of substandard product they could not sell. Several wineries went out of business with the more fortunate ones selling their licence to a more viable winery, all with the encouragement of the Government that permitted the buyer then to expand its own retail store system: one store for each licence purchased. This clean-up of the wine industry was long overdue, eliminating several wineries in a dramatic descent of the roller coaster that would continue until the early 1970's and leave only seven wineries remaining in business. From the end of Prohibition until this time, there would be no new grape winery licences issued in the province.

From the birth of the industry, through the initial growth spurt of adolescence, and the challenges of World War One, Prohibition, and the Depression, Ontario wineries had produced a wide range of inexpensive wines, a few table wines and 'Champagnes', but primarily sweeter wines and high-alcohol ports, sherries, and communion wines, all from labrusca-based American grapes like Concord, Catawba, Delaware, and Niagara: unique vines that for more than half a century had made wines which were popular with Ontario consumers. Originally, they were highly recommended by doctors, the clergy, private clubs, and hotel owners. The industry's reputation suffered considerably when quantity, not quality, became the motivation for winemaking during Prohibition, but even then there was no change in the raw material producing the wines – perhaps just a little more water, sugar, and a few chemicals!

In truth, there had been little incentive to change the nature of grape growing in the province, although by the end of the 1920's the Horticultural

Research Station in Vineland was busy trying to develop new and 'better' hybrids without any wild labrusca in their make-up. Some may have heard about the 'new' French Hybrids, which continued to be developed in France, but few people in the industry seemed to be paying attention and there was simply no track record of winemaking with them in eastern North America. Making wine from any vinifera grape was still out of the question, leaving the wineries with no other option than to use those grapes which had already established a basic reputation for winemaking.

A change in the ownership of one Ontario winery in 1933 would provide the motivation at last for positive developments in the somewhat stagnant Ontario grape and wine business: radical changes that would eventually propel the industry forward and upward for the third time in its history, but this time to world-class status.

CHAPTER THREE

A radical change: French-American Hybrids and...Chardonnay!

"Whatever his reasons, Hatch brought his resources to bear in his quest to make better wines. Harry's ambition inspired the turnaround of the Ontario wine industry." Linda Bramble, "Niagara's Wine Visionaries"

"The two men (Dr. John Eoff and Adhemar de Chaunac from Bright's Wines) virtually single-handedly were to turn the Canadian Wine trade around and create the basis of the industry we know to-day." T. Aspler, "Vintage Canada"

"De Chaunac spent a lifetime devoting himself entirely to the betterment of Canadian wines". Percy Rowe, "Red, White, and Rose: Enjoying wines in Canada"

By the early 1930's, a self-made millionaire named Harry Clifford Hatch had become a titan of Canadian business. Through Prohibition, he had made a fortune as the so-called 'King of Distillation' while buying two Ontario distilleries in the process. He then set his sights on acquiring Bright's Wines in Niagara Falls which had the largest privately-owned cellars in the British Empire (one of the largest wineries in the world at the time!) capable of holding 4 million gallons (18 million litres) of wine. Most people would have seen only problems in buying a large winery at this difficult time, but Harry obviously saw an opportunity once again to obtain another business at a good price and in 1933 he became the owner with a plan to reorganize the business and bring needed improvements to the company's portfolio of wines. Bright's Wines was retained as the winery name.

Over the next 10 years Harry Hatch set in motion the innovations that would take both his winery and eventually the industry in a new direction. His first step was to hire Dr. John Eoff, an American food scientist with experience at the U.S. Food and Drug Administration, to address winemaking issues. As the new winemaker, John applied his regulatory background to introduce new sanitation procedures along with an emphasis on quality control. He hired another microbiologist, a Frenchman named Adhemar de Chaunac, who, after World War One, had been working as a chemist in Montreal with the Lallemand Yeast Company and who also had expertise in quality control. With these two professionals in charge, the winery created a plan to work on new table wine production which De Chaunac estimated would cost over $500,000 and require a commitment of twenty years.

Before this time, Bright's had purchased all its grapes from growers; but in 1934, Hatch decided to invest in vineyards of their own and bought 1400 acres of land in the peninsula on which Bright's could start its own grape research program. Soon a considerable number of older vines would be torn out and replaced with grapes that would help make more appealing dry table wine. De Chaunac chose two grapes which were in short supply in Ontario vineyards and which he felt lacked obvious foxiness, Catawba and Delaware, along with Elvira and Agawam, that could all be used to make a better white wine. The management at Bright's had come to realize that they needed to improve the quality of their dry table wines even though this was not a significant part of their sales at the moment. But this was an opportunity to grow another part of their business.

De Chaunac had been very critical of some of his company's wines, describing the red wines as "sweet" and the whites as "undrinkable" and he decided to begin trials in the hopes of making a better white table wine. Hatch was impressed with the results and asked his winemaker to make a commercial volume of a dry table wine. This experiment evolved into the first new Ontario table wine since Prohibition with the introduction of Manor St. David's Sauternes in 1941 made from the Agawam grape, one of the more highly rated American hybrids.

Continuing his research, De Chaunac became aware of new Hybrids that had been created in France over the previous half century in an attempt to deal with the phylloxera crisis there. Like the American hybrids, these were also crosses of European Vinifera vines and native American species, but not the labrusca species whose character was not to the liking of the French. Created by a small number of French hybridizers, they produced vines that would provide a better level of resistance to the devastating pest phylloxera.

As a less expensive alternative to grafting vinifera cuttings onto more resistant American rootstock, these "French Hybrids" as they came to be called (or French-American Hybrids) also produced good crops with the potential to make very acceptable wine, perhaps not as 'fine' as many vinifera varieties but certainly a far 'better' quality of dry wine than the available American hybrids. They were identified by the name of the hybridizer (e.g. Seibel for Albert Seibel) along with a number to differentiate the original seedlings (e.g. S-1000 or S-9110). De Chaunac knew about these grapes through his association with colleagues and friends at the Research Station in Geneva, New York, who believed that they offered significant potential for making European-style table wines in eastern North America. Bright's planted some Seibel 1000 vines (this grape would later be given the name "Rosette") in 1938, the first and only French Hybrid planted in Ontario before World War Two and followed this up by making an experimental batch of red wine from the grapes when they became available. De Chaunac, who apparently was not known for his modesty, called it "the first acceptable quality red made in Canada"!

The difference in the wine when compared, for example, to a red wine made from Concord, would have been astounding for the time and De Chaunac must have realized he had come upon something extremely worthwhile. Certainly, there were many other similar hybrids to work with, and who knew then what their potential might be? It was time for further experimentation with these hybrids, if only he could obtain them!

Others at the management level must have been impressed as well for at this point Bright's decided to establish commercial plantings of several French Hybrids, a propitious decision that would eventually have an impact on the rest of the wine industry. Unfortunately, the outbreak of war in 1939 meant that grapevines could no longer be shipped from Europe and further work with them would have to be delayed.

After Dr. Eoff passed away in 1940, De Chaunac was named the next Director of Research with a new young assistant, George Hostetter, son of Bright's vineyard manager, Jacob Hostetter. It would prove to be an ideal partnership. Later in his remarkable career with Bright's, Hostetter would prove invaluable in the grape breeding program as Director of Viticultural Research and would assume De Chaunac's position in 1961 when Adhemar finally retired. Unfortunately, in 1946 Harry Hatch himself passed away at the age of 62 without seeing all the amazing results his investments in grape research would produce. But he had positioned Bright's at the forefront of what would turn out to be an epic shift in Ontario winemaking.

On September 21, 1945, De Chaunac attended a meeting of wine industry people in Geneva where a 'blind' tasting of experimental wines was held that included some French Hybrid wines made by Philip Wagner, a leading American proponent of the grapes. Wagner's wines were a revelation to De Chaunac and he returned to Bright's determined to inform others of the high quality of what he had tasted. When he was authorized to order some, he worked with Hostetter and J.R. Van Haarlem from the Vineland Research Station to select what they felt could be the most promising from the hybridizers' catalogues they had.

On April 11, 1946, the shipment arrived from France containing 20 different varieties, 13 of these from Albert Seibel, 4 from 3 other hybridizers as well as some Muller-Thurgau, a Germanic Hybrid, and two Viniferas, Chardonnay and Pinot Noir, an interesting and fortuitous inclusion at this time. These were entrusted to Hostetter for planting. Considering the unfortunate history of Vinifera in eastern North America there was more skepticism than optimism over their chances of success and little was known about the winemaking quality of most of the Hybrids which at this time even lacked a proper name. The French had already identified a few of the more popular ones, like Marechal Foch for Kuhlmann 188-2 or Baco Noir for Baco 1, and these names would be used later in Ontario as well, but at this early date most of them continued to exist as simply mysterious numbered Hybrids. In 1948 Bright's decided to begin commercial plantings with 40,000 vines and 4 years later introduced some of the varieties to their growers, taking the first major steps in establishing a new direction for Ontario viticulture.

The same year that the first Hybrids came to Bright's, the Horticultural Research Institute purchased a 35 acre property on Cherry Avenue in Vineland to serve as their research vineyard intending to plant some of the French Hybrids themselves. Approximately 7,200 vines were ordered from France later in the year and they arrived in Vineland in early spring, 1947. Oliver Bradt, the grape specialist at H.R.I.O., was in charge of dealing with the shipment that contained both rooted vines and cuttings consisting of approximately 200 each of 35 different Seibel varieties and 5 varieties from 2 other hybridizers. Included in this shipment were the very first Seibel 9549 vines to come to Ontario, a new grape that in 30 years would become Ontario's most widely planted red Hybrid.

From this very inauspicious beginning before 1950, with only a small number of various vines planted, Bright's would proceed to make the first trial batches of different French Hybrid wines. These first wines won high ratings in blind tastings and inspired Bright's to release their first red hybrid wine, a blend of S-10878 (it would receive the name "Chelois" later and was a personal favourite of De Chaunac) and S-1000 (Rosette), which they called Manor St. David's Claret, the first such wine produced commercially in Canada. This was accompanied by a bottle fermented sparkling wine named President Champagne, that resulted from a blend of both American and French Hybrid grapes. An impressive list of 'firsts' was beginning to accumulate for both De Chaunac and the winery – and more were to come! In 1958 Bright's introduced a wine made from the Marechal

Foch grape, calling it 'Canadian Burgundy', much to the annoyance of the French who were upset that anyone would label a wine "Burgundy" that was made from a hybrid grape, and in Ontario yet!

Although almost one million acres of French Hybrids had been planted in France by the 1950's, there was the belief, not yet evident in our industry, that the Hybrids were actually a threat to their traditional viniferas since they made wine that was considered somewhat inferior to their classic wines. Some of the French called them 'bastards', or worse, 'American' Hybrids, and they were outlawed for use in table wine production at this time. They would come to be more appreciated in Ontario although it would take some time for growers and other wineries to grasp the significance of the achievements at Bright's. They would be the grapes responsible for transitioning our wine industry from its labrusca past to an amazing future, serving as a stepping-stone to the use of preferred vinifera grapes, while making wines like Vidal, Baco Noir, and Foch, Hybrids that continue to be valued highly by consumers to-day.

In 1951, defying conventional wisdom, Bright's planted 10 acres of Chardonnay, convinced that this vinifera could indeed grow in Ontario if planted with a rootstock that was more resistant to phylloxera and maintained with an innovative spray program that George Hostetter had devised to control powdery mildew. His technique consisted of spraying the vines in the Fall and then as a dormant spray in the Spring before the mildew started and it worked! These vines produced the first vinifera wine made in Canada in 1955, a Pinot Champagne, and the following year the first vinifera table wine which Bright's called Pinot Chardonnay (it would be over 20 years before our industry dropped the 'Pinot' when it was realized that Chardonnay did not belong in the family!).

Attempting to grow vinifera grapes that had only a history of failure in eastern North America was indeed a display of courage on the part of Bright's and represented a technical achievement in viticulture, a long-sought after goal to grow vinifera vines in this part of the world and have them survive, that would ultimately enable the wine revolution in Ontario that was still 25 years in the future.

This was indeed a defining or watershed moment in the history of Ontario winemaking, marking the quiet beginning of our modern wine industry! To-day, those working in the wine industry would be hard pressed to recall this achievement which has been overshadowed in recent years by an amazing growth in numerous vinifera plantings that some now take almost for granted. And even at that time the impact of these new developments went largely unheralded, not only with most consumers who knew nothing about the new grapes but with many wineries in the industry itself who continued to pump out their traditional ports and sherries.

Sales of Ontario wine had bounced back after the end of World War Two and it was easy to question the need to make any changes in our winemaking. This was especially true for growers who were not yet convinced that the time and expense involved in replacing their vineyards with new vines when their old vines continued to provide a good livelihood was a sound investment. After all, the French Hybrid and Vinifera vines had little track record in North America and required a different method of viticulture. But the successful planting of vinifera in this part of North America was a remarkable breakthrough considering their past history and the fact that such progress was able to be accomplished after only 10 years of experimentation.

The initial plantings at Bright's and Vineland through the late 1940's and the 1950's marked the beginning of real change for our grape and wine industry by introducing the vines that, once established, would prove to be a game-changer for Ontario winemaking. In many ways this was the legacy of one man, Harry Hatch, whose investment and commitment motivated a team at Bright's Wines, led by Adhemar de Chaunac and George Hostetter, to revitalize their winemaking, taking the initial steps that would enable the future grape and wine industry to compete in the global wine industry.

In considering their importance to the history of our winemaking as the initial pillars of our modern industry, knowing that it is impossible to think of Ontario wine over the last 30 years without vinifera grapes, one has only to ask where would the Ontario Wine Industry be to-day without the contribution of those visionaries at Bright's Wines?

CHAPTER FOUR

And then there were eight...seven...six! Sustaining a corporate wine industry

"The early years of Ontario wineries are one long history of small fish being swallowed by bigger fish who are in turn swallowed by even bigger ones." T. Aspler, "Vintage Canada"

"In the years that followed VE Day came an explosion of new ideas, new grapes, new wines, new concepts by governments and new lifestyles that made the days when 'Catawba' was a bad name nothing but a memory most Canadians were happy to put behind them." W.F. Rannie, "Wines of Ontario"

"Obtaining suitable recognition of Ontario wine is a never-ending struggle...Grape producers, to-day, are on a vicious treadmill. In order to compete with imports, we must exercise every efficiency." Ron Moyer, Chairman, Ontario Grape Growers' Marketing Board, January 1972.

At the end of the Second World War, the Ontario wine industry appeared ready for 'business as usual' with 19 wineries still operating although it would not take long for the downsizing that had started after Prohibition to continue and reduce this number. One of the first to sell was the J.S. Hamilton Winery in Brantford which sold out to London Winery in 1950. The Hamilton winery had evolved from the Vin Villa Winery on Pelee Island dating to the late 1860's and could legitimately claim to be Ontario's oldest operating winery. In total, 10 wineries would go out of business before 1960 including five located in Toronto, the Twin City Winery in Fort William, Kitchener Wines, the Dundurn Winery in Hamilton, and 2 in Niagara, the Fred Marsh Winery and the St. Catharines Winery.

Not only did most of these smaller operations have no vineyards of their own to ensure a supply of grapes but, unlike the larger players with their own retail store network, they found it simply too difficult to compete in the changing environment. Faced with a challenging future that posed serious threats to their established business model, they decided to sell their assets, including their valuable store licence, to another winery. Bright's alone acquired 4 more licences as they continued to lead the industry with 13 retail stores and their on-site winery outlet while London Winery was able to enlarge its business by buying eight other wineries. In total, the remaining Ontario wineries were operating 51 retail stores spread across the province in addition to supplying the LCBO system which continued to open new stores annually.

With further consolidation occurring in the business, Ontario wineries became larger and more corporate in nature. Already in 1948, Jordan's, after the death of longtime owner W.B. Cleland, had been purchased by the Distiller's Corp./Seagram's and the Torno family, merging with the Danforth Winery as Jordan-Danforth Wines. Five years later this conglomerate purchased the St. Catharines Winery and renamed itself 'Jordan Wines'. This business in turn would be sold in 1971 to Canadian Breweries Ltd. (Carling-O'Keefe) and blossom into Jordan-Ste. Michelle Cellars shortly afterwards.

In the same vein, in 1966, Parkdale Wines in Etobicoke purchased the Grimsby Winery and then was itself purchased by brewer John Labatt who renamed it Chateau Cartier. In 1973 Labatt's took over Chateau-Gai in Niagara Falls where it centralized both operations as Chateau-Gai, leaving the Cartier name as a marketing brand. And Barnes Winery would join the corporate game in 1973 when it was purchased by Reckitt & Colman, exactly 100 years after its founding. Subsequently, the business would be acquired by Gilbey's, a well-known brand in the alcohol business that would bring additional marketing expertise in promoting what was now Canada's 'oldest operating winery'.

But the one sale that would eventually turn out to have the most impact on the Ontario wine industry itself came in 1964 with the purchase of the Welland Winery by Imperial Tobacco. Six years later, the business now renamed 'Beau Chatel' and moved to new facilities in Winona alongside the Queen Elizabeth highway between Grimsby and Hamilton, was sold again to Hungarian born Andrew Peller who had emigrated to Canada in 1927. Peller had established several businesses in Hamilton including a brewery (1946) which he would sell for a profit 7 years later. He then attempted numerous times to obtain a new winery licence but was refused each time due to the continuation of government's strict post-Prohibition 'no new licence' policy but also, apparently, because Peller constantly broke advertising rules with his brewery and upset the government. In frustration he moved to British Columbia and opened Andres Wines in Port Moody in 1962. A few years later, with his son Dr. Joe Peller as President, Andrew tried again to obtain an Ontario licence and was again rebuffed, with the suggestion that the only way this would happen was if he bought an existing winery. At last he had found a way to enter the Ontario market. Peller would re-name the Beau Chatel winery, whose original licence dated back to 1930 as the Victor Subosits Winery, "Andres Wines" with the opening taking place on January 1, 1970.

With this transaction, an end finally came to more than 40 years of winery consolidation in the province as it would be the last of the 'old' winery licences to change hands. By 1970 the Ontario Wine Industry was now left with only 8 larger wineries, Andres, Bright's, Barnes, Chateau Gai, Chateau Cartier, Jordan's, London, and Turner's, and that number would drop to 7 with the merger of Chateau Cartier and Chateau Gai in 1973, and then to 6 with the closure of the smallest member of the group, the Turner Winery in Toronto at the end of 1977. The Ontario Wine Industry was now essentially a Niagara-centric one with only London Winery operating away from the peninsula.

The largest of these wineries either already owned or planned to build branch plants in other provinces across Canada to increase their listings with the Liquor Boards there. Bright's had operated a bottling plant in Quebec since 1934, while Jordan's and Andres would eventually establish operations in 5 provinces to gain better access to the provincial liquor boards. Barnes enjoyed the unique distinction of having at least one wine represented in every part of the country. Led by Bright's with almost 9 million gallons of storage, the total capacity of the industry at this time had reached over 20 million gallons of native wine!

After years of repeated growth and downsizings, Ontario's native wine industry had managed to reach its centennial in the 1960's, an amazing milestone given all of its tortuous history, and was preparing to enter its second century with its new 'corporate' look. Clever and inventive winemakers were now making sizeable volumes of several brands as part of a full range of wines including red, white, and rose table wines, numerous ports and sherries, and Champagnes and sparkling wines, while a few also specialized in appetizer wines, dessert wines, Kosher and Sacramental wine, and flavoured concoctions, amazingly all from only a small number of 'native grape' varieties. Sales had now become the realm of marketing executives tasked with building their 'brands' and maintaining market share with product lines that continued to expand as wineries, fully aware of the need to stay competitive, tried to be all things to all consumers.

Looking back, it is easy to forget that our native industry was still in its infancy compared to the 'Old World' where some wineries had been making wine for centuries and that our wineries, without any significant volume of Vinifera or French Hybrid grapes available at this time, were handicapped, limited for the most part to the Ontario grown, native hybrids they had used since the beginning. As a result, Ontario wineries offered very little that could be considered a source of pride to connoisseurs and had little potential to change their portfolios. Thus, when consumer demand for decent dry table wines began to manifest itself after World War Two, our wineries could only rely on the status quo, wine styles like ports and sherries that were now losing popularity.

In truth, there had never been anything fashionable about these wines, certainly nothing 'classic' in nature or even vintage-dated, but they had served a purpose with their higher alcohol levels ideal for soothing the ills of drinkers during the Depression, and their sales had sustained the industry for a long period of time. However, the lights on these high-alcohol products by this time were beginning to flicker, suggesting further issues down the road. Clearly indicating the shift in consumer taste, the table wine category, which was less than 1% of the market in 1946, had grown to 32% of all wine sold in the province by 1968, but Ontario table wines still made from Concord, Elvira, and Niagara, disappointing for the most part, were hurting the industry's reputation.

Needing to fight for acceptance, the industry had modernized after the war with costly expansions and with a renewed emphasis on wine palatability and quality and ongoing experimentation. The Canadian Wine Institute, an association of Canadian wineries formed in 1946, conducted monthly 'blind' tastings in Vineland at the Horticultural Research Station through an industry Quality Standards Committee to monitor the quality of Canadian wines (including imported 'ringers') to benefit all concerned. A new product introduced by Jordan's in the early 1960's called 'Zing', with 20% alcohol and flavoured with juniper, became an overnight sensation. By the end of its first year it turned out to be the largest selling wine in Ontario at 120,000 gallons and this figure would increase to 350,000 gallons the following year. Typically, when one winery comes up with a winning new product, everyone else joins in but this time some wineries, like Barnes, Bright's and Chateau Gai, refused to make these inexpensive, 'gin-like' products, feeling they degraded the industry. Other wineries did follow the leader, introducing wines with names like Riki, Tini, Zoom, Zip, and Zest, following the fad for flavoured wines that lasted until the end of the decade even though some liquor boards refused to list them.

But such a product was not going to save a wine industry that was encountering headwinds of an ever-increasing strength. The change in consumer taste for dry table wines for use with meals and on social occasions - with Ontario's efforts faring badly by comparison - had resulted in a significant increase in listings in the LCBO of imported brands, a trend that would continue to strengthen until imports heavily outnumbered Ontario wines in the ever-expanding LCBO retail system (in 1969 there were 210 Canadian wines and 417 imported wines listed in Ontario), although Ontario sales still dominated at 73% of the market with imports at 27%). Eventually this would eat into the market share of local wines and reduce this so dramatically that it would leave us as the only wine-producing country in the world that does not consume predominantly its own domestic wines.

And, just as worrisome, was the increasing public criticism of our native wines, seemingly initiated by wine 'gurus' who found our traditional wines, stigmatized by their 'foxy' parentage, unacceptable to their palate. This was not just a display of our typical Canadian 'inferiority complex' when it comes to local products (except for maple syrup or Canadian whisky) but a festering fashion to put down local wines in light of the perceived superiority of imported brands. And, unfortunately, there were not enough French hybrids or vinifera yet planted in the province – by 1966 the "Seibels" as they were called, represented just 10% of Niagara plantings - to make significant commercial quantities of 'new' wines which could provide any alternative.

Adding to winery concerns was the increasing amount of 'homemade' wine that was being made mainly by an ethnic population that had burgeoned after the war, people who were used to wine with their meals and on social occasions, and preferred their own wines, usually made with vinifera grapes imported from California like Alicante or Zinfandel, to table wines made from domestic grapes like Concord, Elvira, and Niagara. Estimates for the amount of product turned into such wine ranged from 50 percent to 100 percent of the tonnage used by the commercial wineries. The industry could do nothing about this, only observe the considerable volumes involved and their impact on Ontario wine sales.

In spite of this difficult environment, Ontario's wineries continued to sell millions of gallons of wine, 8,406,720 gallons in Canada in 1970, which represented a 10% increase over 1969. Since 1965 the average annual growth rate in sales stood at an impressive 8.1% with the average price of a bottle of wine about $1.20-$1.40, the same as the minimum hourly wage at that time.

Ontario wine was successfully exported to countries far and wide including the United States, Britain, the Caribbean, Japan, and even Europe. The LCBO was continually adding new stores to the mix opening 362 outlets by 1966 and the restrictive attitude of government to alcohol (an early example of 'social engineering') was slowly changing to a more consumer-oriented sales philosophy, including opening the first self-serve liquor store in 1961 along with abolishing the sales permits which had been in place for 34 years. More good news for the wineries was the rapid growth in the per capita consumption of wine by our 20 million Canadians from about one bottle in 1964 to four just six years later.

Thomas Comery, President of Chateau-Gai Wines in 1965, while noting the competition from home winemakers, was happy to remark that his winery was having difficulty in meeting the demand for some of its more popular brands. On the surface you could say that the corporate nature of our wine industry was one of success, although with consumers developing an ever-increasing awareness of the world of wine, reflected in increasing sales of imported wines, some were beginning to question the long-term sustainability of an industry with an aching Achilles heel – American hybrid grapes!

In the Grape Marketing Board Annual Report for 1970, Chairman Ron Moyer outlined two themes that would become more and more important for the future success of the Ontario Grape and Wine Industry. He explained the need to make the public more aware of the industry and the steps being taken by the Board through a public relations program to better educate consumers and enhance the sales of Ontario wine. This was needed in light of LCBO policies that were developing into an advantage for imported wines with more listings and displays for imports helping to increase their market share. At the same time the government had refused to allow any increase in the number (51) of winery-owned retail stores. Moyer well knew that any downturn in Ontario wine sales would mean reduced grape purchases by the wineries and this would have a disastrous impact on his grape growers.

The Grape Growers were also concerned about the production of grapes now exceeding the processing demand and the threat of a looming surplus of labrusca varieties. Wineries were insisting that by 1974 the demand would exceed supply but the Growers wanted the wineries to tell them which grapes they were going to require to ensure that there would be no surplus of anything. While commenting that relations between grape growers and processors were quite good, Moyer made it clear that they had to work to-gether for their mutual benefit – a hint of the tension that existed in the business between sellers and buyers of a crop that varied so much in volume from year to year.

For 1970 the corporate wineries processed 42,445 tons of grapes into wine, an amount representing 67% of the total harvest with the balance taken by other food processors and domestic needs and a significant amount exported to the U.S. (6,775 tons). Moyer feared a diminishing trend in these latter uses would soon see a surplus of grapes remaining and serious problems for the province's grape growers. His point was that the wineries and the growers were part of the same team facing a menacing opponent in imported wines (with government regulators acting as the bureaucratic referee and consumers involved as spectators wanting to be entertained) and the game was in danger of being 'lost'.

Yet even in 1970 the majority of Ontario's grape growers were still convinced that there would always be a market for their labruscas with the result that many simply refused to consider planting French Hybrids or Viniferas, the so-called 'preferred' varieties. With a better crystal ball, they would have known that within 20 years their labrusca vineyards would be 'obsolete', with consumers almost completely by-passing the wines those grapes were producing, but at this very moment they had good fortune on their side. A brand-new wine style was about to hit the shelves and it was destined to become the most successful labrusca-based product ever developed in Ontario and would help save the Ontario corporate wine industry!

Ironically, the wine was initiated by Andres Wines, a business that had had such a difficult time with the government in obtaining a winery licence only a few years before. And it could not have come at a better time for the wine industry, now drowning in Concord after a huge harvest in 1971 of 84,000 tons. As Keith Wiley, Chairman of the Ontario Grape Growers' Marketing Board admitted at the time, "Until Andres hit the market our wines were dead"! While that was hardly true, it was also a fact that Andres' arrival in Ontario was a godsend for the industry.

In Ontario, the new wine style had actually been initiated by the Fred Marsh Winery in Niagara Falls at the beginning of the 1950's. This winery was attempting to produce a sparkling wine at the low alcohol level of only 7% but was having difficulty with the stability of the product. Bright's Winery bought out Marsh in 1953 and inherited the evolving concept, giving the stability issue to Adhemar de Chaunac to resolve successfully. Bright's then introduced the new wine as their 'Winette', which sold in half-bottles and as Du Barry Sparkling Vin Rose. The products were inexpensive to make, and the government was convinced by Bright's to reduce the champagne tax of $2.50 per gallon to just 25 cents in consideration of their low alcohol level. The idea proved to be a winner, especially as Bright's would have the market to themselves for several years.

In the 1960's Andres Wines in B.C. was the first in Canada to make a wine called 'Cold Duck', a name that was proving popular in the United States with huge sales, a kind of sparkling burgundy with 12% alcohol. The name was based on a 200 year-old German legend that credited a Prince of Saxony with creating a beverage from the dregs of unfinished wine bottles mixed with other wine with the blend given the name 'Cold End'. It became the practice in Bavaria then to mix cold sparkling burgundy with previously opened bottles of wine, and since someone had too much of this to drink, he pronounced the German word 'end' as 'duck', which is quite similar. The name 'duck' stuck forever as 'Cold Duck'!

In Ontario, Chateau-Gai produced a sparkling blend of two labrusca grapes, Concord and Elvira, in 1971 which they also called Cold Duck and which was taxed at $2.50 per gallon as a Champagne style. Andres had made a similar product but with only 7% alcohol called Chante that their winemaker in B.C., Guy Baldwin, had developed in 1967, creating a red, a white, and a rose. The new Andres winery in Ontario was inspired to create a similar product of their own by blending the red and the white Chante which were made from Concord and Niagara grapes. The resulting blend would be taxed at only 25 cents a bottle because of its lower alcohol – an immense benefit to the winery. The new wine was called simply "Baby Duck", a true inspiration as it would turn out!

Introduced in 1971 with some clever marketing, it was an astounding, over-night success. Aimed initially at young people 'graduating' from pop to their first wine, this inexpensive, 5% sweetness, 7% alcohol, frizzy, purple concoction with a tiny yellow duckling on the label eventually took over the entire market. By 1974 Andres' Baby Duck was achieving sales of 9 million bottles annually, 1 out of every 24 bottles of wine sold, and by the time its sales peaked in 1983 it had reached over 80 million bottles becoming the top selling wine in all of Canada two years in a row.

To-day, those who recall 'Baby Duck' will do so with nostalgia and a chuckle, for it is difficult to explain the appeal of a wine which few serious wine drinkers would ever admit to drinking…but did! Certainly, the giddy nature of the wine added nothing to the unfortunate reputation of the corporate wine industry for derision and snorts of laughter were common at the mere mention of the name Baby Duck for years. But more Canadians on a per capita basis than anyone else on earth were drinking and, obviously, enjoying it at the time. Even to-day, while Baby Duck no longer 'quacks' as loudly as it once did, almost 50 years after its introduction to the market, it continues to sell in significant volumes! (the winery is now known as "Peller Estates" and the production formula has changed but the wine will always remain Andre's Baby Duck!)

Perhaps its major claim to fame was the trend it initiated for what came to be called 'refreshment' or 'contemporary' wines by the industry (or 'pop' wines to everyone else since the wine opened with a 'pop' and tasted like pop). Most of the other wineries followed the leader and created a plethora of similar products with a menagerie of copy-cat names like Gimli Goose,

Pussycat, Luv-a-Duck, Fuddle Duck, Baby Bear, Baby Deer, and Pink Flamingo, in a wide range of colours. Per capita Canadian consumption increased to 7 bottles by 1977 while total wine sales in Canada shot up from 1968 to 1977 from 100 million dollars to 300 million dollars, a phenomenal increase. These sales propelled the corporate industry through the decade, sustaining the wineries and keeping growers in the labrusca business happy while diverting attention away from other developments that were causing a stampede away from the traditional market.

Unfortunately, the industry was really only ducking the inevitable!

CHAPTER FIVE

From prose to poetry: Embracing change in Ontario winemaking

"A global revolution in wine began in the 1970's. Countries that had made mainly mediocre wine began to produce quality wine that could compete on world markets….The winds of change that began to rustle the leaves in vineyards around the world stirred the foliage in Ontario too." Rod Phillips, Ontario Wine Country.

"Labrusca wines? My God, they're terrible. I had a glass on the train from Montreal and my arm nearly fell off." Christopher Plummer, 1974.

'Ontario Wines? Hah! I wouldn't even wash my car with them." Satirist and Comedian, Henry Gibson

"In a chronically leaking boat, energy devoted to changing vessels is more productive than energy devoted to patching leaks." Warren Buffet

The 1970's will undoubtedly be remembered as the most amazing decade of all in the history of Ontario winemaking, ten years when our wines could be said to have changed direction from rejected to respected. Coinciding with the arrival of the 'refreshment' wines came a turmoil of other industry activity featuring "new" at every turn, wineries, winemakers, vineyards, grapes, wines, and numerous changes in regulations. So many things happened so quickly, unusual for an industry focused on the business of agricultural where changes usually take time to implement, that by the end of the decade it would be appropriate to talk of a paradigm shift in our winemaking. This has been called the 'watershed' decade for our grape and wine industry, for by 1980 it would be well on its way to re-inventing itself. And for myself, it was truly a fortunate co-incidence that this was also the time that Ontario wine and winemaking became a major part of my life.

During the 1960's, like many of my generation, for my first serious exposure to 'wine' I had found an abundance of tasty offerings from Europe that were pleasing to our palates as we 'graduated' from the soft drinks of our teenage years to the much more intriguing tastes of wine. This meant a visit to our local LCBO outlet to purchase social wines like Mateus, Castelvetro, Black Tower, Blue Nun or more 'serious' wines from France that were not that much more expensive. We had little interest in most of the offerings from Ontario wineries until the arrival of Baby Duck and company! Thinking I needed a hobby as a diversion from my occupation as a Latin and French teacher and knowing that I enjoyed wine, in 1970 my wife Charlotte gave me two winemaking kits for Christmas complete "with instructions for little engineers" and suitable equipment, and I became a 'winemaker', i.e. an amateur winemaker. I quickly learned that (a) you cannot fool with Mother Nature and (b) there is only one way to make wine – the right way – which involved a little more science than was at my disposal. The resulting wines were predictable - cloudy, unstable, and far from drinkable. Such was my rather naive initiation into an activity that would in short order take over my life.

When my next effort to make wine from Concord grape juice only resulted in another 'failure', I vowed to do better by learning more about 'wine' from its history to the science of winemaking itself. My next steps led me to join a local wine club, the Hamilton Wine Circle, a group of welcoming individuals with a similar interest in all things vinous who belonged to a province-wide association of forty clubs known as Amateur Winemakers of Ontario (A.W.O.). How I looked forward to our collegial monthly meetings where we would taste and comment on each other's most recent creation along with some 'professional' products. Sooner than I realized I was inspired to begin the serious study of grapes and wine, tasting through the LCBO shelves and reading whatever seemed appropriate. I ventured to Niagara to talk with growers and met Bill and Helen Lenko in Beamsville who became good friends and a future source of premium grapes. I quickly learned the difference between our old labrusca grapes and the 'new' French Hybrids and Viniferas and I began to realize that the 'new' varieties could make very decent wine, especially grapes like Chardonnay, Merlot, and Gewurztraminer which the Lenko family was growing.

As a club we planned visits to wineries in New York State on weekends and trips to the annual A.W.O. convention to meet like-minded 'oenophiles'. By the mid-1970's my interest had evolved into a passion and then obsession to know everything about winemaking. Unknown to myself was the fact that other wine enthusiasts were planning on starting their own wineries to take advantage of changes in the industry driven by the availability of the new grapes that had the potential to make wine which consumers were eager to try.

In the 25 years since the end of World War II, French Hybrid varieties had developed from the first few vines imported by Bright's Wines for their own experimental use into an ever-increasing percentage of vines planted in Ontario vineyards. At first, growers had been unwilling even to consider planting these grapes as they had a market already established for what they were growing but after on-going experimentation and further learning they gradually began to realize that 'the Seibels' and even some vinifera varieties could grow well in our environment and be a sound investment. Thus, by 1970, a survey of our vineyards would have shown that there was now an amazing variety of different grapes available for winemaking where, before World War Two, there had only been a small number of different native American vines. To be sure, many growers still depended on the older varieties for their living, but plantings now also included numerous French Hybrids, a much smaller number of Vinifera varieties, and additional new hybrids that had been developed by the scientists at the Horticultural Research Station in Vineland.

Many growers continued to avoid planting viniferas in spite of the higher prices they were bringing as there was still considerable doubt about their ability to grow successfully here, a belief that was reinforced by some of the research scientists in Vineland who were skeptical about their future. But there were increasing plantings of Riesling, Chardonnay, and Gamay, that would soon offer opportunities for the wineries. There was considerable support for most of the French Hybrids which were growing well and did offer much better winemaking potential than grapes like Concord or Niagara although these same French Hybrids had recently been banned from table wine production in France. Vinifera growers in the 1950's had convinced everyone there that they made wine which was a poor substitute for their traditional grapes. This was not yet an issue in Ontario since neither Vinifera vines nor French Hybrids had been grown in any meaningful way here in the past and no one at this point could really forecast what the future had in store.

Several of the more popular French Hybrids had already been given names in France and these would be used by our industry as well including Baco Noir (Baco 1), Marechal Foch (Kuhlmann 188-2), L'Aurore (Seibel 5279) or Aurora, Seyval Blanc (Seyve-Villard 5276), Chelois (Seibel 10878), and Chambourcin (Joannes-Seyve 26-205). Seven other varieties which were growing successfully here also received names in 1970 from the American Finger Lakes Wine Growers' Association including Rosette (Seibel 1000), Chancellor (Seibel 7053), Verdelet (Seibel 9110), and Cameo (Seibel 9549). When the Canadian Wine Institute voiced an objection to the naming process, after discussions with the Americans, it was agreed in 1972 to change the name Cameo to De Chaunac, in honour of Adhemar de Chaunac's contribution to our winemaking, while retaining all the others. The major varieties now had the credibility of a name and this allowed the growers to identify more efficiently what they were growing and provided the wineries with appropriate names for any new varietal wines.

Rather than promote Vinifera at this time or even individual French Hybrids, the Horticultural Research Station scientists preferred to attempt to create their own new varieties, crossing French Hybrids with the hardy traditional American Hybrids in the hopes of developing "near vinifera" style grapes that would produce more tonnage, make better wine with less of a 'labrusca' character, and be sustainable in the challenging Ontario climate. After WW II, they created several new varieties and introduced many of them in the 1960's with names beginning with "V" for Chateau Vee (the HRIO experimental 'winery' name) – eg. Vintage, Veeport, Ventura, Veeblanc, Vincent, and Vivant. Although some of the Vineland creations were planted successfully in Niagara vineyards, mainly Veeport and Vincent, they failed to generate a lot of interest within the industry and would not be important in taking our viniculture in a new direction.

Ironically, one of the creations which was not well received in Ontario, would later go on to become a top-quality grape in Nova Scotia where it has helped establish a solid wine industry there under the name 'Acadie Blanc'!

There is a saying that 'real wine is red wine', a maxim that the local wine industry, both growers and wineries, accepted at face value. Concord had predominated historically as the grape of choice with the result that Ontario red wines in the past outnumbered whites five to one. Although it's percentage of vineyard vines was now falling from a high of over 70%, Concord would continue to be heavily planted through the 1970's and have an important role to play in our winemaking for several more years. In 1979, for example, Ontario processors purchased 23,414 tons of Concord, almost 3000 more tons than 10 years previous, an amount which represented 39% of purchases as the primary grape. But through the 70's there had often been unfortunate surpluses of the grape, a concern for the Grape Marketing Board which had been obligated to buy them for conversion into Brandy at Rieder Distillery in Grimsby (founded 1973) or into grape concentrate and juice. As well, the Ontario Government had agreed in 1975 to help growers remove up to 3,000 acres of labrusca grapes over 3 years and replant with 'preferred varieties'. The support was labelled the Ontario Grape Conversion Assistance Program and it offered growers 5 years free of interest and principal payments, the time needed for new vines to develop a good crop.

Unfortunately, growers were slow to take up the assistance as labrusca grapes continued to be of value in 'refreshment' wines, an ongoing success story for the corporate wineries, and were often in demand for export to the United States. But no one could dispute the significant downward trend in sales of Ontario ports and sherries, wines made from these grapes, whose sales from 1969 to 1974 had fallen from 67% of the market to less than 40% and a similar disappointing trend for Ontario wine sold to other provinces, with a decline of 32% in volume by 1979 from 1969. And in 1973, for the first time ever, sales of imported wine in Canada, after 10 continuous years of increases, surpassed sales of all Ontario products. These were clear indications that something was amiss, even though purchases of American hybrids in 1979 still represented 80% of processed grapes. Both growers and wineries could sense that time was beginning to catch up to the labruscas and it was now a matter of when, not if, they would become history.

During this same period, production of French Hybrid grapes had increased from just over 9% to almost 17% with the leading variety being the red De Chaunac at 4,727 tons in 1979. Growers had opted to plant far more red varieties than white, with the result that wineries were obligated to pay a bonus for white grapes. At this time consumers were showing a definite preference for white wines and our industry found itself with too many red grape varieties in the ground. De Chaunac had been so heavily planted (some called it the "new Concord") that its price was only $275 a ton in 1979 compared to $330 for most other red varieties and $440 a ton for whites which now included Seyval Blanc, Vidal, and Aurora, in addition to the longer established Verdelet. Some wineries saw an opportunity in the pricing and made valiant efforts to make a white wine out of De Chaunac by 'decolorizing' the juice and blending it with a variety of white grape juices.

It is more difficult to obtain accurate information on vinifera production in the 1970's as the Grape Marketing Board did not list varieties separately but in 1979 there were approximately 1426 tons of viniferas sold to processors from a total of 59,665 tons (just 2.4%), representing approximately 100,000 cases of wine. For an entire industry this was not a lot of wine even if it represented a considerable increase in volume from the beginning of the decade and with the hope of more to come from ever-increasing plantings. Growers were becoming more comfortable trying Chardonnay, Riesling, and Gamay, and a few even attempted to grow very cold-sensitive varieties like Gewurztraminer, Merlot, and the first Cabernet Sauvignon grapes in Ontario, planted by John Marynissen who would eventually open his own winery in Niagara-on-the-Lake. While the word 'vinifera' associated with Ontario winemaking was drawing more and more attention, who would ever have thought at this time that this species would come to dominate our industry in just 20 more years!

It is interesting to note that over 50 different grape varieties, now divided into 10 classes for pricing purposes, were purchased in 1979 by the wineries, a dramatic increase over the relatively small number of different labrusca grapes used in the past.

By this time, the corporate wineries had already seized on the momentum of the new grape varieties and were experimenting with small lots of both Hybrid and Vinifera table wines in addition to their refreshment wines and various sherries and ports, putting one foot forward into the future while still keeping the other foot firmly anchored in the past. The first table wines to appear on the market were blends featuring a combination of American and French Hybrid grapes or 100% French Hybrids to which they attached a proprietary name, like Bright's popular Manor St. David's Claret, Burgundy, and Sauterne wines or Chateau Gai 'Seibel' (De Chaunac and Chelois). After 1972, with varietal names now available for the most important hybrids, some of the wineries now introduced new, vintage-dated varietal wines, the first to appear as such in Ontario.

Chateau Gai, which was destined to become the leading seller of these varietals, introduced a vinifera red made by their French winemaker Paul Bosc as early as 1973 labelled Gamay Beaujolais (for both Chateau Gai and Chateau Cartier) and would follow them up with a varietal Marechal Foch they described as Canadian Burgundy. Chateau Gai, believing that future winemaking would target higher class table wines, started a $45 million winery expansion program in 1975 to accommodate the increasing production of their premium vinifera and vinifera hybrids. And it was Chateau Gai that took the lead in formulating "Ontario Wine Standards" for its own business while encouraging the rest of the industry to 'sign on'. Progress in this area would come but it would take a few more years.

Most consumers at this time would probably not be aware of the significance of such wines, made from grapes they had never heard of before, but this was indeed an exciting time for those who had been following the development of the new grapes. I well remember the first releases by Bright's beginning in 1974 which they called their 'chateau wines', outfitted with rather garish, bright red and green labels that had the wine name in very bold print. The first wines to appear included Baco Noir, Marechal Foch, Chelois, and De Chaunac, all red wines, and the white Verdelet. These were followed in 1975 by limited releases of two whites, Aurora and Gewurztraminer, the first in Ontario, as well as a Villard Noir and in 1976 by a truly excellent Pinot Chardonnay. Realizing the importance of these wines to the future of their business, Bright's reduced their purchase of Concord grapes by 50%, once the mainstay of their core brands, deciding to produce these specialized wines in greater volume.

All the other corporate wineries, with the exception of Turner's which would go out of business in 1977, developed their own varietal programs as well. Andres would have a series of 'Richelieu' wines including a Marechal Foch and a De Chaunac, while Dieter Guttler, the German winemaker at Jordans produced a wonderful 'Selected Riesling". Barnes Winery would develop their 'Ontario Country' series and a varietal Chelois they preferred to label S-10878 while London Winery introduced their 'Bellevista' line with a solid De Chaunac.

In Ontario it is customary to talk about the activities of the grape growers and the wineries as a single industry because of the close relationship that exists between grapes and wine. Historically, however, growers and wineries had often been at odds, usually over the price of grapes, and government had to step in on occasion to ensure that growers received a fair price for their product. After 1947, with the creation of the Ontario Grape Growers' Marketing Board (OGGMB) to protect the interests of growers, a system of annual price negotiations was started to establish minimum prices and price increases and help ease the tensions involved in the buying and selling process. Gradually the concept would develop that 'wines are made in the vineyard' and that the quality, rather than the quantity of grapes was the most important issue, putting pressure on growers to re-think their methods of operation and become more efficient. Wineries, who in the past could use additions of sugar and water to 'ameliorate' the quality of their juices, were now paying more attention to the actual quality of the raw material, insisting on minimum standards for grapes, including sugar levels and ripeness, and monitoring the number of tons per acre while agreeing to pay prices that would still allow them to compete against imported wines. Growers needed wineries to continue to sell their wines in order to ensure annual grape purchases at fair prices and hopefully without any crop surplus.

Urging co-operation between the two parties was the theme that Ron Moyer, Chairman of the OGGMB, repeated in almost every Annual Report through the 1970's, attempting to remind both sides that grape prices had to be fair for everyone and that there needed to be mutual understanding and trust in the relationship, which would take precedence over self-interest, or there would be no grape and wine industry. In theory this made a lot of sense, but in reality, the list of obstacles in the way of achieving this two-part harmony was lengthy.

Government could, and did, occasionally raise taxes on the sale of wines which always threw a curve in the way of marketing with a negative impact on sales. And the matter of 'importing' wine from one province to another, an artificial barrier enforced by provincial liquor boards, was a long-standing issue that no one outside of government could understand or find a way to change and this resulted in challenges in selling wine freely across Canada. There were even times when various levels of government refused to serve 'Canadian' wine at official functions because someone in authority feared embarrassing the government by serving wine that was considered less than 'world class'. This resulted in constant efforts by wineries and the OGGMB with governments to be more receptive to the 'local product', and especially in the LCBO system to be more proactive in promoting it. On occasion these efforts sponsored by the Winery Association and by the

OGGMB paid off, but on some issues there never seemed to be progress. The request to increase the number of winery-owned retails stores from the historical 51 continued to be denied although 20% of Ontario wine was sold in this market and the wineries persisted in vain in trying to develop it further.

And then there was the consumer whose tastes could change much faster than growers could replant grapes. This had already been shown in the enormous upswing in table wine sales and preferentially imported table wines by consumers who were buying into the 'if it's imported, it's got to be good' concept with its serious impact on local wine sales. Even though sales of all wines in the province by 1979 had increased significantly from 1969 when Ontario had almost 73% of the market, by 1979 wine sales in the province showed the imports now leading with just over 50%. Near the end of the decade, Ontario wine sales were increasing again after the LCBO initiated a program to delist poor selling imports and offer more shelf space to Ontario wines, but these increases paled in comparison to imports which showed an almost 400% increase in sales over the ten years!

In spite of continuing optimism in the industry, the trend was certainly not Ontario's friend and with the LCBO believing it was obligated to entertain wines from every wine region around the world, there seemed little hope of reversing it. From the 1960's the industry had laid the 'blame' for increased sales of imports at the feet of the LCBO, which insisted on offering importers opportunities, displays, and shelf space in Ontario stores that our wines did not receive in other countries - a theme that would continue to be played regularly while our wineries themselves conveniently ignored the preferential difference that existed in government mark-ups. At that time, the mark-up on Ontario produced wine stood at only 37% compared to 95% on wine from other regions in Canada and 117% on imported wines, a striking disparity that angered importers as it afforded a tremendous price advantage to all 'local' products. But this was still the 1970's and government was able to 'get away with' such pricing because our industry continued to complain about cheaper labour costs elsewhere in the world and the dumping of inexpensive product into Ontario or subsidies provided to benefit foreign wineries by their governments.

In truth, nothing in the grape and wine business is the same from one year to the next although it seems that there is always something to be concerned or complain about - which is especially valid for areas where Mother Nature plays a controlling role. In Ontario, the volume of the annual grape harvest can vary tremendously, as can the quality of grapes which are very weather-sensitive, throwing a wrench into the most meaningful obligations. A grower may plan to machine harvest his grapes and then end up with grapes that need to be hand-picked due to sour rot from excessive rain, a more costly and time-consuming process. And growers at harvest time live in fear of having unwanted grapes left hanging on their vines or having their grapes rejected by a winery for less than satisfactory quality. Wineries as well need healthy grapes and a dependable supply to satisfy their requirements.

To help alleviate the concerns of growers, the OGGMB had expanded its role to include the purchasing of surpluses in certain years to make grape concentrate and juices and brandy which could be sold later; but still there were times when not all grapes were sold. 1971, for example, produced a record crop of 84,175 tons that resulted in a surplus of 6,000 tons and 1976 generated again over 80,000 tons (when a 'normal' harvest by now was closer to 65,000 tons), leaving 4,000 tons of grapes hanging on the vines.

Demonstrating how fragile the life of a grape grower in Ontario can be, 1971 was followed by an extremely poor harvest of only 52,141 tons, a record short crop that not only caused immediate supply problems but would prove to have significant consequences for the entire wine industry in the future. The shortfall in raw material in 1972 provided the wineries with an opportunity to change the nature of Ontario winemaking, a chance to justify their case to use imported material to make 'Ontario wine'. This was not a precedent, for imported material had been allowed in local wines for four years near the end of the 1920's but importing had been outlawed after Prohibition in 1931 to protect the livelihood of Ontario grape growers. For over 40 years they had enjoyed some reassurance that their grape crop would 'find a home' each year while guaranteeing that all Ontario wine was 100% Ontario content.

Although many were not happy with the decision that was made, finally the growers acquiesced to the winery request to import grape concentrate to help deal with a shortage of raw material predicted by winery forecasts of increasing wine sales. There was a strict limit attached to the amount of concentrate allowed to be used for winemaking and this usage would be allowed for one year only, while at the same time it was agreed to create a Grape Development Program that would assist growers who were finding it difficult to fund additional plantings needed by the wineries. Significantly, the growers refused to extend the agreement in 1973 but this was a foot in the door for the wineries and in short order the door would be opened even further.

At times, the winemaking business takes on the character of a battlefield, with man pitted against the elements, or with growers at odds with wineries over pricing, or wineries struggling with the LCBO for shelf space, or with each other for market share, or with imported wines that take on the role of 'the enemy' of the industry as a whole in a 'them' versus 'us' scenario.

In the latter case, unfortunately, foreign wines had been winning the 'war' since the mid 1960's with their sales now surpassing local wines every year. It had taken some time for Ontario's corporate wineries to understand that the consumer was really the critical factor in all of this and that consumers had been demonstrating more and more a general lack of involvement with Ontario wines. The first sign was a striking movement away from traditional Ontario wines, the myriad ports and sherries and concoctions based on our labrusca grape varieties – a trend that meant far less demand for grapes like Concord which, surprisingly, continued to be planted in significant numbers. And just as surprising, swimming against the tide, the wineries continued to bring to market new sherries and ports through the 1970's.

A second trend was the love affair that had blossomed for imported wines of almost any kind but especially table wines which were considered so much 'better' than the local product. The wineries had tried to compete by creating both varietals and blends from the newer grape varieties but even by the mid 1970's there were simply too few of these grapes available to them to have an impact on the market.

In 1976, although faced with the second largest grape crop in history, the wineries purchased less than 55% of the harvest and more and more Concord grapes were destined for distilling into brandy. The real issue for the wineries was the lack of sufficient quantities of the 'preferred' varieties resulting in a shortage of the kind of products in demand by consumers. The wineries asked the government to consider allowing them to import raw material to make up for the shortfall in their requirements of 'better' raw material. The government responded with the Wine Content Act of 1976, to allow up to 15% grapes grown outside Ontario or imported wine or a combination thereof of a winery's total production to be used in blended products.

While this was hardly welcome news to the Grape Growers who naturally perceived it as a threat to their livelihood, the wineries indicated that their sales were increasing and that to take advantage of the 15% limit, they would have to continue to increase their purchases of Ontario grapes. There was the added proviso that the change would not reduce the use of Ontario grapes in their winemaking although any one winery product would now be able to contain up to a maximum of 30% imported material. As well, a new limit of 225 imperial gallons (950 litres), down from 250, was established as the maximum amount of wine that could be made from a ton of grapes – a small concession to the growers! On December 16, 1976, Bill 135 was passed approving the changes and it would stay in effect for 5 years, until the end of December,1981.

At the time, no one seemed too concerned that the new rules brought the meaning of the term 'Canadian' wine into question. Is a wine containing 30% imported material really a product of a particular wine region or country, a product that can be a source of pride for a winery, or is it simply a commodity, an alcoholic beverage in a bottle meant to generate revenue for the business? The answer would not be long in coming as almost every corporate winery began to develop new blends using the now available imported components. Winemakers were hired from around the world including Paul Bosc, Joseph Zimmerman, Dieter Guttler, and Ernst Fischer, bringing a true 'European' touch to the winemaking. Almost overnight the wineries presented new brands in imitation of popular French, Italian, and German wines, marketed with blatantly 'foreign' names and 'foreign' looking packages. Chateau Gai introduced 'Alpenweiss', a blend of California grapes and Seyval Blanc that became an immediate success when it won a tasting competition in 1979 over the top-selling Black Tower, while Jordan's found strong consumer acceptance with both 'Toscano' and 'Maria Christina'. In 1973 Barnes winery was still heavily invested in their sherries and ports which comprised 85% of their product line. Ten years later almost 90% of their wines could be considered table wines, a dramatic change, with 'Weinfest' and 'Beauvoir' leading the way. Not to be outdone, Brights came out with 'Entre-lacs', and a host of Germanic sounding names, 'Liebesheim', 'Warnerhof', and 'Baron Ludwig'. And Andres, still basking in the success of Baby Duck, achieved considerable success with 'Hochtaler', 'Auberge', and 'Domaine d'Or'.

Most of these wines contained 30% imported material and relied on the European-like brand name, not the name of the winery, to achieve sales. Paul Bosc from Chateau Gai appeared in television ads promoting his new wines telling us "We can change your mind!", and it worked. In truth, the quality of Ontario wine was perceived to improve and wineries now added another arrow in their portfolio quiver, with considerable volumes of import blends to go along with their new hybrid and vinifera products, in addition to all the other ports, sherries, sparkling, refreshment, and other labrusca products they continued to make.

Thus, by the end of the 1970's, Ontario corporate wineries, anxious to develop appealing table wines to compete with big-selling European brands, had seemingly found a way! Many Ontario consumers, impressed with the style and flavour profile of these new offerings, eagerly bought them, overlooking the fact they were not 100% Ontario products. Our government had come through with needed help for our wine industry inspiring the 'Blended in Canada' category, obviously more concerned with short-term substance than the optics of the solution. Indeed, at the time, few seemed aware or concerned that this might become a matter of credibility for an industry which still lacked real wine standards or an appellation system, or that 'blending' would come to be a divisive issue in the future, pitting new, small wineries and those advocating for authentic 'Ontario' winemaking against the established corporate wineries and their business needs.

As remarkable as this development was, coming along with the refreshment wines, and the exciting French Hybrid and Vinifera wines, and ever-increasing consumer wine consumption statistics (by 1978 this now stood at 7.5 bottles per person), they would all have to take a back seat to the most exciting and important change that our wine industry experienced in the decade – the arrival of the 'cottage' winery!

CHAPTER SIX

When dreams come true! Ontario's first 'cottage' wineries

"Perhaps it is not too much to hope that the best days of the specialist, the small individual wine maker producing superior wines for an increasingly sophisticated clientele, still lie in the future." William Rannie, "Wines of Ontario", 1978

"On that day Karl Kaiser swore he would never move to Canada, it would have been inconceivable that he and Donald Ziraldo would someday be regarded in the evolving wine industry of Ontario as critical to the ushering in of a new and irreversible change." L. Bramble, "Niagara's Wine Visionaries", 2009

"A vinifera vine is like a sexy woman: take her to bed with you but never marry her." Anonymous scientist from Bright's Wines.

The first 'wave' of cottage wineries in the decade --

- 1975 Inniskillin House Wines Inc. (later Inniskillin Wines Ltd.)
- 1975 Podamer Champagne Company (later Montravin – then Magnotta)
- 1977 Charal Winery and Vineyards (licence later sold to Magnotta)
- 1978 Chateau des Charmes
- 1979 Newark Wines (later Hillebrand/Trius)

Up until 1975 Ontario had never had a 'vintage' year in its wine history. Other than for the beginning and the ending of Prohibition and the creation of the Liquor Control Board of Ontario, for wine drinkers no date in our vinous history had ever really had any significance attached to it. But that was all changed on July 5, 1975, when two friends finally received their commercial licence to make and sell wine. Since 1930 there had been a government-imposed ban on the issuing of winery licences and so after 45 years a new licence could be considered a 'big deal' in its own right. But the arrival of this new winery in Niagara, named Inniskillin because it was located on land settled originally by a member of the Inniskillin Fusiliers after his service in the war of 1812, was particularly significant as it provided the first glimpse into what the future of Ontario wine could be, "ushering in irreversible change" as our original 'cottage' winery. This one winery blazed a path which others would be quick to follow in wave after wave of oenophiles driven by passion and ambition and inspired by wine's appeal to their intellectual curiosity.

While there had been many 'small' wineries in Ontario's past producing numerous wines of dubious quality, Inniskillin would come to define the term 'cottage winery' for the emerging wine industry as a quality-driven, limited production boutique making small lots of wine mainly from the newer French Hybrid and Vinifera varieties with a substantial amount of these grown by the winery itself. Unlike most corporate wineries, the winemaker, who was often the owner, stood out as the face of the business, in a sense the 'star' performer, who was always very accessible to consumers at the winery and at off-site events and tastings, pouring his own wines. This allowed the public to identify with the winery in a very personal way and helped the winery develop a loyal following of customers who propelled both the business and the entire industry to new heights.

Reading the fascinating story of Don Ziraldo and Karl Kaiser, the two men behind the name Inniskillin, as told by Linda Bramble in her profile of "Niagara's Wine Visionaries", one has to be amazed at the role that "chance" played in their ending as partners in a winemaking endeavour that would make an indelible impact on our wine industry. In 1969 Don Ziraldo, only 21 years old and still attending the University of Guelph, was running a family farm and nursery in Niagara-on-the-Lake with his brother Robert that sold fruit trees and grapevines. Donald's father had planted some French hybrids including Chelois and De Chaunac which were being sold to Chateau Gai. Karl Kaiser, 7 years older than Donald, was an economics teacher in Zistersdorf, Austria with no desire to live in Canada although he was about to marry a Canadian girl whose grandfather still lived in Austria. The chances of these two men with very different backgrounds ever meeting, never mind forming a successful partnership, were simply astronomical! But after the Russians occupied neighbouring Czechslovakia, Karl promptly decided to move to St. Catharines where his wife Silvia's parents lived – just a few vineyards away from Niagara-on-the Lake! Without the Russian threat, who knows if Karl would have ended up in Canada at all and it is likely then that there never would have been an Inniskillin! Looking back to-day one might even say that fate had intervened, providing a stepping-stone to the 'new' wine industry that was to come!

Just two years later, Karl met Donald when he went to the Ziraldo nursery to buy some French hybrid vines for his father-in-law's garden. They enjoyed a bottle of a homemade Chelois which Karl had brought along and discussed how different this wine was from the generally available Ontario red table wines. That meeting sparked the beginning of a friendship that would soon lead to a bold and surprising idea – their application for a winery licence. Donald, a dynamic entrepreneur, was growing the necessary French hybrid grapes and had a dramatic vision of a winery which would make the best wine possible from the newer grape varieties in Niagara while Karl brought a modicum of experience in winemaking from helping his wife's grandfather make wine in Austria, a love of good wine, and a keen desire to improve on Ontario winemaking. He quickly enrolled in a chemistry program at nearby Brock University to deepen his knowledge.

Fate again entered the picture with the arrival of a new Chairman of the LCBO, Major-General George Kitching, appointed in 1970 by then Ontario Premier John Robarts who was looking for a knowledgeable and able individual to improve the operations of the Board. Kitching had proven himself a charismatic and talented leader from his experiences in World War II and his selection would be fortuitous for all concerned, the LCBO, wine importers, and the Ontario wine industry. During his 6 years at the helm, he would increase the number of stores by almost 70% to 500 in the province, introduce wine 'consultants' in some stores, and increase LCBO profits considerably. Kitching quickly realized that consumers were looking for more table wines and believing that Ontario wineries could not yet compete, he promoted hundreds of new listings of European wines. The local wineries were not happy with Kitching but in short order they too were provided with a means to improve their situation when changes in the wine content regulations allowed them to import concentrate, grapes, and wine for use in blending with Ontario raw material to make better table wines.

In 1973, Kitching took another controversial step in providing a supporting hand-up to three individuals who were seeking to enter the Ontario wine industry, a Hungarian named Karl Podamer who wanted to produce European-style Champagnes from Ontario grapes and who received a sympathetic ear from Kitching because of his European background, and the duo of Karl and Don. The latter two had only recently had their initial application for a winery turned down at the LCBO but Kitching saw to it that it was put back on track, helping them secure a trial licence to produce up to 10,000 gallons in 1974 while providing expertise for them in acquiring financing and even helping them get started with some used oak barrels. It is sobering to think that if Kitching had not been at the helm of the LCBO providing this kind of support, these projects might never have seen the light of day and the future of Ontario winemaking might have remained solely in the hands of the corporate players. However, winemaking with these fresh faces was indeed set in motion and the rest of the story is history, as they say, or perhaps destiny!

The first Inniskillin wines were made in a rustic fruit packing shed at the nursery, a far cry from the larger corporate entities which were its peers, and in very limited quantities, 600 bottles each of Foch and De Chaunac and 5000 bottles of a blend of French Hybrids called Vin Nouveau, all red wines. In total that is just over 1000 gallons of wine, a tiny amount that would hardly draw the attention of the larger wineries and most consumers. But the wines sold out almost overnight and everyone suddenly seemed to become aware of this new 'cottage' winery whose reputation blossomed out of all proportion to its size. Inniskillin would quickly grow with the unprecedented demand, producing 12,000 gallons in its second year and reaching 70,000 gallons in 1977 just before moving into a magnificent new winery on the Niagara Parkway.

As a creative winemaker, Karl Kaiser would go on to introduce several wines that had not been made commercially in Ontario before including red wines from Chambourcin, Leon Millot, and Chelois, and white wines from Couderc Muscat, Welschriesling, Gruner Veltliner, and New York Muscat, all of which attracted even more interest in the winery while adding to Karl's personal reputation.

Inniskillin's arrival marked the birth of the 'boutique' wine industry while becoming the standard bearer for the 'new' Ontario industry. In short order, it would be followed by numerous other small wineries intent on producing high-quality, world-class wine that would bring attention to what had been a long-suffering industry. Inniskillin was the first to truly revolutionize the industry with the overall nature of its winemaking and for me to-day it seems that through the years Inniskillin has always remained 'first' for its style and leadership industry-wide and especially in the affection of Ontario wine drinkers, due to the fine wines produced by Karl and his successors and so brilliantly marketed by Don, and a great winery team led from the beginning by Deborah Pratt.

As a true 'founding father' of the modern Ontario wine industry, Karl would go on to an outstanding career acquiring numerous awards including an Order of Ontario achievement in 1993, an honorary doctorate from Brock University where he would teach in the COVVI Winemaking program, and Her Majesty Queen Elizabeth II's 50th Anniversary Golden Jubilee Award. Karl would pass away in November 2017 at the age of 76, but he will long be remembered for his unmatched impact on Canadian winemaking.

With all the excitement involving the arrival of Inniskillin in Ontario, almost lost in the aftermath was the opening of a second new winery in Beamsville in a sprawling, ground-level industrial type building on Ontario Street, close by the Queen Elizabeth Highway. A group of 13 Niagara area businessmen had formed a partnership with a third-generation Hungarian champagne maker named Karl Podamer to produce sparkling wine and had actually been given a provisional licence in 1973, a year before Inniskillin but it would take two years for the sparkling wine to be made. Their commercial licence would be granted on July 29, 1975, just a few days following the approval of Inniskillin's licence.

Karl Podamer's family had been making champagne in Hungary for half a century and Karl himself had worked in the family business since the mid 1920's after studying winemaking in France. After the winery was destroyed by bombing in the Second World War and with the Communist government in Hungary taking control of the winery when it was rebuilt, Karl emigrated to Canada where he met his partners and received his initial licence. Their intention was to produce 'Champagne' from Niagara grown Vinifera and French Hybrids and the better American hybrid grapes like Delaware and Dutchess which Karl proclaimed would be "the equal in every way of the best French champagne". The base wines would be made in 1000 gallon casks of white oak which were brought in from Austria as staves and assembled in the winery. Respecting the traditional French 'methode champenoise' style, the second fermentation would take place in bottles which would be riddled by hand in 'pupitres' and disgorged manually with a top-up of sugar, brandy, and wine, producing an authentic 'Champagne'. In all, Karl made several different wines, one varietal Chardonnay called Blanc de Blancs Brut, and blends named Brut, Extra Dry, Special Reserve, and a Rouge.

Although the wines were well made and of excellent quality, perhaps they arrived a little before their time and unfortunately the winery itself never received anywhere near the attention of Inniskillin. Before long, it ran into financial trouble and a new ownership led to a changed portfolio of wines although the Podamer brands were retained. An Austrian named Ernst Fischer, recently head winemaker at Chateau-Gai, and with champagne experience in Germany and in the Finger Lakes, became the new winemaker and in 1983 introduced new varietal table wines including a Foch, De Chaunac, and Seyval Blanc along with a blended red and white wine named Concerto bearing the new winery name Montravin Cellars.

However, even with well-funded owners and a talented European winemaker, Montravin was never able to shed its basic industrial image and convey a sense of the 'romance' of wine, and the Montravin wines failed to achieve the success needed to survive the challenging market in the latter 1980's. The winery would eventually be sold to the Magnotta family who continue to operate it successfully to-day.

Before the end of the decade, three additional new wineries would surface in Ontario, all family-run businesses growing their own grapes. The first of these started on a farm in south-western Ontario, a micro-climate favourable to grapevines, where grapes and wineries had once proliferated until their demise in the 1930's following Prohibition. Charlotte and Alan Eastman had pioneered trial vines as early as 1968 on their property near Blenheim in Kent County, eventually developing almost 100 acres of 30 different varieties of American and French Hybrids and Vinifera vines most of which had never been available to earlier growers. In his book "The Wines of Canada", John Schreiner commented that their efforts were "not for the romance about wines but because they wanted more profitable crops". However, in 1975, the Eastmans impressed the LCBO with their plans to make Estate Grown wines of exceptional quality and were granted a provisional licence. The business would be called Charal Winery and Vineyards, a combination of their first names. That first year they made only 2 wines, just 1000 gallons of a Dutchess and a Chardonnay, hoping for the best! Their Chardonnay won a gold medal and best of class in an American competition two years later when they received their commercial licence and they were off to an impressive start!

By 1982 they were up to 50,000 gallons and advertising on television, with a second retail outlet in London, Ontario, where they sold fifteen different wines. One of Alan's techniques was to ensure freshness in his grapes with the use of a crusher/destemmer attached to his mechanical harvester, a process which allowed crushed grapes to be pressed or directed to a fermenter almost immediately – the first Ontario winery to do so. White wines, which represented the preference of consumers at this time, comprised almost 85% of their production and included Chardonnay, Riesling, and Siegerrebe among Viniferas, Seyval Blanc and Vidal as French Hybrids, and Dutchess and New York Muscat as American Hybrids, while the reds were made solely from the French Hybrids Baco Noir, De Chaunac, Villard Noir, and Foch.

Unfortunately, continuing success as a small producer far from the main Toronto market even with a range of quality wines proved an elusive target and the winery would eventually close its doors. In 1989 the Magnotta family purchased the Eastman's licence in order to facilitate the development of their own operation north of Toronto, recycling an older licence to save the time and red tape involved in applying for a new licence. The fate of the winery would have disappointed Major Kitching who had believed that wineries based on vineyards of their own would all succeed (a requirement for any winery starting to-day), but it has become a truism in the Ontario wine industry that it is harder to maintain a winery profitably in our highly regulated environment than it is to start one.

The arrival of Chateau des Charmes in 1978 as Ontario's fourth cottage winery provides another intriguing example, similar to that of Inniskillin, of an unexpected and dramatic change in the life of an individual, in this case a man named Paul Bosc, which would lead to his playing a major role in the Ontario wine industry, a scenario that would never have happened without that life-altering event. Paul was born in the French territory of Algeria into a family which traced its involvement in vineyards and winemaking back 4 generations to 1840. He grew up working on the farm and attended agricultural school in Algeria before moving to Burgundy to attend the University of Dijon to develop his winemaking knowledge. When he returned to Algeria, he found a job working as the winemaker for a local co-operative where he might have remained forever, with no thought of ever coming to Canada.

However, six years later, Algeria was granted independence from France and the Bosc family lost everything, all their property and livelihood, in the ensuing government turmoil. They moved to France where, unfortunately, there was continuing hostility against the Algerian colonials and Paul was forced to make a decision that would alter his family's life. They moved to Quebec where he was able to find employment with the Quebec Liquor Board. In short order, as a result of the work he was doing dumping bottles of defective product, he decided to write a letter to Chateau Gai because of its French sounding name, informing them of a problem with their wine, adding that he could help them solve it. He was invited to meet the president of the winery, Alex Sampson, and made such a favourable impression that he was hired immediately. That was the beginning of a second very successful career in winemaking at Chateau Gai, then Ontario's third largest winery, one that would last 15 years with Paul becoming the chief winemaker. In 1975, complete with a definite French accent, he became the visible spokesman for the winery in a series of television commercials promoting their limited-edition hybrid and vinifera wines and a new product that he had developed called Alpenweiss, a tremendous retail success, while promising that there were "more good things to come".

Just three years later the irony of those words would resonate loud and clear, not so much for Chateau Gai as for the Bosc family itself as Paul decided to leave a well-funded corporate winery to establish vineyards and a family-run winery of his own in Niagara. This was truly a 'leap of faith' as Ontario wine was still not generally appreciated or considered fashionable, but Paul believed that he could grow vinifera grapes which would make very marketable wine. One could say that the achievement of this was a fitting tribute to his industry, talent, and foresight, but it might never have become a reality if Charles de Gaulle and French politics had not intervened in the life of one family living in Algeria!

By 1974 Paul had bought his first vineyard near Lockport in New York State where he and his two young sons, Paul-Andre and Pierre-Jean, were able to grow vinifera grapes including Cabernet Franc, Cabernet Sauvignon, and Merlot and where Paul could continue his experiments with grafting viniferas onto sustainable rootstocks, experiments he had started much earlier at Chateau Gai. Following that, with two partners he bought another vineyard on Creek Road in Niagara which he decided to underdrain and replant with vinifera vines provided to him generously by Chateau Gai from their experimental farm in Grimsby which he himself had planted. He was risking this third career on the largest planting of sensitive vinifera vines ever in the province, some 50 acres/20 hectares, after his earlier experiments in grafting had strengthened his belief that these would grow successfully for him. A winery was built on the property, a functional, non-descript concrete block building, to which they rather immodestly gave the name "Chateau des Charmes", hoping that one day their operation would indeed become much more impressive. The "Charmes" was inspired by their life in Algeria where they had owned a sea-side summer home they affectionately called 'Villa des Charmes'.

The initial wines from Chateau des Charmes were well-received, although Paul made only 3000 cases the first year and 6000 the second. He had planted not only more familiar varieties like Chardonnay and Riesling but also ones that were completely unknown here before this time including Savignin, Auxerrois, and Aligote, and his portfolio would attract consumers who were becoming more curious about new Ontario wines. With his previous television exposure, he was already a 'wine personality' and this helped establish his credibility, but it was his leadership role as an innovator which would set him apart from others in the industry and assure his future success.

Paul was the first to begin serious work on clonal selection using different clones of grape varieties, a type of mutation within a vine, and different rootstocks, in an attempt to discover the hardiest and most productive vines for our climate. In the early 1980's this project would lead to a significant government grant, the first of several that Chateau des Charmes would receive, in support of the innovative research he was doing and allow him to hire the ebullient Dr. John Paroschy, a research scientist, to continue with further experimentation. The winery would become a model for his iconic statement that there would be "more good things to come" in our wine industry. Included in a long list would be hundreds of award-winning wines, honours for Paul from both government (Order of Canada in 2005) and the wine industry (Winemaker of the Year in 2007), a number of 'firsts' like his installation of wind machines to protect vineyards in the winter, and a $6 million cutting-edge winemaking facility completed in 1994 on his York Road property, the fulfillment of a dream for a world-class Chateau-style winery! Under Paul's leadership, Chateau des Charmes has made its mark as a pillar of Ontario's modern wine industry, and this continues to-day with his son, Paul Junior, very capably directing the business.

Before the end of the 1970's Ontario's fifth boutique-sized winery would welcome the public to its cellar door in Niagara bringing the total number of wineries in the province to eleven. Joseph (Joe) Pohorly had planted French Hybrid and Vinifera vines on his 35 acre property on Highway 55 near Virgil in the late 1960's while at the same time teaching for the Lincoln Board of Education and developing a talent as a self-taught amateur winemaker. In 1979, with a desire to turn his hobby into a business, he made the decision to leave teaching for the risky life of an entrepreneur and opened Newark Winery– the name originally given to Niagara-on-the-Lake in the 1790's - producing 5,500 gallons of wine as Ontario's smallest winery. This was a true 'family' winery, with Joe as winemaker and his wife Betty and three teenage daughters wearing many other hats. One of their wines would acknowledge the contribution of his wife to the business with the name 'Elizabeth Rose', the first winery in the province to do this, setting an example for other wineries.

Over the next 3 years Newark's production increased dramatically to 13,000 gallons in 1980 and 47,000 gallons in 1982 with a portfolio that included French Hybrids like Foch, De Chaunac, Seyval, and Seyve-Villard, as well as Chardonnay and Gewurztraminer, and various blends called Wellington, Chevalier Rouge and Comtesse Blanc. Joe also experimented with 10 barrels of Sherry in two styles made from the American hybrid Agawam grape. Unfortunately, his growth came at a time of double-digit interest rates in Ontario, and this put his operations in jeopardy. When an offer to purchase his winery came from a German wine and spirits group called Scholl and Hillebrand, Joe decided to accept, staying on for a while as President and winemaker and proceeding to make one of Canada's first icewines in 1983 from frozen Vidal grapes. That year the winery would be renamed Hillebrand and would begin a transformation to a corporate entity aided by the participation of a Toronto wine merchant named Peter Mielzynski.

The purchase of Newark could be considered the first foray into our winemaking by a foreign buyer, a sign of interest in the potential of the wine industry which would intensify in the coming years and help propel it forward with the development of new vineyards and an influx of winemaking talent. Joe Pohorly would eventually find a new career operating a hotel in Niagara-on-the-Lake called the Colonel Butler Inn (which he designed himself). Then, to the surprise of many, he and his wife purchased an 8 hectare peach farm on Highway 55, not far from his original site, replanted with several varieties of grapes, and re-entered the wine business in 1996 as Joseph's Estate Winery with Kathie Reid becoming winemaker.

Capping off a fascinating career, Joe created a new company in 2003 called 'Joseph's Natural Products' to market a pure grapeseed oil which he created from grape pomace, the skins and seeds remaining after pressing the fermented grapes, inventing his own equipment to separate the seeds and press the natural oil. After selling the second winery in 2014, this true 'pioneer' of the modern Ontario wine industry, sadly passed away in September 2020, at the age of 88, after a life-long dedication to Ontario agriculture and winemaking.

As it turned out, the 1970's proved to be a decade of tremendous innovation in Ontario winemaking which, along with a more liberal attitude from government to the use and advertising of alcohol, changed forever the face of our local wine industry. In truth, by 1980, we had two wine industries, the established corporate companies still producing their traditional ports and sherries, refreshment or 'pop' wines, other labrusca-based products, a small number of French Hybrid and Vinifera wines, and the new category of import-Ontario "blends", as well as the five boutique wineries producing primarily limited edition, vintage-dated varietals.

The market was still dominated by the large wineries that purchased most of their grapes from numerous growers while the cottage winemakers focused on wines they made mainly from French Hybrids and Viniferas they were growing themselves. In a sense they were 'farm wineries' with the owner making the wine from his own grapes, a new development that would become the trend for winery development in the next decade. This would hi-lite the importance of the vineyard in the changing winemaking philosophy, introducing the concept that "wine is made in the vineyard" by an individual who was deeply concerned about the quality of his raw material and resulting wine, a belief which helped to create confidence for these wineries among consumers who became very loyal to them, identifying with the winemaker on a first-name basis. Such a development would become so significant for the success of the industry that the government would soon mandate that any new winery had to have a minimum of 5 acres of planted grapes in order to operate.

At this time in the industry, almost all the wineries, including the boutiques, ventured into the world of 'blends', wines made from imported material and Ontario grapes which any winery could legally produce. This change in regulations allowed the smaller operations to increase their production and help cash flow and gave the corporate wineries the opportunity to develop a broader portfolio of higher quality wines that enabled them to compete with imported products. When the blending regulation was introduced, no one seemed concerned that labelling these wines "Product of Canada" was somewhat misleading or that it would cause a backlash in the future from more chauvinistic consumers who wanted their Ontario wines to be 100% Ontario grape. As we shall see, this would become an issue in the 1990's and afterwards when new wineries were forbidden by law to make them while a small number of wineries in a 'grand-fathered' position were allowed to continue with less expensive "Cellared in Canada" blends that cannibalized sales of 'Ontario' wine.

However, at last Ontario was producing wines of a style and quality that were 'better' than before and appealed to more and more consumers, generating a happy buzz for what was yet to come in the industry. This positive feeling would soon translate into increased investment, more grower-winemakers and ever-improving wines. Such a frenzy of activity had left in its wake what 100 years of local winemaking had failed to achieve, a nascent wine culture and a sense of pride in Ontario wines, helping to end the ridicule and criticism that had shadowed our native wine industry and the excuses that had always been necessary for its deemed poor quality. The corner was turned in 1976 when well-known wine authority Hugh Johnson, who had left Canada out of his World Wine Atlas only a few years before, commented on his amazement at the change in our wines at a tasting in England. In particular, he singled out the 1974 Inniskillin Marechal Foch as his favourite, a comment which had a telling impact on industry sales, driving that grape to the forefront of consumer demand for several years.

Suddenly, leading Toronto restaurants like La Scala and the Windsor Arms and well-known chefs were ordering Ontario wine and charities were eager to have Ontario winemakers at their special events. It became the fashion for a number of individuals to come out of the closet as 'wine writers', with the likes of columnist Michael Vaughn of the Globe and Mail who now began to focus his attention on Ontario wines. Our first wine magazine, appropriately entitled "The Wine Press", became a required read. Author Tony Aspler would be motivated to produce the first book to discuss the 'new' industry and the first of several wine books he would write, entitled "Vintage Canada", which he dedicated "to all those who have found pleasure in Canadian wine…and to those who have yet to discover them".

So much had changed, almost overnight, and it was obvious that even better things were indeed to come!

CHAPTER SEVEN

The 1980's: A decade of expansion, excitement, and...anxiety!

"The industry is embarking on the most exciting phase of its history. Now it is up to the consumer to forget, or at least forgive, the past." T. Aspler, "Vintage Canada", 1983

"You worry about whether you can ferment the juice because it is so sweet... but, quite often it is a higher quality product (than German Eiswein). It hits you like a two-by-four!" Klaus Reif, reported in "Icewine – The complete story", John Schreiner, 2001

"Some degree of protection, through preferential pricing, will be necessary if our industry is to survive...however, as customers become more sophisticated, quality will become the most compelling factor." Professor J. Tanner, "Report of Ontario Wine and Industry Task Force", May 12, 1986

"Just as Ontario's wine industry seemed to be taking off in the 1980's with new wineries, vineyards newly planted with vinifera, and the new icewines, a new threat loomed – the 1989 North American Free Trade Agreement (NAFTA)." R. Phillips, "Ontario Wine Country", 2005

New Wineries: The "Sweet Sixteen" – 1980 – 1989 and original winemakers

1980: Colio, Harrow - Carlo Negri

1982: Reif, Niagara-on-the Lake - Ewald Reif, Klaus Reif

1983: Vineland Estates, Vineland - Dieter Guttler, Alan Schmidt

1983: Pelee Island, Kingsville and later, Pelee Island - Walter Strehn, Walter Schmoranz

1984: Culotta, Oakville (out of business, 1991) - Rudi Mueller, Bob Claremont

1985: Willowbank, Niagara-on-the-Lake (out of business 1987 with wine sold to Bright's and equipment sold to John Marynissen) - Ray Cornell

1985: Stoney Ridge Cellars, Vinemount - Jim Warren, Bryce Weylie, Brian Alexander

1986: Konzlemann, Niagara-on-the-Lake - Herbert Konzlemann

1986: Cave Springs, Jordan - Angelo Pavan

1987: De Sousa, Beamsville - Dieter Guttler

1987: Paul Masson, Beamsville (out of business, 1990) - Tom Challen

1988: Henry of Pelham, St. Catharines - Dave Hulley, Ron Giesbrecht

1988: Quai du Vin, St. Thomas - Roberto Quai

1989: Stonechurch, Niagara-on-the-Lake - Dave Hulley

1989: D'Angelo, Amherstberg - Sal D'Angelo

1989: Vinoteca, Woodbridge - John Follegot

By the early 1980's, new vineyards planted with Vinifera grapes were beginning to dot the landscape throughout Niagara and South-Western Ontario, confirming the trend for the wine industry's future. It had taken several years since the first plantings of Vinifera by a handful of courageous growers but now more and more people in different parts of the province, having become more knowledgeable about suitable rootstocks, spraying regimes, winter survival techniques, and vine management, were feeling confident that success with these sensitive vines in our 'cool climate' was indeed possible. Yet, after 3 years of very good harvests, 1981 would prove a deadly winter for them, killing countless vines in Niagara and indicating that there could still be problems attempting to grow this species as some of the sceptics owning labrusca vineyards were saying. Fortunately, an increasing number of individuals, some planning to open their own winery when their vines were ready, believed that planting viniferas was the only direction to go. A world-class wine industry, producing top-quality, varietal wines, would require nothing less!

The number of Vinifera vines planted in Ontario increased significantly in the early 1980's, from 5.6% of all vines in 1981, to almost 10% just five years later, a number that would continue to go up, with many established growers leading the way like Bill Lenko in Beamsville (Merlot, Chardonnay, Pinot Noir, Gewurztraminer), John Marynissen in Niagara-on-the-Lake (Merlot, Chardonnay, Cabernet Sauvignon), the Hunse family in Niagara-on-the-Lake (Riesling, Chardonnay, Morio Muscat), and the Pennachetti family on the Beamsville Bench (Riesling, Chardonnay), whose philosophy was simply "vinifera only!". This trend would continue to the end of the decade with grape growers John and Mary De Sousa on the upper Beamsville Bench and the Speck Family who took over an ancestral property on the rolling hills west of St. Catharines in 1985. After the untimely passing of their father, Paul Speck Senior, his three young sons, Paul Jr., Matt, and Dan, set out to make their winery, Henry of Pelham, one of Ontario's most successful operations. In short order, all these growers would add their names to the list of trailblazers and establish wineries of their own.

At the same time, some enterprising grower/winemakers came from Europe to Ontario in what might be called the 'Germanic invasion', purchasing and planting or replanting vineyards which would become the basis for new wineries here. Ewald Reif moved to the Niagara Parkway in 1977 from the Rheinpfalz and purchased a property near Inniskillin which he replanted with vinifera vines. Soon he would be joined by his nephew, Klaus Reif, who had trained as a winemaker at Geisenheim planning to take over winery operations in 1987. Two years later, Herman Weis, whose family owned a winery named St. Urban in the Mosel region of Germany and operated that country's largest private vine nursery, bought 200 acres below the escarpment in Vineland. This property, the future Vineland

Estates, was planted extensively in Riesling, including the Weis clone (21-B) which would become the source of many of Ontario's finest Riesling wines. Dieter Guttler would make their first wines in what at the time was an old barn, a very rustic foundation for the ultra-modern facility in place to-day.

In 1980 in Essex County, a winemaker from Austria named Walter Strehn, planted several different vinifera, mainly Germanic varieties, on 100 acres, a significant investment at that time, prior to opening Pelee Island Winery, renewing a winemaking tradition on the island that stretched back to the late 1860's, but this time with much better grape varieties. Herbert Konzelmann, whose family had been making wine in Wurttemberg, Germany since 1893, moved to Niagara-on-the-Lake in 1984 and purchased a 40 acre property fronting on Lake Ontario where he planted vines with the intention of opening a winery on the site. To-day his winery has become a 'must visit' facility, renowned especially for its icewines but also as our foremost producer of Pinot Blanc.

By 1987, these operations would be established successfully, bringing years of experience growing Vinifera vines to our developing cottage wine industry. Their impact would be felt in other ways as well, with their fresh thinking and a tremendously positive outlook that would lead to further innovation and help stabilize the industry in the challenging years that were waiting down the road. They planted a considerable amount of Chardonnay, which was becoming Ontario's premium white wine grape, but just as important, they also planted thousands of Riesling vines and a variety of other vines new to Ontario, like Kerner, Pinot Blanc, and Zweigelt, adding to an expanding industry portfolio of Vinifera grapes.

In South-western Ontario along the north shore of Lake Erie, where once many of Ontario's labrusca grapes had flourished, numerous new plantings of 'preferred varieties' would confirm the previous efforts of grower and winery owner Allan Eastman in renewing a local wine industry. A group of Italian businessmen headed by Enzo De Luca opted to develop a vineyard in Harrow, near Windsor, that would become the site of Colio Wines in 1980. Their business set the example of an "Italian focus", with a talented winemaker from Italy named Carlo Negri dedicating himself to making good quality commercial wines aimed at an 'average consumer'. Mention has been made of Walter Strehn and the extensive Pelee plantings which inspired other individuals to do the same. A teacher and amateur winemaker named Sal D'Angelo planted a vineyard just east of Amherstberg in 1983 prior to leaving teaching and opening his winery in 1989. In St. Thomas, another amateur winemaker named Roberto Quai took over a vineyard planted by his father in 1968 and opened a small winery to serve his local community. Others would quickly follow making it possible for Ontario to establish a second official vineyard and winery region in addition to the Niagara Peninsula, that would be called appropriately "Lake Erie North Shore".

Aside from the European winemakers who had the confidence to establish a winery in the new environment, the others in this group of sixteen who made the decision to invest in the industry each had their own motivation propelling them forward. At this time Ontario wines still enjoyed a preferential mark-up over imported wines, and this edge could be deemed a financial incentive for opening a winery, but in truth this business still existed very much in the shadow of its unfortunate past, and when it came to sales, many Ontario consumers were still definitely prejudiced against the local product.

Considering the significant investment required to plant vines and wait 3 or 4 years at further expense for them to produce, the restrictive control of all aspects of the alcohol business by various governments, and the challenging competition from the established corporate wineries as well as imported wines, it is a wonder that there was so much boutique winery activity in the province. But there was a definite feeling that the labrusca industry was in decline, along with an overwhelming optimism as well that a 'new' wine industry was very much alive, and no one was aware of any immediate threats on the horizon. Much to the surprise of everyone in the business, especially those who started in the late 1980's, this optimism would be challenged and converted to pessimism before the end of the decade.

I am sure that many of them, like myself with Stoney Ridge, were too pre-occupied with their own business to indulge in any negative thinking. As well, from my own experiences in amateur winemaking, I knew that good wine, certainly an improvement on many of the offerings from the larger wineries, could be made with the newer grape varieties. While I knew very little about viticulture and did not grow any grapes myself, since the mid-1970's I had become familiar with many of the available French Hybrids and Vinifera as an amateur winemaker, buying them from many independent growers in Niagara. My plan was to continue teaching while operating a tiny, 'hobby' winery with my wife Charlotte, and partners Bryce and Jennifer Weylie, who were growing grapes on their farm in Vinemount, a small community on top of the escarpment near Stoney Creek and Brian Alexander, a fellow amateur winemaker. It is also fair to say that my interest in winemaking had become an obsession, and perhaps this was indeed influencing my thinking, clouding the reality of the risks we were taking. I imagine that people like Sal D'Angelo, also a teacher, and Len Pennachetti, who was teaching at University, might have felt the same way although they also owned vineyards of their own which they believed could be the basis for a winery. For some, there was no other option but to make their business work and maybe we thought we had something to prove. Perhaps we were simply bent on dancing with Bacchus!

Our first vintage at Stoney Ridge came in 1985 with plans to make a very small amount of wine in a barn on Bryce's property, 500 gallons or so, including Vidal, Baco Noir, Chardonnay, Merlot, and Couderc Muscat, a grape that had won numerous awards for me in amateur winemaking competitions. This wine was a real delight and became the winery's first ever 'medal winning' wine when it was awarded a bronze in the Intervin Competition held in 1986. This inspired our growth over the next three years to 4,000 gallons as we re-fitted the small barn to house a lab, sales counter, cold storage, barrel room, working area, and case storage. I am not sure that any other Ontario winery had started in such a challenging fashion with only well water and no sewers and with very minimal and primitive equipment, featuring a labour-intensive bladder press and a de-juicer that made more mess than juice, two stackable poly tanks imported from Germany, one 'large' 450 gallon stainless steel tank, a collection of demi-johns and smaller carboys, and a tiny pump, borrowed from one of Bryce's friends, that moved all our wine through a one inch line – until we could afford an upgrade! When it came time to bottle our wines, we would drive down the mountain to Andres Wines where our bottles were very kindly received, load them in a van, drive up the mountain and hand load them, case by case, in a small shed next to the main building. Bottling was all done with a manual filler and corker with labelling performed by our entire family by hand, one bottle at a time. But we sold a lot of juice to other individuals and made wines that attracted people from Toronto and Ottawa. And we began to make our mark in our own way as a member of the Ontario wine industry!

As Ontario's smallest winery, at least for a while, with myself still teaching full-time and unable to participate at times in industry activities, Stoney Ridge continued to fly under the radar until the first "Cuvee", a Competition and festive Awards evening for Ontario wines sponsored by Grey Gables School in St. Catharines. Our winery won the white wine competition, and we were runner-up in the red category, results that would set the 'winning' direction for the winery for the future. Yet, this came with a price, for we realized with the increasing demand for our wine that we were limited in the current location and facility and that the work involved here was becoming excessive. Bryce, Jennifer, and Brian would sell their shares to Murray Puddicombe, a grape and fruit grower with an extensive farm just below the Weylie farm on Highway 8. After 4 vintages in Vinemount, Stoney Ridge found itself in a new home in Winona in a new winery building with a new partner who was prepared to allow the business to grow. It was at that time that I realized I had to retire early from teaching for the demands of this business had decidedly changed.

As the regulations for starting a winery at that time still did not require ownership of a vineyard with the obligation of making the wine on site, you could open a winery almost anywhere in the province, even where there were no vineyards. Cave Springs had its vineyard on the Beamsville Bench with the winery, which opened in 1986, located in Jordan, some 5 miles away. Len Pennachetti, the driving force behind the winery, with a long-time friend Angelo Pavan as partner and winemaker, had purchased the old Jordan Winery Plant in Jordan, an amazing, sprawling building which they would soon convert into a winery, retail, and restaurant hub.

Pietro Culotta was involved in a business that imported grapes and grape juice from California to sell to home winemakers when he decided to open his winery in Oakville on the North Service Road opposite the Ford Plant in 1983. In this location his winemaking might be considered 'industrial' in nature although he focused on affordable blends produced "in the style and character enjoyed by our European ancestors...utilizing premium off-shore varieties (60%) to complement superior Ontario hybrids and limited local viniferas".

John and Rosanna Follegot had also been importing material from California to sell to local winemakers in Woodbridge, north of Toronto, when they decided in 1989 to make wines that would sell only at their winery which they named 'Vinoteca'. To complement this business, they purchased an 18 acre vineyard on the North Service Road in Beamsville, a considerable distance from their winemaking! Two additional wineries would open without vineyards, Willowbank, started in 1985 in a small industrial mall near Hillebrand Winery by a Niagara lawyer named Tony Doyle, who hired Ray Cornell from Bright's as his winemaker and a winery named Paul Masson, located in a large facility on the South Service Road in Beamsville by the QEW with Tom Challen as winemaker. Although the first wines were well received, the winery decided to cease business shortly afterwards and auctioned off its equipment. Before long, the building was reconfigured and to-day has found new life as the headquarters for the local Lincoln Town government.

In total, between 1975 and 1990, 21 new wineries opened in the province, 14 in Niagara and 7 between Toronto and Windsor. A small number of these would grow very quickly beyond their original 'cottage' designation (Inniskillin, Chateau des Charmes, Hillebrand, Colio, and Pelee Island) developing off-site retail outlets and enjoying a national and international status. This was certainly a tribute to their marketing efforts but especially to the talent of their winemakers. Our industry had benefitted immensely from several winemakers who had come from Europe to work originally at one of the corporate wineries, like Paul Bosc, Dieter Guttler, Rudi Mueller, Ernst Fischer, Joseph Zimmerman, and Carlo Negri, or who had started their own winery, including Karl Kaiser, Ewald Reif, Walter Strehn, Herbert Konzlemann, and Paul Bosc, bringing their learning and expertise with them. Ray Cornell, Ron Giesebrecht at Henry of Pelham, with a degree in microbiology from U. of Guelph, and Tom Challen at Paul Masson, had previous experience with a large Ontario winery, while Alan Schmidt had been making wine in British Columbia for Sumac Ridge Winery and David Hulley had recently graduated from the oenology school at Davis in California. All were young winemakers very eager to make their mark in the changing environment.

Of the remaining group, some had 'amateur' winemaking experience and a familiarity with grapes, but for the most part had no experience as a commercial winemaker. Since I was included in this group, I have always felt a special connection to these people who were as eager to learn as they were willing to experiment. In spite of their being what some might consider 'handicapped' for this very competitive business, as individuals they made a wonderful difference in the emerging industry, adding a natural, creative flair from which flowed numerous innovations. For them, winemaking involved using 100% Ontario grapes, without the addition of water in order to make the best wine possible, introducing the term 'hand-crafting' to commercial winemaking and producing wines that helped take the industry in a different direction. In every case these neophytes went on to considerable success, helping to propel Ontario winemaking to its present world-class reputation.

Unfortunately, not all the new wineries would be able to find continuing success with their business model, proof that the wine business is as challenging as any other and certainly no guarantee of quick and easy riches. Three wineries, Willowbank, Culotta, and Paul Masson, following on Charal, would add their names to the list of 'ghost' wineries in the province, disappearing completely from the scene with the winemakers moving on to other wineries.

They would not be the only ones to meet this fate as there would soon be another 'downsizing' in the industry involving several of the older corporate players who would become the victims in a business that was transforming out of their control, caught in a web of dramatically changing regulations from which they were unable to escape.

Ontario Icewine: A local curiosity becomes a global treasure

It is impossible to talk about the success of the reborn Ontario wine industry without including the word 'icewine' for it has become the star in the extensive portfolio of world-class wines we produce and its reputation as one of the most delicious and decadent dessert wines made in the global world of wine is undeniable. As much as we have to credit the arrival of French Hybrid and Vinifera grapes for the overall new direction of our 'table' wines, we also must recognize our debt to the category of sweet wines for bringing the attention and respect of the entire wine world to Ontario and to all Canadian wines that now have this wonderful elixir as its flagship. Indeed, icewine is truly a national treasure.

By tradition, and now by law as well, icewine is made from grapes that are picked long after their normal harvest time and only when the temperature remains below minus 8 degrees Celsius for a few consecutive days and they freeze like marbles while still on the vines. The grapes are usually protected from birds and wild animals by nets while they wait, through rain and freeze-thaw cycles, at great risk of rotting, or dessicating beyond use, or dropping off, a nerve-wracking time for both grower and winemaker because of the dollars involved. And when the time does arrive, sometimes as early as November or as late as March, it requires a horde of hardy souls to endure brutally cold, hard work, picking the frozen grapes perhaps through the night (although now a lot of the harvesting is done by machine) and then pressing them in a difficult, frigid environment.

The result is worth the effort as the juice that drips from the press will be at least 35 degrees Brix (the minimum VQA standard) but even higher if the temperature is colder when the juice drips out like a syrup, almost against its will. Most of the water in the grapes remains behind frozen as ice, resulting in much less than half the volume of juice compared to a normal harvest with the juice containing virtually twice as much sugar. Fermenting at these high sugar levels, with much higher acidity as well, is the final challenge in making a wine that will have intense and vibrant aromas and flavours, often described as honey-like, tropical, and exotic, with an opulent fruit character of peaches, apricots, mangos and pineapples, enriched and concentrated by the extra hang-time. The alcohol tends to finish between 9 and 11 percent as much of the sugar remains unfermented.

The idea to turn our wonderful, cold winters to vinous advantage and make a wine from frozen grapes is said to have originated during the summer of 1983 from a chat between two friends in Niagara, Karl Kaiser and Ewald Reif, winemakers who would have been familiar with such a wine from their European background. Such a wine had been made in Germany and Austria for a long time, beginning as an accident of nature some 200 years ago when a sudden freeze caught a winemaker by surprise before he could harvest in his normal fashion, and then afterwards only in rare years when the weather would co-operate. The wine was called "Eiswein", and it was usually made only for family and friends as a remarkable, prestige product. For Kaiser and Reif, this seemed like a worthwhile experiment, and they planned to leave several rows of a grape called Vidal for the wine. Vidal was a hardy French Hybrid grape that had become widely planted in Ontario in recent years as it made a very pleasant white wine. The grapes normally ripened in October, which was later than many other white varieties, with good acidity, very pleasant aroma and fine flavour, and with a very thick skin which the friends believed was suitable for resisting disease and hanging longer on the vine. For their innovative effort they could not have chosen a better grape!

No winery in Ontario had ever made this product in a commercial sense before although through the years there were some historical references to experiments involving the same concept. In the mid 1860's, one of our pioneer winemakers at Clair House in Cooksville, Justin de Courtenay, made both a red and white 'congealed wine', as he called it, with the amazing prophetic comment "I have always considered the exportation of congealed wines to Europe as the great future of both Upper and Lower Canada!" At that time, the Vidal grape had not yet been created and no one knows for sure which grape or grapes de Courtenay really used, but his vision was amazing!

Almost a century later, George Hostetter, who was Director of Research at Bright's Wines, would relate a story about their winemaker Adhemar de Chaunac who apparently was inspired to use frozen Vidal grapes in a personal experiment making a luscious wine which he liked to share with friends, including at the 'Alliance Francaise' in Hamilton. There is no record of how this German innovation was received by a group of French speaking oenophiles! De Chaunac was never able to interest the owners of the winery in developing his project commercially, but it is interesting that he chose to use the very grape that would become the basic icewine grape in Ontario shortly after he had passed on.

A few years later, a young Ontario graduate student named John Paroschy went to Germany to complete his doctorate working with the famous Helmut Becker at Geisenheim where he helped picked grapes for an 'eiswein'. When he joined Bright's in 1979 as a research scientist four years later, he decided to conduct an experiment along the same lines using frozen Vidal grapes. Apparently, it turned out so well that the winery owners took it all for their own use!

It is not surprising with so little previous experience with frozen grapes and no reference manuals on how to make wine following the 'eiswein' model, that things started on the wrong foot! It is not always easy being a pioneer! In fact, the first efforts by three different wineries seem like a comedy of errors, with a strange mix of comic and tragic outcomes. When Karl Kaiser's grapes finally froze in December 1983, he was away at a wine conference. As the rows of Vidal he had left to be used were not netted, a flock of hungry starlings arrived and literally devoured the grapes before any picking started, leaving nothing for the winery's experiment but a lesson for the future.

On Pelee Island, Walter Strehn did net over several rows of vines and ended up trapping a number of birds while protecting his grapes. This brought an immediate response from ever-vigilant Ministry of Natural Resource's conservation officers who charged him with trapping birds out of season! Apparently, no one in government had the common sense to understand why the nets were in place and ordered that they be removed! Once again birds were able to feast on the overripe grapes. Eventually the charges against the winery were dropped and Walter was able to rescue enough grapes to make some icewine. He sold the wine in half-bottles (375 ml.) to the LCBO where it retailed for $12.50 a bottle. At this price, and because it was indeed a 'novelty', the wine did not sell, and the LCBO delivered it back to the winery. Walter ended up sending it to the US where it sold for more than $100 a bottle. Of course, the LCBO wanted to buy it back, but they were now frozen out!

With its new German ownership, Hillebrand Winery decided to make an icewine in 1983 as well after their new German winemaker noticed the rows of vines left with grapes at Inniskillin. They picked their grapes in October before any freeze and while they were still healthy and put them in cold storage. When the deep freeze came in December, they brought the grapes outside where they froze and then pressed them. As there were no 'rules' for making icewine then, the winery considered this an acceptable technique although the grapes did not benefit from the extra hang-time they missed. Hillebrand insisted that their grapes were frozen "naturally" but others in the industry did not consider this a legitimate way to obtain the special character of icewine. Others had picked up on the Hillebrand technique and were simply freezing their grapes artificially, then pressing them to extract a sweeter juice, a process known as cryo-extraction. Some were even using concentrated grape juice at high brix to make an 'icewine'. Four years later, when the first draft of the VQA standards was formulated, it was generally agreed that such shortcuts yielded an inferior product and regulations were conceived that eliminated all artificial production of icewine juice with the decision that the grapes used for icewine had to be frozen naturally on the vine.

From that point on, what had been inspired by a "what if…" question among two friends, rapidly developed from an artisanal, experimental innovation to an exciting commercial category, with our harsh winters ideally suited for making icewine regularly every year. Kaiser and Reif netted their vines in 1984 and produced their first icewine. Inniskillin made only 66 cases but the wine was entered in the Intervin Wine Competition later and won a gold medal! Hillebrand repeated their experiment the same way as the previous year but decided to net their vines the next year to improve quality. At Bright's, a young assistant winemaker named Ray Cornell would make Vidal icewine as a research project in 1983 and 1984 as a prelude to the winery's first commercial icewine in 1986 which they, like others, labelled after the German example as 'Eiswein'. Herbert Konzlemann made his first icewine in 1986 and Klaus Reif followed the next year, with both wineries producing luscious and refined Vidal icewines that won them gold medals annually in international competitions.

Vineland entered the field in 1988 as did Chateau des Charmes, following the "German group" as Bosc called them, producing 200 bottles (375 ml.) of a Riesling icewine. At Pelee Island, winemaker Walter Schmoranz produced a 'red' icewine in 1989, the first of many red icewines that would follow in the industry. That year both Henry of Pelham and Cave Springs would make their first efforts in very small quantities while the following year, Stoney Ridge made just 54 litres of the first Gewurztraminer icewine and the same amount of New York Muscat and it would not be long before we could enjoy an icewine made from several different VQA-approved grapes. This would lead to further innovations with barrel-aged and barrel-fermented icewines, sparkling icewines and sparkling wine with an icewine dosage. Icewine would be used to flavour truffles, or jams and jellies, or to make delicious syrups, while Kittling Ridge cleverly created an icewine and brandy beverage that attracted attention from consumers and the industry alike. Icewine was proving to be the "real deal"!

However, it would take a few years for icewine to establish its credibility in spite of its seductive nature as some producers discovered the wine was as difficult to sell as it was to make. For many wine lovers it was a mystery which made for some resistance to buying the new product. People did not know how to serve it or with what food or with what part of a meal it was meant for. No one knew if or how well an icewine would age. And sales were slow to develop as some consumers found the wine simply "too sweet" on tasting it for the first time, while others, who did not understand the complex process behind it, believed that it was just a money-making "gimmick" or "too expensive" for a local wine.

Fortunately, more and more consumers began to realize that the prices asked for icewine represented wonderful value when compared to other prestigious wines that were far more expensive. We learned that Vidal icewine would last nicely for 5 years before changing its personality, darkening in colour and becoming more toffee-like, while Riesling, with higher acid levels, produced a more refined icewine that could age considerably longer. Winemakers quickly realized that juice which was exceptionally sweet was not an advantage, producing a wine that was cloying on the palate, and changed their ideas on picking and pressing temperatures. Where icewine was first sold as 'dessert in a glass', others discovered that it went well before and during, as well as after a meal and paired nicely with a variety of foods from cheeses to hors d'oeuvres to chocolate and desserts (not sweeter than the wine itself), and as a tasty balance to salty, acidic, or spicy foods.

While icewine still remains a mystery to some Canadians to-day, such feelings have essentially evaporated with the passing of time, with the knowledge that our industry has the strictest production standards in the world, with extensive positive media coverage, and as the winemakers have improved their techniques producing ever more elegant and beautifully balanced nectars. And both production and sales would begin to soar when the quality of Canadian icewine was validated by the Asian market, especially Japan and then China, which deemed them to be luxury products and worthy of similar pricing.

However, the real turning point in this success story can be pin-pointed to one event that happened in 1991. That year, Inniskillin entered their 1989 Vidal icewine in a prestigious competition at the VinExpo Show in Bordeaux and won a Citadelle d'Or Grand Prix d'Honneur, one of only 19 awarded out of 4,100 entries. That brought the attention of the world to Inniskillin and to Ontario icewine. Over the next three years production of what was now considered the world's most special sweet wine would increase dramatically by over 500% and there would be no looking back. In just a decade, Canadian icewine had become the industry's signature wine and the world leader in both volume and quality, and it was a wine we could expect to make every year!

Considering the game-changing impact that the creation of icewine has had on our entire wine industry, with just the idea of making a wine in winter called 'ice'-wine attracting attention, the almost innocent nature of its beginning seems particularly sweet, certainly as sweet as this unique wine itself!

Problems mount for the "Corporate" wineries

As the 1980's began to unfold in the wine industry, the increase in Vinifera plantings and the growing number of cottage wineries were helping to stimulate both an interest in a local wine culture and a hope for better quality wine. Although the residual market resistance to Ontario wine in general was beginning to wane, our corporate wineries were finding it difficult to maintain real growth in terms of sales in spite of their efforts to entice consumers with a new offering of 'lite' wines and a plethora of affordable blends which occupied considerable shelf space in the LCBO system. Traditional ports and sherries were continuing to lose market share while in the LCBO the larger wineries found themselves losing needed shelf-space as well. The Ontario government had allowed an influx of imported wines that more than doubled their listings in the LCBO and there was added pressure from the 'new kids on the block', many of whom were in a growth mode of their own, seeking additional listings. Colio, for example, had in only five years managed to own the best-selling red and white Ontario brands, Bianco Secco and Rosso Secco, and several of the new players including Hillebrand, Pelee Island, Colio, Inniskillin, and Chateau des Charmes, were at the same time adding new off-site stores to their winery retail system in order to reach out to more consumers. In the six years between 1982 and 1987, the sales held by the large wineries at the LBCO would drop by 15% to less than 40 percent, an all-time low, leaving several of them in financial distress. This was the beginning of a complicated divisive relationship between the large and small wineries that would see them become opposing forces in the same industry.

Although the Ontario wine business had lived with confrontational attacks throughout its history, the challenges facing the larger wineries became overwhelming in this decade. The attacks began with the Temperance movement of the late 1800's and blossomed into Prohibition and its aftermath with a new provincial regulatory board appropriately named the Liquor 'Control' Board (LCBO) regulating all aspects of the alcohol business. In economic terms this amounted to onerous taxes, fees, and mark-ups while in social terms this meant ongoing efforts by dedicated groups to curtail consumption of alcohol, to limit its availability, and to pursue legislation tightening advertising and demanding warning labels on bottles. A consumer health movement would eventually lead to serious concerns about the excessive use of alcohol, its consumption during pregnancy and to organizations like Mothers Against Drunk Driving (MADD), all with a negative impact on wine drinking.

For the Ontario corporate wine industry, involved in producing numerous high alcohol ports and sherries to drive its financial well-being, these threats were as serious as increasing competition and diminishing sales and obligated the wineries to be more concerned about promoting themselves and their products in a socially responsible manner. Thus, when a totally unexpected health issue involving wine came to light during some LCBO lab testing, the livelihood of the wineries was suddenly thrown into jeopardy.

In 1981, the LCBO Quality Control Department began to investigate whether a carcinogen named ethyl carbamate, found to cause cancer in some animals, was produced in wine. It was established that it was indeed present, formed during the fermentation process and especially when urea was used as a yeast nutrient. Testing showed that the amount of ethyl carbamate was related to the concentration of urea and ethanol and increased exponentially with increases in temperature and in storage. Wineries used urea abundantly to push the yeasts to produce more alcohol and then often "baked" the wines to make sherries and ports. Although the risks to human health had never been established, it was suggested that 10 parts per billion would be a safe level, considering that the chemical was found naturally in the environment.

When it was discovered that the levels in many of the products of the large wineries were far higher than 10 ppb, with some in the hundreds of ppb and even higher, suggesting there might be some potential for harm to human health, the LCBO was caught in a dilemma. If they exposed the results and removed numerous products from their stores, this would hurt the business of the wineries at what was proving to be a difficult time. If they did not inform the public, there could be considerable political embarrassment or worse. At first the matter was kept secret among LCBO Quality Control management and individual wineries were contacted quietly and encouraged to solve the problem as best they could while the offending products "worked their way through the system". The six large wineries were informed not to use urea as an additive in any product but otherwise the matter was kept confidential.

A new CEO for the LCBO, Jack Ackroyd, showed an immediate interest in health and safety issues after two scandals involving European wine came to light, leading him to request a report from his executives. When he discovered the nature of the Ontario problem, he contacted the Minister of Consumer and Commercial Relations who immediately called a Royal Commission, November 20, 1985. The outcome in early 1986, while exonerating the LCBO in spite of the 'coverup' that had taken place, established that public health was the priority in the matter and that mistakes had been made which would now be corrected. The LCBO was quick to respond with a revamping of their internal communications system, making changes which resulted in improvements to their Quality Control operations as well. But, when the full story came out in the media, the perception was that the larger wineries had been producing wines that were contaminated and potentially harmful to human health, leaving them the villain in the matter.

The scandal damaged the reputation of the industry leaving the corporate wineries to weather the storm. But the damage was done and within a year another period of downsizing in the industry would begin with the closing of Jordan's Wines in 1986, a winery that had prospered since Prohibition, the business purchased by Bright's Wines, Ontario's largest winery. Bright's closed all the Jordan's & Ste.-Michelle Cellars' plants, consolidating production at its own winery.

In 1985 we had just started our winery, Stoney Ridge Cellars, and I was unaware of the ethyl carbamate scare. I was still teaching full-time in Hamilton, and this often left me in the dark about happenings in the industry. However, I was invited to become a member of the Wine Council of Ontario and went to my first meeting in Mississauga where I listened with considerable concern to other industry members talking about the activity that was ongoing relating to winemaking including at least one potential threat to the survival of the entire wine industry. I left the meeting wondering what I had done in rather naively starting a winery at what had become a time of such worrisome uncertainty.

The nature of the problem was so serious that the Ontario Government had created a task force to consider the status of the grape and wine industry and make recommendations that would help ensure its long-term viability. The Minister of Agriculture appointed Dr. Jack Tanner, a professor in the Department of Agriculture at Guelph University, to head the task force which included seven representatives from the growers, the wineries, and the LCBO. The Tanner Task Force discussed everything from the need for research and education to sugar standards, new vineyard plantings to bulk wines, and the sensitive issue of unfriendly relationships between all facets of the industry.

When the report was released on May 12, 1986, it presented 29 recommendations with the preface that the future of the industry would depend on improving the quality of all Ontario wine, "equivalent in quality to foreign wines at a lower price or better in quality at the same price". Recommendation 5 dealt head-on with an issue that had proven divisive in the industry for years, calling for the phasing out of "the production of labrusca grapes for use in table wines, including light table wines" until December 31, 1995. Considering that labruscas were still a mainstay for most Ontario grape growers and that the large wineries continued to use these grapes, to implement such a proposal would be a daunting task!

Fortunately, the cottage wineries could take some comfort knowing that labrusca grapes were not involved with their own survival and were already meeting to discuss a future where 'achieving top quality' would differentiate their wines from the commercial products of the larger wineries. But they were still a part of the wine industry and vulnerable to some of the changes that were being considered.

Robert Carman, the Provincial Secretary of the Cabinet, had contacted the Deputy Minister of Consumer and Commercial Affairs, Valerie Gibbons, to inform her that the Wine Content Act was terminating and needed to be renegotiated. She assembled industry stakeholders from the growers, wineries, and the LCBO to come together in 1987 to reconsider "under a common vision" issues relating to blended wines, the matter of 'stretching' volume with the use of water, and the role of labrusca grapes. The larger picture included achieving some form of harmonious agreement between growers and wineries that would confirm that the industry was worth saving.

The comment has often been made that politics and the Ontario wine industry have always gone hand in hand, usually in the form of a hand-out or what is sometimes called a hand-up. Growers had benefitted from this policy since the beginning of Prohibition and the Ontario Government had always been ready with an 'Assistance Program' to support wineries, as it was recognized that the industry played a significant part in the Ontario economy. However, the year 1988, which Tony Aspler declared would go down "in the annals as a watershed year for Ontario wine" in his book "Vintage Canada" (1993), left the industry struggling to believe this.

On September 1, 1988, the government introduced a reformulated Ontario Wine Content Act that would swamp some wineries in its wake. Labrusca grapes were banned from all Ontario table wine, restricting them for use in ports, sherries, and the refreshment category, while the LCBO declared that it would no longer retail table wines with labrusca content. For Ontario grape growers this was a moment they had feared, but the wineries agreed to purchase at least 25,500 tonnes of grapes from them annually until 1999 by which time the expectation was that growers would have planted more preferred varieties. The amount of water that could be used in 'stretching' production from a tonne of grapes was reduced by 13% to 885 litres from 1022, ostensibly as a step in the direction of improved quality. Yet, considering that a normal tonne of grapes would yield only approximately 700 litres of juice per tonne, this meant that some water could still be added in production (ironically called 'amelioration').

To deal with the decrease in the use of labrusca grapes and resulting shortage of wine, a significant change was made in the blending category with new blends allowed to contain up to 70% import material, purchased from wine regions like Chile, South Africa, California, France, and Australia. Blending had started in 1972 in response to a shortage of grapes in Ontario with a change made in 1980 allowing 30% maximum import material in any wine, but 70% represented a remarkable change. That would be a blessing for the larger wineries to help them make necessary volumes of better wine and retain market share. Yet, for one large winery, the changes came too late, and Barnes Wines decided to close in 1988, the second established corporate winery to cease business within two years. This closure would see the end of Canada's oldest continuously operating winery with a history dating back to 1873. Hillebrand would scoop up 12 off-site wine stores operated by Barnes as it continued to expand its own retail system.

Competition in the industry had never been more severe and to help the wineries remain competitive in the emerging new environment, the Ontario government introduced a "Grape Price Support Program". The average price per tonne of a variety grown in California was compared to the Ontario Marketing Board price for the same or equivalent variety grown in Ontario. Since the local grapes were usually more expensive, an Ontario winery would pay the California price and the government provided the difference to the grower as a "transition subsidy" which would decrease annually until the end of 12 years. The growers received appropriate money for their grapes, and this helped stabilize the industry for a while.

While work on the Wine Content Act was still in progress, another set of talks between the Federal Government and the American Government intersected with it, and it would place everything in jeopardy when it was discovered that the Canadian negotiators were preparing to trade away the entire wine industry for the sake of "Free Trade"!

The concept of a 'free-trade zone' between Canada and the United States had been suggested by our Federal Government as a response to a growing protectionist sentiment in the United States that had generated import restrictions and/or duties on such Canadian goods as softwood lumber. The topic was introduced when Brian Mulroney met with Ronald Reagan in Quebec City prior to St. Patrick's Day in March 1985, hoping to mend relations in the post-Trudeau era, and the two, with their wives, ended up singing "When Irish Eyes are Smiling". Not everyone was pleased with the outcome of what then came to be called the 'Shamrock Summit'- they achieved an agreement in principle to begin Free Trade talks - and when the wine industry eventually heard what was being contemplated, the smiling eyes would turn to tears.

To protect the sales of the Ontario wineries, the mark-up on foreign wines coming into Ontario had previously been set at 123 percent, significantly higher than for Ontario wines at 58 percent, with the difference making imports more expensive. This blatant, preferential treatment was justified according to the government because it was believed that grapes and wines were highly subsidized by many countries in the European Economic Community (EEC) who were exporting to Canada which allowed these wines to be sold at a reduced price. Wines from the United States, especially California, were considered 'foreign'. During the Free Trade discussions, the Federal Government decided to end the competitive advantage enjoyed by Ontario wines and allow American wines to be treated exactly the same as domestic. Later in time, the chief Canadian negotiator, Simon Reisman, admitted that Canada had originally been prepared to sacrifice the wine industry to achieve other goals, believing that the wine industry was no longer sustainable anyway.

On October 4, 1987, details of the agreement were released, and it was revealed that the protective pricing would indeed be lost, phased out over 7 years. Brian Nash, Chair of the OGGMB and Jan Wescott, Executive Director of the WCO, predicted that the consequences would be disastrous for the industry. Ontario wines had enjoyed a long ride, over 120 years, but were now being taken for a ride of a different kind and the destination was not a happy one. Compounding the problem was a General Agreement on Tariffs and Trade (GATT) Panel preliminary ruling that came out in October 1987, declaring that the higher mark-ups which the provinces placed on foreign wines was an unfair trade practice. The Europeans had been worried that preferential treatment would be extended only to American wines, and this prompted the GATT challenge. Now the industry faced losing their pricing advantage entirely, with the result being higher prices for Ontario wines, or there would be potential retaliation from the twelve countries in the EEC.

There was another issue involved in the Free Trade talks that was of concern to the Americans, the existence of nearly 350 winery owned retail stores in Ontario in addition to the LCBO system. The Americans declared that they too wanted the right to operate stores of their own, a demand that was deemed unacceptable to our government. To resolve the matter, it was decided, effective October 4, 1987, that any new winery opening in Ontario would be allowed only one retail store and that would have to be at the site of the winery. The off-site stores currently in operation, owned primarily by larger wineries, would be "grand-fathered" and allowed to remain open. In practical terms, this meant that a small number of established wineries would retain multiple stores while over 90% of Ontario wineries, including many cottage wineries that had never opened even a second store, could never have any other retail outlet.

This discriminatory decision effectively split the wineries into two camps, referred to as the 'haves' and the 'have-nots', creating an inequity that was obvious and damaging to the 'disadvantaged'. The bad feelings would only mount with the ever-increasing number of new small wineries who simply had to accept a situation that denied them potential access to the local market. The discrimination would become even worse in the 1990's.

On November 22, 1987, the Wine Council, Grape Growers, and the Ontario Government responded to the Federal Government with a "Framework for a Response to the GATT Panel Ruling" attempting to manage a situation that they could no longer control. The most important commitment concerned the removal of labrusca and additional undesired French Hybrid vines from Ontario vineyards, a figure that would exceed 8,000 acres of grapes. In addition, the Federal Government was made aware of a new organization that was in the works, an association of cottage wineries that was currently drawing up a set of regulations that would bring an appellation system to Ontario, enhancing the industry with high quality wines that would make it worth saving. Impressed and encouraged by the development, the Federal Government attempted to negotiate with the EEC on the wine issue but were unsuccessful. On March 12, 1988, the final GATT ruling was announced giving Canada until December 31 to indicate how it would respond. The die was cast!

The Free Trade Agreement was ratified by the US Senate in September of 1988 and the GATT Agreement was signed in Brussels on December 17. A Canadian election held on November 21 would see Brian Mulroney and his Conservatives win, leading to the Free Trade Agreement receiving Royal Assent from Governor-General Jeanne Sauve on December 30. All Canada woke up on Sunday, January 1, 1989 to a new relationship with the United States. Overall, the wine industry had been treated like a puppet on a string, its movements depending on one or other puppeteer, and it was now facing a state of crisis.

Many grape growers were looking at a loss of livelihood, beyond the normal risks of growing grapes, or, if they were willing to pull-out and replant with preferred varieties required by the future industry, they would have to make an enormous, upfront investment and then survive with no income until the new vines were producing. It could be argued that growers had been given a chance years before to begin replanting when very few took advantage of the funding provided. And some would say that they had kept their bets on a losing horse by maintaining their labrusca vineyards when demand was falling. But, in truth, they had only continued to provide grapes that several wineries required, and given the expensive alternative, who can blame them for staying the course and trying to make a living?

In the span of just a few years, the large wineries and labrusca grape growers had been victimized for attempting to maintain their business growing the native grapes and producing wines from these grapes to the best of their ability. But time and the arrival of new grapes, along with changing consumer tastes, had caught up with the industry and now two trade agreements had made it impossible to sustain the 'old ways'. Some blamed the OGGMB for conceding on the issue, but over the years this organization had done its utmost to keep growers in business. The Chairman at that time, Brian Nash, himself a labrusca grower, had put up a vociferous defense throughout the negotiations, refusing to go down without a fight, and his efforts on behalf of the growers were highly appreciated.

Fortunately, the Mulroney government had promised help to anyone hurt by the Free Trade Agreement and the provincial government was working on a compensation package with significant financial support that would help growers deal with their losses and at the same time move the entire industry in a new direction. Ironically, the forced changes would stimulate improved vineyard activity, an impressive number of new wineries, a dramatic leap in wine quality, and a fiery competitive spirit, hardly the disaster that had been predicted, with the result that after a transition period of only 10 more years, the wine industry would be able to say with confidence that it was "poised for greatness"!

The end of the 1980's: A is for an Assistance program and an Appellation system, at last!

The loss of our original grapes, historical wines, preferential mark-ups, and two long-established wineries was the price the industry paid for its survival – that is the corporate wine industry. With import blends now able to contain 70% 'foreign' material, the larger wineries would essentially become 'blenders', producing large volumes of inexpensive 'Product of Canada' blends needed to compete with other imported wines in the LCBO system. Very few of the cottage wineries were involved with 'blends', primarily because this type of wine was not their focus, and they did not value them as Ontario wines. Blending was 'big business', necessitating the purchase of import material in large volumes to reduce costs but at huge upfront expense, along with the marketing ability and sales force to move these volumes as bottled wine. Most of the smaller wineries were content to produce 100% Ontario Vinifera or French Hybrid wines which continued to sell well and at higher prices.

Blends were critical to the larger wineries to sustain their business and help them overcome the stigma of 'mediocre' wines which had shadowed them before. Ontario chauvinists and wine connaisseurs were put off by these pseudo-Ontario wines believing that the overall profile of our wines was tarnished by them, but that criticism was unfair. It did require expertise to source quality wine as well as considerable winemaking talent to achieve a consistent, pleasing, and good value blend, and the wineries did purchase a lot of Ontario grown grapes to make them. The real problem was in the marketing of the wines, especially as they appeared to masquerade as a Product of Canada. Some consumers might have been confused, but others simply did not care, believing the price was right and they were supporting an Ontario business. The change to the Wine Content Act allowing up to 70% import material in a given wine was a logical step to ensure the survival of some wineries but the government should never have allowed any bottle of wine with more import material in it than domestic to be sold as 'Canadian'. That was an unfortunate mistake, and it would have to change!

Our winery, Stoney Ridge, was expanding in volume and about to move to a more mainstream location on Highway 8 in Winona. We had no desire to use labrusca grapes or become a "blender", although I had that right, and I had no intention of opening another retail store as our production could not justify that and the change in mark-ups was of little concern even though we were starting to sell some wine in the LCBO system. And for most of the small wineries the situation was essentially the same. We began to enter our wines in competitions where the success we achieved brought unexpected benefits. The first 'Cuvee' competition was held in Niagara Falls in early 1989 and Stoney Ridge won first place in the white category with our Chardonnay and second place in the red category with a Merlot, both grapes sourced from Lenko Vineyards. This was a 'coup' for our winery and brought immediate consumer attention. The very next day, a Saturday, Niagara was shut down with a ferocious ice storm, yet customers were lined up down our laneway off Ridge Road following an article in the newspapers about Cuvee. Within a week, two prestigious Toronto restaurants had ordered our wine and people were phoning to reserve wine. In short order, we were sold out and I decided then that entering competitions would become a major part of our 'marketing strategy'!

Other wineries were discovering that awards in competition helped to attract customers to their cellar door. Hillebrand had grown into a 200,000 case winery in just a few years, becoming at the same time one of our foremost multi-awarded wineries. Konzlemann and Reif were producing award-winning Icewines, Vineland Estates was leading the way with outstanding Rieslings as was Cave Spring with their Rieslings and Chardonnays, and Henry of Pelham would soon become known for their Baco Noirs. The 'rivalry' between the smaller wineries was intense but friendly and meant dedicated hard work with 'quality' being the target but I could not have been enjoying myself more. I was still able to produce 'blends', but for Stoney Ridge this meant making small volume, unique wines from premium California grapes and juices which we imported frozen to sell to home winemakers. If there was any remaining unsold, we would use this to make special wines for our Barrel Club members. Thus, the fall-out from all the recent negotiations had not dampened the enthusiasm of the cottage industry with its new breed of winemaker even though it had confirmed the division in the overall Ontario industry that was now its basic operating mode.

Reflecting all the upset of recent developments, Ontario wine sales for the end of the decade decreased by 7.5% each year from 1988 to 1990, marking an industry low point. And the pessimism generated by increased mark-ups for Ontario wines, up from 1% in 1986 to 60% in order to create the infamous 'level playing field' with imported wines, would cast a gloomy shadow a while longer but the promise of financial assistance from government provided considerable hope for the entire industry, and to the surprise of many, recovery would happen quickly.

The "Grape and Wine Adjustment Program" that was unveiled, with funding shared by both levels of government, would benefit all the industry's stakeholders in business when the Free Trade Agreement was signed. It was quickly named the "Pullout Program" as individual growers were compensated to pull out grape varieties deemed surplus to industry needs, essentially unwanted labrusca varieties and some French Hybrids like De Chaunac that were in oversupply or deemed less suitable for quality winemaking. Some 8500 acres were removed in the end, a significant percentage of Ontario's vineyards, most of this between 1989 and 1991 with growers compensated at $1,100 per acre. The program, which was provided on the widespread belief that local growers could not possibly compete with California growers in a free trade environment, was not perfect as there was no incentive provided to replant, and many growers were expected to use the windfall revenue to get out of grapes and try other crops. As well, the program rewarded those growers who had not previously planted the preferred varieties and gave those who had already planted them no support at all. But many growers did replant, moving to Vinifera varieties that would make the kind of wine consumers were demanding. In 1980, there had been 800 tons of Vinifera harvested, a figure which would increase to 4,000 tons by 1990. Just 10 years later this volume would surge to 20,400 tons and the industry could feel that the program, valued at $100 million, had been a remarkable success.

The remaining $100 million went to the wineries in what came to be called the Ontario Winery Assistance Program (OWAP) to help make them more competitive. I recall having to spend money upfront on marketing, consulting, research, and capital purchases, to the limit that Stoney Ridge was given, and then we received 75% of our costs back from the program. This allowed us to purchase a new press, more tank capacity and new barrels, and hire a salesman to develop LCBO and restaurant business.

Other wineries benefitted greatly as well, and by 1991 sales of Ontario wine were once again on the increase! Government had managed to rescue the wine industry, assisting growers and the large wineries to stay in business and providing a means for the cottage wineries to improve their reputation and their sales of 100% Ontario grown wines.

Donald Ziraldo is undoubtedly the most well-known Ontario and Canadian wine industry personality, recognized primarily as the co-founder of Inniskillin Wines, the first of the modern cottage wineries, and as a leading producer of award-winning Ontario icewine. Not a winemaker per se but a talented marketer of his own wines, and an assiduous promoter of the Ontario grape and wine industry, the charismatic Donald has devoted his time and energy for over 40 years to putting Ontario on the map as a proper wine region. This serious adventure started when he found himself unable to deliver wine to France that he had sold in 1982 because Ontario at that time had no regulatory basis for establishing the authenticity of any wine produced by our wineries and thus the French would not do business with him. From that time on, he became a 'man on a mission' to develop an "appellation system of origin" for 100% Ontario grown wines that would guarantee the source of all the grapes used to make a given wine was a particular location in Ontario.

Donald began by talking with other cottage winery owners trying to form an alliance of like-minded individuals, holding meetings to discuss a framework for a regulatory system along the lines of the appellation systems developed in other world wine regions. In Ontario, blended wines would not be eligible as only 100% Ontario grown grapes could be used and only the 'preferred varieties' (no labruscas). I remember attending my first meeting in 1985 where the discussion centred on whether the wineries that produced blended wines would be allowed to participate or not, with some in agreement and some not. Some wanted to deny French Hybrids any place in the developing system, but others insisted they be retained. There were so many issues that had to be talked out in order to reach a consensus and move on. Soon Donald's vision would expand to include stringent winemaking standards, authorized grape varieties, recognized viticultural areas, appropriate labelling, and a stress on 'quality', that would make Ontario wine respected and saleable anywhere in the global wine world.

To-day, few people would appreciate the challenge inherent in attempting to implement such an innovative concept for Ontario wines. Our wine region had not been blessed with indigenous grapes of any real value for world-class winemaking as in Europe and our wine industry was still young, with no venerable vineyard sites or 'old vines' as in other countries to point to, or 'classic' terroirs which were highly esteemed by sophisticated wine drinkers. A few Ontario wines had won awards in competitions over time, but high quality was simply not the hallmark of an industry which produced mainly generic port and sherry style wines. In fact, we had little in the way of a 'wine culture' at all up to the 1980's. What we did have was an industry obligated from its beginning in the 1850's to use the only grapes that would grow in our cool climate, American Hybrids, which were considered to be sub-standard for fine table wine, and by the 1970's a very limited acreage of French Hybrids and Vinifera which some growers continued to fight planting. To attempt to present the image of a 'quality wine industry', therefore, might have seemed rather brash to some, but this small group of dedicated individuals believed strongly that this was the right time to challenge traditional notions of Ontario winemaking – and they would be proven right!

By 1986, with an assist from the LCBO, an independent, competent tasting panel had been formed using LCBO professionals and this would be followed by numerous drafts and revisions of a set of rules and regulations/standards/terminology assembled by a dedicated team aligned with the industry including Donald Ziraldo, Dr. Vicki Grey from the Horticultural Products Lab at HRIO, professor Peter Peach from Brock University, Leonard Pennachetti, president of Cave Springs Winery, Leonard Franssen from the Quality Control Department of the LCBO, and lawyer and keen Ontario wine advocate Ken Douglas to provide the legalese. A Board of Directors was chosen, and they met for the first time on December 19, 1989 to approve the initial draft of the regulations for what was now known as the Vintners' Quality Alliance (VQA). The Board included eight directors from the wineries and one each from the LCBO, the growers, from research, and from the hospitality industry. The final draft of the Regulations was approved on June 27, 1990, and on March 18, 1991, Peter Gamble, formerly with Hillebrand Winery, would become the first Executive Director. Perhaps without even realizing it, all these people and others who were working so hard to bring the VQA to fruition, were truly making history!

Ontario would now have three 'designated viticultural areas', referred to as a DVA, the Niagara Peninsula, Lake Erie North Shore, and Pelee Island, which were linked to Vinifera grapes, as well as a less restrictive 'Ontario' appellation that would permit the inclusion of Vinifera hybrids. A list of 'approved' grape varieties was accepted for producing varietal wines grown in the designated areas. All wines would be made without the addition of any water, a dramatic change from the past. Standards for minimum 'brix' levels in grapes were set as a guideline with floating prices for higher brix to compensate growers who attempted to produce higher quality grapes. Labelling rules were designed to provide complete transparency to consumers while guaranteeing authenticity for the contents of the bottle. And all wines had to 'pass' a tasting at the LCBO and receive a Certificate of Analysis from the LCBO lab to establish that the wine was considered a product of quality which lacked any wine faults.

At this early stage in the life of the VQA, all members of the Alliance were committed to ensuring its success, although complying with the rules would be 'by gentlemen's agreement' as government legislation binding members by law was not yet in place. Still, this had been a tremendous accomplishment and would serve as the stepping-stone to the immediate recognition of Ontario as a world-class wine region with its VQA wines approved for international trade.

As the 1980's came to a close, there would be one more surprise in store for the Ontario wine industry, a development that in itself was of little concern for most wineries but would serve as a prelude to further major change in the 1990's. Chateau Gai Winery in Niagara Falls, which traced its roots back to the days of Prohibition, was put on the market by its current owner, John Labatt, Ltd., a large conglomerate that had operated the business since buying it in 1973. Concerned with the potential negative impact of the Free Trade Agreement, and with its stock falling on the Stock Market, Labatt's wanted to exit from the wine industry in order to focus more on their core business and become more competitive selling their beers. A willing buyer appeared to have been found when Joe Peller, President of Andres Wines, made an acceptable offer which would see him acquire the business and leave Andres as the largest winery in Canada. However, a group of Chateau Gai employees led by Allan Jackson, V.P. of Operations, who had worked there since 1977, decided to pool their resources and attempt a management buyout of the business. They believed that in spite of the obvious challenges at the moment there was a great opportunity for the winery to carry on successfully in the rapidly changing wine industry. To overcome the Andres' offer they needed help and they turned to a former Senior V.P. with Labatt's who had left in the early 1980's and was now a partner in an investment firm, a man named Bob Luba.

Luba could sense the enthusiasm of the group but felt they needed someone with skills in running a large business, someone with expertise in marketing, business finance, and the matter of mergers and acquisitions to assess the business. He decided to contact an individual that he thought perfect for the task, another former employee of Labatt's, Don Triggs, who had been hired in 1971 to develop their wine business in Ontario and then in California. Although Triggs had just been promoted to a very responsible position with his present company, Fisons, PLC, which was based in the United Kingdom, he received permission from them to investigate the potential of the investment in Ontario. Triggs, whom Linda Bramble describes as a true 'visionary' in her book on key industry players, must have felt that here was a chance for him to run a business of his own, and one that certainly appealed to him, if he could see a promising future in it.

After doing their due diligence, Triggs, Luba, Jackson, and two other managers were convinced that the business could be profitable and they, along with sixteen other employees, agreed to pool their resources with many going out on a limb to come up with the needed cash. They found a bank willing to provide them with a substantial mortgage and were able to match the Andres' offer. Their fortitude and courage in the face of the risks involved convinced Labatt's management to sell the business to their employees for $28 million in July 1989. Don Triggs as the largest single shareholder became the president and CEO of the new business which, as a first step, changed its name to Cartier Wines. The winery team had stayed the same, but with a new entrepreneurial leader the winery would almost immediately go in a new direction, and there would soon be other surprises as a result!

The 1980's ended with a transformed wine industry, or perhaps two industries with a handful of wineries focusing on the blended wine business, which represented over 80% of Ontario wine sales, and numerous smaller wineries positioned to take advantage of the changing vineyard landscape and the introduction of an appellation system. Of the 25 wineries in business, 18 were located in Niagara, 5 in South-Western Ontario, and 2 outside of a DVA with only 4 remaining as 'large' wineries. Of real concern, in spite of the increasing number of wineries, was the trend in wine sales with imports continuing to add market share. The high point in the decade for Ontario wines had been 49.5% sales by volume, falling to just over 40% at the end and this was also intensifying domestic competition.

Once again, the provincial government had shown dedicated support for the grape and wine industry, relieving much of the pressure exerted by the imposition of difficult trade agreements, although there would be ongoing complaints about the inequities that had resulted. Where a level playing field had been achieved for the sale of wines in the LCBO system between Ontario and imported wines, there was far from a level playing field within the industry itself, inspiring one wine writer to picture the small wineries as tiny mice scurrying around the feet of three or four large elephants, eager to gather up the crumbs they were leaving and being careful not to be squashed in the process.

All the threats aside, many of the changes were not only long overdue they were also absolutely needed, and consumers would be the winners as all wineries were now committed to the improvement of wine quality for Ontario wines, no matter their origin. Vinifera acreage was on the increase with a growing list of new varieties, like Pinot Gris and Sauvignon Blanc and Syrah, and the dreams of the pioneers were at last bearing fruit as most wineries, including the large operations, anticipated making premium VQA wines. The real issue was whether consumers would forsake some of their appetite for established 'Old World' wines still deemed to be superior in quality and other 'New World' wines, from places like California, Chile, and Australia, that were enticing with their flavours, and buy more Ontario wine!

CHAPTER EIGHT

The 1990's - Building a wine business with courage and unsung heroes

"By 1996 our wines were at parity with American and European wines... it was becoming increasingly clear that the playing field on which Ontario wineries were competing was neither level nor fair." Linda Bramble, "Niagara's Wine Visionaries", 2009

"The philosophies and practices of these new vintners were enshrined in the regulations of the VQA, the single most important piece of legislation to save the industry from extinction." Tony Aspler, "Canadian Wineries", 2013

A smorgasbord of wineries: 1990 – 1999

1990: Magnotta Winery Estates Ltd. – Vaughn (bought Charal Winery licence in 1989)

1990: King's Court Estate Winery - St. Catharines

1991: Marynissen Estates – Niagara-on-the-Lake

1991: Lakeview Cellars Estate Winery – Vineland (now part of Diamond Estates, NOL)

1992: Merger of Inniskillin and Cartier Wines – Cartier-Inniskillin Vintners

1992: Southbrook Farm Winery – Richmond Hill (now moved to Niagara-on-the-Lake)

1992: Lauro & Burden - Mississauga (closed)

1992: Kittling Ridge Estate Wines & Spirits – Grimsby (licence bought by Magnotta, 2013)

1992: Sunnybrook Farm Winery – Niagara-on-the-Lake (Fruit Winery)

1993: Hernder Estate Wines – St. Catharines

1993: Pillitteri Estates Winery – Niagara-on-the-Lake

1993: Domaine Wagners – Niagara-on-the-Lake (closed)

1994: Merger of Cartier-Inniskillin Vintners and Bright's Wines results in Vincor Canada

1994: Thirty Bench Wines – Beamsville (originally French Oak Vineyards)

1994: Willow Heights Estate Winery – Vineland (now Green Lane Winery)

1994: Milan Wineries – Toronto (closed)

1994: Hillebrand purchased by Andres Wines (Peller)

1995: Norfolk Estate Winery – St. Williams (Fruit Winery) (closed)

1995: Ocala Orchards Farm Winery – Port Perry

1995: County Cider – Waupoos (Fruit Winery)

1995: Walter's Estate Winery – Beamsville (became Eastdell Winery, 1999) closed

1996: Bright's merges with Cartier-Inniskillin to become Vincor (then bought London Wines)

1996: Culotta Wines purchased by Kittling Ridge Wines and Spirits

1996: VP Cellars - Jordan (became Creekside Estate Winery, 1999)

1996: Joseph's Estate Wines - Niagara-on-the-Lake

1996: Magnotta Winery – Beamsville (purchase of Montravin Cellars)

1997: Cilento Wines – Woodbridge (closed)

1997: Archibald Orchards and Estate Winery – Bowmanville (Fruit Winery)

1997: Rush Creek Wines – Aylmer (Fruit Winery)

1997: Strewn Winery – Niagara-on-the-Lake

1998: Meadow Lane Winery – St. Thomas (Fruit Winery) (closed)

1998: Cox Creek Cellars – Guelph (Fruit Winery)

1998: De Sousa – Toronto (second winery)

1999: Harvest Estates Winery - St. Catharines (Hernder Winery)

1999: Thomas and Vaughn Vintners - Beamsville (bought by Diamond Group) closed

1999: Malivoire Wine Company - Beamsville

1999: Kacaba Estate Winery - Vineland

1999: Thirteenth Street Winery - Jordan Station (sold 2008 – moved to St. Catharines)

1999: Royal Demaria Wine Company – Vineland

1999: Maleta Vineyards and Estate Winery - NOL (sold 2004 to Cadenza Wines)

1999: Daniel Lenko Estate Winery - Beamsville

1999: Leblanc Estate Winery - Harrow (closed)

1999: Featherstone Winery - Vineland

1999: Scotch Block Winery – Milton (Fruit Winery) (new ownership 2019)

1999: St. Jacob's Country Winery and Cidery - Waterloo (Fruit Winery) (closed)

All of Ontario becomes a wine region!

The last decade of the century marked the coming of age of Ontario as a bona fide and respected world wine region, albeit a very tiny one! From cult and garagiste wineries producing only a few hundred cases of wine annually, to small and mid-sized boutique wineries and all the way up to the extensive operations of Vincor and Andres (Peller), and with native ports and sherries and refreshment wines, Ontario/import blends, VQA wines, and fruit wines, our wine industry covered all the bases.

In total, forty new wineries opened their doors during the decade, starting up both inside and outside the designated viticultural areas, including eleven denoted as "Fruit Wineries" that grew a variety of fruits other than grapes for most of their wines. One third of the wineries developed as an extension of an already existing grape farm with the grower now becoming a winemaker as well. The industry also attracted businessmen who had made their money in other fields, and they would buy a producing vineyard or a property for planting grapes to start their own winery and undertake a new career. Other entrepreneurs with no experience in the grape and wine business bought wineries that were put up for sale for various reasons, believing such a purchase would give them an immediate foothold in the industry. Of the new operations, twenty-three developed in Niagara, six in the Greater Toronto area, four in Lake Erie North Shore, with the rest located all over the province including one in Prince Edward County, the first in a region that would soon blossom as a new Ontario DVA.

Considering the challenges facing the industry at the beginning of the 1990's and the ongoing changes in government policies and regulations intended to exert some bureaucratic control over the rapidly expanding industry, it may seem amazing that anyone would want to start a winery at this time. But there were definite signs of optimism in the air including the establishment of the VQA with its rising reputation and increasing sales of icewine, a high margin product. Or perhaps some of these individuals believed there was a good business case and future potential in making wine from French Hybrid and Vinifera grapes, with some growers in particular thinking that it made better financial sense to turn their grapes into wine themselves rather than selling them to a winery. And fruit growers were seizing on the opportunity of making 'value added' wine as an additional source of income from their fruit production in places where the preferred grape varieties were difficult to grow. For others who had the means to pursue their dreams, it might have been simply the desire to spend their time in wine country, enjoying a perceived 'romantic' lifestyle that centered on winemaking, having been seduced by the lure of dancing with Bacchus.

Whatever their motivation, they held one belief in common - that the future of the wine industry would be a healthy one - and on this basis were willing to make the significant investment required. As a result, when the decade came to an end, with these passionate newcomers establishing their wineries from Harrow in south-western Ontario to Waupoos in eastern Ontario, as in the Prohibition era, the entire province had become a wine region!

Mergers and Acquisitions: Growing a wine business

In 1984 Gabe and Rossana Magnotta launched Festa Juice in north Toronto and quickly found success selling imported grape juice to home winemakers. The experience they gained led them to believe they could develop their business into a winery, something they could pass on to their children, after the government allowed wineries to make blended wines containing up to 70% foreign material. In 1989 they were able to purchase the assets and licence of Charal Winery, a boutique winery on a farm near Blenheim that had been put up for sale. The vineyards were not part of the sale but everything else was moved to Vaughn and the winery was able to open in December 1990.

Through determined hard work, the Magnottas quickly grew their business purchasing other licences, including the Montravin Winery in Beamsville in 1996 in order to expand the number of their retail outlets, as well as vineyards in Niagara and in the Maipo Valley in Chile to ensure a reliable supply of high-quality grapes. A brewery and distillery would follow as the family continued to build one of the most successful operations in the industry becoming our third largest winery and achieving recognition as 'Canada's most award-winning winery'.

Shortly after taking over Chateau-Gai winery and renaming it Cartier Wines, the group led by Don Triggs began to look for another winery that they could purchase which would give them greater access to the premium wine market. Triggs approached Don Ziraldo of Inniskillin, described by Linda Bramble in "Niagara's Wine Visionaries" as "the jewel in the crown of Canadian wineries". He convinced him that a merger of the two wineries would be a Win-Win opportunity, offering Inniskillin a chance to expand their business with a national sales force and the ability to sell in Cartier's retail network in Ontario while giving Cartier a stepping-stone into the world of premium wines and high-end restaurants and retailers around the world that Ziraldo had cultivated. They would grow the icewine business in which Inniskillin was a world leader and use it as a lead-in for the rest of their portfolios.

The Ontario wine industry was shocked when news of the deal was announced as few could understand why Inniskillin would want to merge with a long-established, corporate winery whose culture and history of winemaking were so different from its own. But Triggs had been determined to lead Cartier in a new direction and the merger was a clear indication that the industry had to consider major changes if it were to prosper.

A year later it was revealed that the Hatch family, who had owned Bright's Wines since the 1930's, intended to put the winery up for sale. In short order it was purchased by Gerry Schwartz, President and CEO of Onex Corporation, for $50 million. Schwartz was aware that Don Triggs had also been interested in Bright's and he invited him to a meeting to discuss an intriguing idea – the merger of Cartier-Inniskillin with Bright's that would make the new company the largest wine business in Canada and one of the largest in all North America. When the deal was completed, Don Triggs became CEO of Brights-Cartier-Inniskillin Vintners a merger that would have a profound impact on the wine industry in the province, in Canada, and soon, internationally. In June 1996, Triggs took the new company public as Vincor International Ltd., preparing to expand the business with the revenue from selling the initial shares. Shortly afterwards, the assets of London Winery, the last remaining older corporate winery in Ontario with its roots traceable to the mid 1920's, were purchased by Vincor and other acquisitions would soon follow in B.C., Australia, New Zealand, and the U.S.

The sale of London Winery brought an end to 10 years of 'downsizing' in the corporate wine business with the closure of Jordan's, Barnes, and London, and the merger of Chateau Gai/Cartier and Bright's into Vincor, all the remaining 'old guard' wineries. This would leave Vincor and Andres as the two largest wineries in our wine industry along with a growing list of much smaller businesses competing for what remained of the market.

Although the evolution of Vincor was far and away the most recognized transaction with the general public, there were other changes of ownership that were also important for the individuals concerned and for the wine industry. In Vineland, the Weis family, who had owned Vineland Estates for several years, decided to sell to businessman John Howard who lived nearby. John began extensive renovations to the business, turning it into what has been called "Niagara's most picturesque winery" while retaining the brilliant winemaking team of Allan and Brian Schmidt.

In Niagara-on-the-lake, Hillebrand Winery, which had grown to almost 300,000 cases from its founding as the tiny Newark Winery, was acquired by Andres Wines in 1994. Andres CEO, John Peller, recognized the attractive location that the winery had on Highway 55 but also wanted to take advantage of the wonderful reputation of the winery and the expansive retail store system that the winery had developed. This would be the first step for Andres in eventually growing their network of Ontario and British Columbia premium wineries, all under the umbrella of a new family name, Peller Estates.

Two years later, Kittling Ridge in Grimsby purchased the assets of Culotta Winery in Oakville which also operated six retail stores mainly in the Toronto area. The creative owner of Kittling Ridge, John Hall, who had been one of the original partners in the Cartier buy-out, set his sights on increasing sales of products like his unique 'Icewine and Brandy' through these outlets.

Three other small wineries changed hands before the end of the decade with two of the three also changing their name. Ron Vidal and Wayne Philbrick, who had opened VP cellars in 1995 in Jordan, sold their farm and winery just 3 years later to Peter Jensen and Laura McCain who renamed it Creekside Estate Winery. The investment allowed Creekside to develop a true barrel cellar and enlarged facility on the way to becoming one of Ontario's most awarded wineries.

Buck and Sadie Walters were grape growers In Beamsville, whose extensive vineyards along the very base of the Niagara Escarpment enjoyed a magnificent view over Lake Ontario. They built a winemaking facility to take advantage of this in 1995 but were convinced to sell the operation in 1999 to Susan O'Dell and Michael East, a couple who had bought a property just down Locust Lane from the Walter's farm. They named their winery Eastdell and it quickly became a tourist destination with its picturesque walking trails and restaurant (above the winery) offering a magnificent view all the way to Toronto.

At this same time, the Puddicombe and Warren families decided to end their partnership after ten years and sell Stoney Ridge Cellars which was located on the Puddicombe Farm in Winona. The assets were purchased by a group of investors from the Ottawa-Hull area who moved the winery to Vineland and began to acquire property for planting vinifera vines on the Bench in Beamsville at what came to be called Kew Vineyards and along the base of the Escarpment overlooking the Twenty Mile Creek in Vineland. The move came with a small change in name of the winery to Stoney Ridge Estate Winery along with ambitious plans to grow production. Under the direction of manager John Belanger, a new winery was constructed, and an old plum orchard was removed to allow the planting of Pinot Noir grapes on site while the grounds themselves were further developed into what would become "Ontario's Garden Winery".

Changing the rules again…and again…and again

At the beginning of the 1990's there were essentially two 'kinds' of wineries in Ontario, a small number of larger wineries owning their own chain of retail stores and a much larger number of smaller wineries operating their one and only retail store at the winery. At this time, all wineries could 'blend' import material with local grapes if they so desired although most produced only 100% Ontario wine. All wineries were deemed to be 'grape wineries' (although some did produce wines from fruit other than grapes), and it was possible for a winery to open anywhere in Ontario, with or without vineyards.

In 1993, the Government introduced a winemaking policy that would change the nature of the industry significantly, with a focus on the role of agriculture in the wine business and brand-new rules for establishing a winery. Criteria were developed concerning 'elegibility' to open a new winery with a serious consideration of the role of an on-site winery retail store (or WRS in government speak).

In Ontario since the 1970's, reflecting the constantly changing wine market, the government had made numerous changes in regulations relating to the production of wine and this was something that wineries simply had to live with. In this case, however, the policy was designed "to preserve agricultural land and promote value-added agricultural activities, rural economic development, and tourism", steps which would "support and enhance the Ontario wine and grape industries" at the same time.

The third intent of this new 'viticultural policy' was more pointed in that the rules were structured "to avoid the proliferation of "store-front" wineries that focused on wine retailing rather than on wine production and value-added agriculture". Presumably, by "store-front" wineries, the government meant wineries operating a retail store at a winery that was not located on a vineyard in a DVA – with a desire to end this type of operation.

The new rules that had to be followed if the winery wanted a WRS would take effect beginning January 1, 1994, and no winery, except for those few with stores already in place, now deemed to be 'grand-fathered', could operate more than this one store.

1. any new grape winery would now have to be located in one of the three DVAs (Niagara Peninsula, Lake Erie North Shore, or Pelee Island)

2. the winery would have to operate a vineyard and the winery would be obligated to produce 50% of its total production from its own grapes grown on site

3. a 'fruit winery' could locate anywhere in the province provided it had 5 acres of planted fruit other than grape (or enough maple trees or beehives to be a maple winery or meadery). Such a winery could even produce up to 20% of its wine from grapes, if it desired, without the need to grow those grapes itself!

While this all sounded agriculturally wonderful, it is amazing that the bureaucrats who devised the rules could not foresee how difficult the 50% restriction would be. The ruling would ensure that any new grape winery would be established with a successful vineyard, but it limited the production of the winery to the output of its vineyard (in this case, a bigger size would be better!), preventing the winery from buying in other grapes beyond this limit. It gave a new winery no ability to grow without enlarging their vineyard! It also required considerable mathematical dexterity in production to ensure that the 50% or 20% limits were not exceeded, for that would, and did, bring down the heavy hand of government on the offending winery!

And restricting new grape winery development to the three DVA's in order to ensure that a winery would now be viticulturally based, while 'reasonable' to the government, overlooked the reality that some people were now planting grapes outside the DVA's with the intention of opening a winery.

Perhaps the most unfortunate result of the new 'policy' was the patch-work quilt of wineries that it confirmed for the industry and several "unhealthy realities" as Richard Johnson of the Prince Edward County Winegrowers Association called them. One of these centred on a relatively small number of pre-1993 wineries enjoying distinct competitive advantages and market-share dominance over the other wineries and certainly any new winery that would now open. Some wineries could legally create 'blends' while the other 90% of the industry was forbidden to use any imported material after 1993. And those who could blend were the same wineries that enjoyed the grand-fathered privilege of owning more than one retail store. A small number of wineries were operating outside the DVAs and without vineyards but with a retail store, mainly in the Greater Toronto Area (GTA), where they had ready access to a large market that was much further away for the 'farm wineries' in a DVA, giving them a significant retailing advantage that the LCBO (also a competitor) wanted to curtail. So much for a level playing field!

From January 1, 1994 on, all new wineries would be in fact 'farm' wineries and this was good news for fruit growers who wanted to extend their farm activity with a 'value-added' winery and wine retail store. But from the beginning, a fruit winery was considered somewhat of an oddity with many 'connaisseurs' questioning whether fruit wine could be considered 'wine' at all. And in truth, although fruit wineries used 100% Ontario fruit, paid the same fees and taxes as any grape winery, obeying the same rules and regulations pertaining to 'alcohol', and could even make up to 20% of their wine from Ontario grapes, unfortunately they would never be considered a part of the Ontario Wine Industry, unable to participate in the activities of the Wine Council of Ontario or enjoy government benefits afforded Ontario grape wineries. Essentially limited to sales at their farms, it was a real challenge for fruit wine producers to market and sell their wines. It would take a long time for fruit wines, no matter their fine quality, to achieve any credibility given the discrimination they faced, being excluded from most wine competitions, as well as from the official 'wine route' map, and from government funding and assistance, all of which were limited to grape wineries only.

With the wine industry now well fragmented, it did not take long for many small wineries to express their unhappiness when they attempted to operate within the 50% rule, an unreasonable restriction on their production, never mind the other inequities in the industry. Grape growers were also unhappy that new wineries would be limited in their grape purchases to half of what they were producing. Realizing that part of the 1993 policy was flawed but convinced that its spirit was sound, in 1997 the LCBO Policy Managers massaged the rules for operating an on-site Winery Retail Store, the heart of the matter. Removing the 50% requirement was the essential change "to enable wineries to increase production and sales by acquiring more grapes from independent growers". This eliminated an unnecessary speedbump for wineries starting up as they could now produce as much wine as they required from grapes grown off-site or purchased from other Ontario growers and at the same time enhance the capacity of the industry.

The other criteria remained the same including the necessity of a grape winery to be located in a DVA on 5 acres of planted grapes and making 100% Ontario wine. Any winery making apple wine was obligated to use at least 70% Ontario apples and all wineries had to ferment on-site the minimum Ontario requirement of each bottle of wine sold in the WRS. New wineries were also required to meet LCBO site inspection requirements, a step which would serve as a prelude to a March 1999 Policy statement on "Compliance with the requirement that an Ontario wine be "made" by a winery" with the key word "made" defined in considerable detail.

Just when the bureaucrats believed they finally had it right, they began to encounter headwinds concerning the rule that discouraged a grape winery from opening outside a DVA. People were starting to plant grapes on a commercial scale in Prince Edward County, on the Oak Ridges Moraine north of Toronto, and in other areas on an experimental basis and they were seeking permission to develop a winery with an on-site retail store. Some of these growers would have to rely on special over-wintering techniques to ensure the survival of their vines while others believed they had discovered a suitable micro-climate which would allow vinifera and vinifera hybrids to grow successfully for them. Although aware of the inherent risks, they were determined to invest in their dream, hoping as well that global warming might have a dramatic impact on Ontario grape growing and work in their favour.

For a while, the government wrestled with the pros and cons, as they saw it. These new plantings would be adding production at a time when there were concerns about grape surpluses. And a winery developing in what could be called a 'marginal' area might have to get by with winter hardy hybrids that were less in demand. If these grapes were in fact of lower quality, would this have a negative impact on the overall reputation of local wine? Such a winery might be able to grow the "Frontenac" grape successfully, for example, but would consumers want to buy such a wine? Another worry reflected how differently bureaucrats think from winemakers. It was suggested that "a major expansion of the number of operating wineries may increase fragmentation in the industry and make it more difficult for it to develop its own identity". Those who worry about such things asked how would this "further the long-term needs of the grape and wine industry"? This was powerful language for a renewed industry that was still in its infancy and with a fractured 'identity' already!

Some, but certainly not all, of these concerns were valid. Others would point out that allowing more wineries to develop outside of the current DVAs would help to increase the visibility of the industry and help enhance its image and increase demand for Ontario wine, surely as important as defining its 'identity'! And this might add to the number of DVAs! In the end, the government agreed that new wineries would be unlikely to develop outside a DVA unless they received permission to operate a winery retail store, and to facilitate this, while maintaining the viticultural direction of the policy, in June of 2000, the LCBO came up with a new 'rule': a grape winery could open outside a DVA with a WRS if it produced at least 50% of its grape wine from grapes grown within the boundaries of the county or region or district in which it was located.

The government had half-opened the door for a new kind of farm winery, allowing for a "measured expansion" of the wine industry and facilitating the development of a new DVA which they believed would "take many years to emerge". With a continuing explosion of new wineries, especially in Prince Edward County, it would quickly be proven wrong on both accounts!

Agri-tourism comes to town!

In Ontario, the government had long been censured for its 'prohibition' mentality in matters pertaining to the advertising and sale of alcohol, maintaining a tight 'control' that periodically annoyed people in the alcohol business. On the other hand, it had always been faithful in its support of the province's grape and wine industry, reacting with a financial hand up when needed to assist both grape growers and winemakers or helping to ensure the survival of the industry when severely challenged. In 1993, the government took a more proactive stance to the wine business, with the introduction of a viticultural policy that would encourage people to visit wineries all over the province. In so doing, it was signaling a much more relaxed attitude to the sale of wine for the public outside the normal LCBO retail system. The term coined for this new hospitality-driven activity was 'Agri-tourism', inviting consumers to visit wine country where they could enjoy a variety of educational and entertaining events, and, of course, take advantage of the opportunity to buy the local wines which might not be available in the LCBO system. Agri-tourism was immediately welcomed by the increasing number of small wineries seeking ways to enhance their individual sales while competing not only with blended Product of Canada and imported wines, but with each other.

Visiting the boutique wineries was not a new activity in the industry but a heightened interest in Ontario wines developed at this time as a result of the number of new wineries, a developing familiarity with the VQA concept, and the perception that the quality of these artisanal wines was worth pursuing. An increasing number of consumers started to take a personal interest in Ontario wine and were anxious to 'try out' each new kid-on-the-block, to discover what wines they were making and what they were like, then to build a relationship with the business if the experience was enjoyable. I remember half-joking at one time that our winery had more customers coming from Ottawa than Hamilton as our 'story' was willingly spread afar by word of mouth by satisfied visitors.

To drive consumers to their cellar doors, the wineries would become creative in their marketing with winery newsletters, 'futures' (a pre-sale of new wines), loyalty clubs, weekend seminars on grapes and wine with food and wine pairings and cooking demonstrations, and numerous inviting attractions from grape stomps to classic car shows to open houses complete with musical entertainment. Any good idea displayed by one winery was immediately seized upon by others and this provided consumers with ongoing opportunities to visit a wine region as a very pleasurable habit.

The activities helped to increase traffic flow for all wineries as they became destinations for repeat visits where you could buy hand-crafted, top-quality wines from people who were passionate about their work, and frequently meet the owners or the winemakers themselves.

I was fortunate at Stoney Ridge to have a loyal following of customers who joined our "Barrel Club", which provided them with special tastings and sales in return for investing in our barrel program. When we moved to Puddicombe Farms in 1989, the winery store was attached to my partner's farm market which offered home-baking, light lunches, and farm products for sale with the added attraction of a petting zoo. My wife Charlotte, as a kindergarten teacher, set up a children's play area in one corner of the retail store which encouraged parents with children to visit and taste knowing their children were safely involved close by. From all of this evolved our Cheese Shop, and at harvest time we became known for our Concord Grape pies, a grape attraction!

In 1990, Vineland Estates winery opened a large patio off their retail store and served hors-d'oeuvres, cold cuts, and cheeses, to customers who could relax and take advantage of the marvelous view overlooking the vineyards and north over Lake Ontario. What was essentially a 'wine bar' would eventually evolve into one of Niagara's finest restaurants. Cave Springs winery developed their winery site in Jordan into a world-class tourist mecca, opening their renowned On The Twenty Restaurant and Wine Bar in 1993 along with a boutique Hotel across the street which could serve as a base for touring the region. Both restaurants became so popular that several other wineries opened their own, ranging in style from casual to upscale, offering visitors an enticing choice of gourmet eating to accompany their wine touring.

By this time Niagara presented a fascinating range of winemaking facilities to visitors, from rustic, barn-like structures, where the winemaking was simply accommodated, to amazing structures that were built as a state-of-the-art winery, complete with barrel cellars, bottling lines, a visitor friendly retail store, and hospitality rooms. The variety of facilities added interest in itself, and every winery had their own 'story' to relate to visitors adding that welcome personal touch.

1994 marked a turning point in touring with the opening of the new and breath-taking Chateau des Charmes winery, a 36,000 square foot production facility that resembled a "chateau" in every way, set back a considerable distance from the road with an impressive winding entrance and surrounded by manicured vineyards. The $6 million investment provided an ideal setting for visitors including rooms to host tastings, a large deck around the back of the winery for outdoor functions, a wine bar, and a theatre. The achievement was taken as an indicator of the direction the industry was heading, a remarkable symbol of success with the potential for growth and even better things in store. And indeed, within a few years it would inspire the construction of other state-of-the-art wineries in what some considered "the dream business". With annual tourism beginning to approach 3 million people, someone had already described Niagara wine country as "Napa North", a fine compliment indicating that our wine industry had finally "arrived" in the world of wine.

The emphasis on tourism had been initiated in 1988 by then Premier David Peterson who realized that with all the growth in boutique wineries, they would depend more and more on retail sales in their on-site store considering the limited shelf space available in the LCBO and the difficulty competing to sell their wines to restaurants. His government established the Niagara Wine Route from Stoney Creek to Niagara Falls providing a brochure and installing bold blue and white signage that directed traffic to the increasing number of wineries. This was followed by a reduction in the fee that wineries had to pay the LCBO on sales in their own retail store from 5% to 2%. In the early 1990's further help was provided when the government finally decided to allow Sunday sales in the winery retail stores and this, along with the ability to use credit cards that soon followed, resulted in a doubling of on-site sales.

With the limited marketing funds they had available, the wineries sought out opportunities to make consumers aware of their existence. Many participated in trade shows where the public had the chance to meet the winemaker, 'discover' the winery, and taste the wines. Our winery went annually to the Toronto Wine and Cheese Show, and the Hamilton and the Ottawa Food and Wine Shows in the hopes of educating consumers about Ontario wine and encouraging them to pay us a visit in Niagara. It was also helpful that these shows held wine competitions for the show participants, providing medals or plaques that could be displayed during the show to entice show goers to your winery 'booth'. As well, wineries attended many charitable events to pour their wines and always benefitted from meeting people who were developing an interest in local wine and were pleased to meet and talk face to face with winery team members. Meeting the public in a very personal way helped establish a new identity for Ontario winemaking, something that was non-existent in the previous period of corporate winemaking, lending credence to the "Buy local!" slogan.

Considering the improving quality of our local wines, it became important for a winery to enter some of the numerous wine competitions that were available for wineries, in the hopes of achieving stellar results and 'free' promotion in the media including wine magazines, radio shows, and newspaper wine columns. The example of Inniskillin winning its special award for its Icewine in 1991 was on everyone's mind, and although the costs were high to enter some of the competitions (fees and product), there could be beneficial publicity if your wines won an award.

Locally, the annual Cuvee Gala which was held in Niagara at a 'quiet' time of year for wineries in March, stimulated keen interest among consumers who had a chance to taste the medal winning wines that had been selected previously in a blind judging by the winemakers themselves. Wine writers were invited to participate in special tastings, gathering the information they would write about in their articles. Cuvee would also acknowledge Ontario Restaurants that promoted VQA wines and honour individuals associated with the industry with an "Award of Excellence" for special achievements in grape growing and winemaking or for service to the industry.

Another major competition was introduced in 1996 through the efforts of Tony Aspler, one of Canada's best-known wine authorities, and David

Rose, a Toronto marketing guru, in conjunction with the Ontario Wine Society, a group of oenophiles who gave tremendous support to local winemaking. Wine judges selected the top Ontario wines in numerous categories and presented awards to the winning winemakers at a lavish dinner served with some of the winning wines. The hi-lite of the evening was the naming of the "Winemaker of the Year" (see Appendix), an individual whose work in the industry had been exemplary and worthy of the respect of the other winemakers. This, my favourite local competition, has developed successfully over the years with 'Tony's Team', including his wife, Deborah, and chief steward, the indomitable Sadie Darby, recently celebrating the 25th anniversary of what has become the equivalent of the Academy Awards for the Ontario Wine industry.

A third competition, the All-Canadian Wine Championships, held annually in Windsor under the auspices of Brian Bannon, a local wine columnist, provided a great setting for wines I produced as we always seemed to have such good luck in it. This was an opportunity to meet consumers and restaurant owners in the Windsor-Detroit area at a sampling of our wines and at a dinner when the awards were presented and always proved to be a very enjoyable weekend.

In addition to these competitions, many wineries chose to enter international competitions for the opportunity to compete with wines of the world and the prestige of winning a 'world-class' award. These included Intervin, VinItaly, Vinexpo, the International Wine Challenge, and several others, where a medal would give a winery considerable exposure in the media and bragging rights for some time. This emphasis on awards through the 1990's shone a spot-light on many wineries and stimulated an interest in our wines that helped elevate the entire industry's reputation.

The Niagara Region, leveraging its natural assets, had made a celebrity of the wine industry, creating what has been called "the most successful Agri-tourism enterprise in Canadian history". Other Ontario regions would follow in step with the realization that tourists love to visit wineries where they can experience not only great wine but things which are natural, the outdoors, vineyards, farm operations, country markets, bed and breakfasts, winery restaurants featuring locally grown food, and events and cultural experiences of all kinds, a travel smorgasbord of delight and satisfaction.

By the mid 1990's, with interest in the grape and wine industry intensifying, a number of individuals believed the industry now required a research institute to provide it with in-depth scientific knowledge on grape growing and winemaking in our 'cool climate' region and to supply outreach services in support of the industry. To accompany this would be an educational program to help with the rapidly increasing number of wineries, filling a need for employees who would be knowledgeable in all facets of the business, grape growing, winemaking, winery sales and marketing, and research.

Once again, Don Ziraldo stepped forward to provide the necessary leadership along with John Howard, President of Vineland Estates Winery. In 1996 they co-chaired a fund-raising campaign that raised $4 million to establish what came to be known as the Cool Climate Oenology and Viticulture Institute (CCOVI), to be built at Brock University in St. Catharines as a partnership between the University and the grape and wine industry. Both the Grape Growers' Marketing Board and the Wine Council of Ontario made significant contributions to the campaign as did many wineries and individuals, but it was decided to name the building "Inniskillin Hall" in recognition of a very generous gift of $600,000 from Vincor International and the amazing Don Triggs. The first eight students entered the program in 1997 as it initiated both undergraduate and graduate degrees in oenology and viticulture.

At the same time, a demonstration vineyard was established on the Niagara College Niagara-on-the-Lake campus that would develop into a 38 acre property to operate in conjunction with a planned undergraduate program that would support expansion in the grape and wine industry and with industry partners. When the program started in 2000 it was titled the Niagara College Winery and Viticulture Technician Program to emphasize the practical learning that would be provided over two years for students intending to become lab or viticulture technicians, sommeliers, retail sales and marketing staff, and winemakers. Management of the program was entrusted to Dean Jon Ogryzlo and operations manager Steve Gill, who both provided a devoted effort to make everything come together.

The centre of the hands-on work would be the teaching winery, described as the first commercial teaching winery in Canada, and the first class hosted 25 full time students (with a waiting list!). It was my privilege to direct the winemaking program whose intent was to provide the essential knowledge of making wine while involving the students as much as possible hands-on in the actual physical process. Other courses covering the math and the chemistry of wine, vineyard mechanics, wine marketing, the history of wine, and an awareness of the modern world of wine, helped to round out the experience. Students also enjoyed the benefit of a Fall 'practicum', working one semester in a winery where theory became practice and everybody had the opportunity to make their own wine, carboy size, for a class competition.

Although we had a rather rustic beginning in a horticultural shed that had to serve both horticultural and winemaking students, I would have to say in retrospect that my participation in the program was the hi-lite of my winemaking career. The program became so highly valued that before long it was necessary to double the enrolment and for the winemaking program to take over the entire 'barn'. This would be followed by the construction of a new winery with a room with a wonderful view over the vineyard for on-site public sales. From the beginning we were able to make several wines that won awards in numerous competitions, including the "Best White Wine in Canada", our 2001 Barrel Fermented and Aged Chardonnay, which the College was able to serve proudly for the grand opening of the program, providing a wonderful foundation for the future.

Since their inception both educational programs would go on to exceed expectations, attracting students from around the world and sending them back trained and prepared for work in their desired grape or wine endeavors in Ontario, in wineries elsewhere in Canada and abroad. The Research Programs at Brock, and to a lesser extent Niagara College, aided by the co-operation and participation of many wineries, would attract world-class researchers and prove to be very successful, providing expertise on priorities of the Canadian grape and wine industry and supportive services for the needs of that community. To-day, one can hardly imagine the industry without them.

Ending the 20th century on a high note!

Not many individuals outside the grape and wine industry have ever had direct dealings with the Wine Council of Ontario, an organization which was incorporated in 1974 to represent the wineries in dealings with the Ontario Government and to handle the administrative needs of the wine industry. It has also acted as the voice of the industry although few consumers have ever been familiar with its work or even aware of its actual existence. Through the years, while the new cottage wine industry was beginning to find its way, the Wine Council (WCO) represented primarily the corporate wineries and it was these wineries who provided the leadership of the group in dealing with the Grape Growers of Ontario, the LCBO, and the LLBO to protect their interests in negotiating grape prices or regulatory matters.

When several smaller wineries became members, wineries with concerns that were quite different from those of the larger wineries, problems began to develop that would eventually lead to frustration and stress among members. The corporate wineries, who sold the lion's share of wine in the province, believed they had the right to 'run the show' while the smaller players felt their voices were ignored in discussions and that they had little ownership of decisions being made. This would entrench a 'them vs us' mentality, especially when it came to dealing with competing interests as in deciding how to handle government funding for marketing activities.

In 1994, aware that help was needed to deal with this problem, the Wine Council decided to hire a new Executive Director, someone who understood the mechanics of government and with the ability to bring opposing forces together. They hired a lady named Linda Franklin who had worked as chief of staff for Conservative Ernie Eves at Queen's Park over a six year stay where she learned 'the workings' of government, and with an additional five years of experience working on behalf of the College of Physicians. Her arrival proved to be more than just a breath of needed fresh air as she immediately took a professional approach to numerous pressing issues providing very competent leadership that would last over her 14 years with the Wine Council.

Acting quietly and efficiently behind the scenes, Linda represented the industry in many different activities, working with a patience and sense of good humour that belied the aggressive drive beneath her always cheerful composure.

Linda was able to develop a solid rapport with everybody in the industry, no matter the size of the business, ensuring that the large wineries were able to operate as they required while developing a wonderful working relationship with the smaller winery owners, business competitors who became collaborators in advancing the interests of that group. The proactive core of this body, who stepped forward on behalf of many others whose face or name might not be as familiar to Ontario wine drinkers, included Peter Gamble, the original Executive Director of the VQA who had been responsible for so much of its structure, Allan Schmidt from Vineland Estates who took on the role of the 'numbers man', and Paul Speck from Henry of Pelham, and Len Pennachetti from Cave Springs who both had no fear in calling a spade a spade using the appropriate, figurative language and were determined that their way was the right way. Not only did they have their own winery business to take care of but in addition they would dedicate hours of their own time in meetings and on the phone putting the plans in place to improve the fortunes of all wineries. Other wineries owe these 'unsung heroes', who played a true 'game-changing' role in the industry, a sincere debt of gratitude for their effort and achievements.

Through the late 1990's they emerged as the leaders of the industry in confronting two issues that were of growing concern with the ever-increasing number of small wineries. The first of these involved the sale of VQA wine to restaurants, a difficult and expensive market for new, boutique wineries to develop, while the second involved the future success of the entire wine industry, the completion of all the work that was pending to establish the VQA as a legislated body. Both issues were extremely complex matters involving intense negotiations with the government, but with Linda Franklin co-ordinating the work involved, the Wine Council would prevail, and the story would have a happy ending for everyone.

Considering the number of taxes, fees, mark-ups, and licences involved in the wine business and the significant amount of their revenue that wineries had to 'remit' for these essentials, it would be understandable that they believed these ranged from onerous to excessive, but if you wanted to dance with Bacchus you had to pay the piper, in this case the government. However, there was one mark-up in particular that the wineries had good reason to complain about because there was no doubt that it was simply unfair to them.

Although large wineries dominated sales of 'Ontario' wine to restaurants with their inexpensive, international blends (and a clever use of their marketing budgets to secure the loyalty of the owners!), some smaller wineries were finding that some restaurants were also interested in their award-winning, limited production VQA wines. Unfortunately, this kind of sale offered little profit for the winery due to the costs of delivering the wine, sometimes having difficulty being paid in a timely fashion, and paying for a salesman to service what were normally small accounts. However, the real issue behind the complaining from the smaller wineries involved the amount of the mark-up that the LCBO demanded from the sale, 58% at this time, which was the same as if the restaurant had ordered at an LCBO store. It was a case of the wineries doing all the work in order to achieve a sale, with the LCBO taking most of the revenue for doing absolutely nothing, millions of dollars over a year for performing no services. The wineries perceived this as unjust, and it was!

After some negotiations with a very resistant LCBO who advanced the excuse that this could not be done as it conflicted with 'international trade obligations', the Wine Council went directly to Finance Minister Ernie Eves (whom Linda Franklin knew very well!) and David Tsubouchi, Minister of Commercial and Consumer Relations, to state their case. In the end, the Government could see spin-off benefits to accepting what came to be called "Direct Delivery" to restaurants and conceded to the Wine Council's request in 1999. However, the concession was for VQA wines exclusively, whether listed by the LCBO or not, and did not include the International blends/ Cellared in Canada wines as the LCBO refused to consider surrendering what was a significant amount of their revenue beyond the anticipated VQA 'loss' already involved. This was an important win for the smaller wineries as it facilitated the development of another meaningful sales channel for them while returning needed revenue (some $12 million in the first year alone) and helped gain credibility with consumers who could now find more VQA wines in their favourite restaurant or bar. Unfortunately for fruit wineries, they also were excluded from the direct delivery agreement, but their justifiable complaints were unfortunately ignored.

The other matter was easier to resolve as government quickly agreed with the Wine Council's planning although at the same time it required dedicated effort and a commitment of time over two years to work out the legalities. A proposal from the wine industry was submitted to David Tsubouchi concerning the status of the VQA, changing it from an association of members who regulated themselves to one that would have the VQA regulated by provincial law. After legislation was drafted to incorporate the Vintners' Quality Alliance of Ontario, Minister Tsubouchi signed the package into law on June 1, 1999.

The primary function of the VQA would be to act as the industry's watchdog on behalf of wine consumers, ensuring the compliance of the members with regulations, with a 13 member Board of Directors (9 from the wineries and the balance from government, the Grape Growers, and the Restaurant and Hotel/Motel Association). On January 15, 2000, Laurie Macdonald was hired to be the first Executive Director of the VQAO, a not-for-profit, independent "wine authority", to administer and enforce the new VQA Act including the power to impose penalties and even lay criminal charges for winemaking or labelling infractions.

This change in status would serve as a magnet for attracting more new wineries to the industry with potential owners feeling comfortable that their investment and efforts would be almost automatically accepted by consumers. And indeed, the legislated VQA did bring a new credibility to the wine industry, one which would soon be reflected in gradually improving sales and overall market share. Consumers might not have been aware of the individual rules and regulations – even wineries had to become suddenly familiar with a host of these – but the presence of the VQA logo on a bottle of wine, a guarantee of authenticity, was now very important in the local market and would serve as a proud brand ambassador abroad. VQA at last signified a belief that quality winemaking was a reality in Ontario, and this offered wonderful hope for the future.

In one of his books on the Ontario wine industry, noted writer Tony Aspler described this time as the "Golden Age of winemaking" in the province, referring to the dramatic change that had happened after the prediction of the demise of the industry. And indeed, there were numerous signs of improvement and prosperity to support his belief.

In our vineyards the tide had turned once and for all with 'labrusca' grapes like Catawba, Concord, and Niagara giving way to a growing number of vinifera including Riesling, Chardonnay, Sauvignon Blanc, Pinot Gris, Pinot Noir, Cabernet Franc, Cabernet Sauvignon, Merlot, Gamay, and several others, all with the potential to make world-class wine. Many French hybrids had come and were now gone leaving only the more successful like Vidal, Marechal Foch, and Baco Noir as suitable for quality winemaking. Grape growing itself was now becoming more of a science than in the past with considerable innovation and new technology touching on all aspects of viniculture from the use of rootstocks to an awareness of grape clones, from vine spacing to trellising to the use of sprays, with greater awareness of organic growing and the first hints of biodynamics in the vineyard (see later). All of this would explain the concept that 'quality begins in the vineyard' along with the development of the notion of 'terroir', stressing the importance of the relationship between the vineyard environment and the ensuing winemaking.

The proliferation of wineries meant a growing need for winemakers, and this provided an opportunity for new talent to come to Ontario from other winemaking regions in Europe, Australia, New Zealand, and South Africa. They came, well-educated and trained, bringing new learning and experiences to our wine industry. Coinciding with their arrival there was an influx of new technology and learning for the making of wine. The use of oak barrels was becoming more prevalent along with increased knowledge about the different kinds of barrels and their impact on wine. The process of fermentation was benefitting from ongoing scientific analysis, resulting in improved yeast strains and fermentation additives that allowed the winemaker to have more control over the product. Some wineries were experimenting with new technologies from the use of carbonic maceration to enhance the fruit level of a red wine to micro-oxygenation to produce more complex red wines to new styles of fermenters, along with new techniques to push the envelope on quality. Winemaking, often described as 'the world's second oldest profession', was being given a new look and Ontario was as pro-active in this regard as any other wine region.

All these innovations helped underline the feeling of optimism that blossomed in the industry along with other developments that had happened over the decade including the opening of educational and research facilities at Brock University, the establishment of Ontario's first wine laws, the emphasis on Agri-tourism along with winery retail store changes, and direct delivery to restaurants. Taken together, these solidified the foundation of a new grape and wine industry that had hit a high note and was anxious to play for the world.

Yet once again, as in the 1970's, so much had happened so quickly that it was easy to overlook some details in the 'big picture' that represented ongoing concerns with the nature of our vineyards, our wineries, and our wines, and the corresponding impact on sales and market share.

In our youthful exuberance we had forgotten just how fragile our grape industry was, attempting to grow sensitive Vinifera grapes in our temperamental, even hostile, cold climate. Grape growers and wineries have to contend with climatic conditions that cause significant variation in quality and production one vintage to the next and which limit our ability to increase production beyond the established micro-climates that sustain viticulture. And by itself, this production is insufficient to support a 100% Ontario wine industry which has been one reason we continue to allow the use of imported material in blended wines.

In the 1990's, production ranged from a high of 64,736 tonnes in 1999 to just 33,929 in 1993 with most years producing 47,000 to 50,000 tonnes. However, the severe winter and resulting crop failure in 1993 led the government to alter the Wine Content Act, reducing the amount of Ontario wine required in a blended wine from 30% to as little as 10% while changing this again to 25% a year later. Most wine regions would never take such action, making their wine from what Mother Nature has delivered, but in Ontario it was considered acceptable in order to allow for as much production of VQA wine as possible. There is no doubt that making consistently high-quality wine in Ontario with our unique climatic and geographical conditions, is as challenging as in any other wine region in the world, if not more, and not something that can be taken for granted.

At just 0.13% of total world production at this time our wine industry was indeed a small player and with its growth restricted by climate, 'small' would continue to be the case. Indeed, the majority of our wineries were small, described as cottage or boutique or farm wineries, and most would remain small with their operations focused almost exclusively on the local market and tourism. Recent developments in the industry would ensure this as they had to operate without the ability to produce international blends or to open additional retail stores to increase sales. Developing export markets for these small wineries with limited product availability was expensive and required expertise and was simply not yet considered a priority. Even with icewine as a featured product, our wine exports were less than $10 million, at a time when both Australia and the United States were doubling their exports to Canada and the European Union was making it virtually impossible for our wines to achieve entry into their market.

Anyone planning on starting a winery at this time needed to be aware of all the regulatory conditions which made the Ontario environment so different from other winemaking regions, and so difficult, because of the impact these would have on a winery's ability to sell its wine. With all their inherent advantages, including their dominant LCBO presence and their own retail stores (Vincor owned 165 retail outlets and Andres just over 100), Ontario's five largest wineries accounted for almost 90% of the market, leaving very little for the smaller wineries to share amongst themselves. And, with more and more wineries coming on stream, the tourism market was intensifying as consumers had more wineries to visit and had to allocate their purchases accordingly. Working in our retail store at Stoney Ridge I could see this change taking place as customers who normally would buy a case or more of our wines on each visit were now buying just 4 or 6 bottles because they were also going to visit some of the 'new kids on the block' and make purchases there.

Wineries who wished to test the restaurant market were finding that there was still a reluctance among many restaurateurs to add Ontario wines to their wine lists and that this was, as a result, an expensive channel to pursue. The larger wineries had a sales force to make restaurant calls and connect with buyers, but smaller wineries were limited in their ability to pursue this as they lacked sufficient marketing funds to hire staff or to help 'convince' restaurant owners to consider their wines by offering 'special' considerations. With their value-priced Cellared in Canada wines, the large wineries were able to secure 'house wine' business but more expensive VQA products were a more difficult sell unless the owner or chef was developing an 'eat local' program (the beginning of the locavore movement in food and drink), was aware of the winery's quality, and usually sought out his or her favourite VQA winery as a supplier. Fortunately, the arrival of the 'direct delivery' program would be a boon for such business and it would be only a matter of time before more restaurants recognized the accomplishments of VQA producers.

Yet, in spite of such challenges, an increasing number of enthusiasts were planning to build a winery, perhaps in the belief that "if you build it, they will come", or feeling that the LCBO, our monopoly when it came to controlling the sale of all alcohol in the province, would come to the rescue. Most new wineries could find a competition somewhere where one or more of their wines achieved a medal and they were "award-winning" almost from the moment they opened their doors. But, to their dismay, they would find that 'award-winning' was not enough to obtain a listing with the LCBO that found itself with an enormous number of customers to please including numerous importers, Ontario wineries producing both international blends and VQA wines, and other Canadian wineries.

As appealing as your wine might be, the LCBO might not be interested in selling it for any number of reasons, but primarily because of limited shelf space in their stores, where there was already a preponderance of imported products, and with an increasing number of wineries seeking new listings. At this time, if LCBO staff felt your product might not sell well or fast enough or perhaps was too expensive or if you were unable to support the listing with a marketing plan, your request could be easily rejected; or, you might be accepted if you agreed to unfavorable terms, like an extended time for payment or the need to discount the wine at your expense if it did not sell.

The LCBO wanted the wine to sell, but if it did not, there was no effort made on their part to promote it or place the product in a 'better' location, and eventually it would be 'delisted'. Some wineries found this also meant 'black-listed' and decided to forsake selling in this channel. But for the many wineries who chose not to sell to the LCBO, the real issue was the pricing structure which provided very small margins in return for the risk – and at this time it was a risk, not a guaranteed sale, in attempting this channel. It was not without good reason that the wine industry was constantly complaining about the LCBO, our 'arbiter of elegance', that essentially decided what wines the people of Ontario would have access to while choosing the most likely to generate the hundreds of millions of dollars required by the government.

Sales of Ontario wine through the 1990's did show a marked increase – from 32,957,000 litres in 1990 to 39,671,000 in 1999 – with the confirmation of the VQA program and with more wineries opening everywhere and perhaps there was a hope that we could increase our per capita consumption which stood at just over 8 litres per person (in France this was 60 litres and in Australia 20 litres!). But, imported listings still far exceeded the number of local wine listings in the LCBO, 1085 to 538 in 1999, and the reality was that imported wines sales were continuing to outpace Ontario sales annually, leaving us with a shrinking overall market share. This was an obvious indication that many consumers were still not convinced that the industry was able to produce wines worth trying or that they simply preferred what the imports had to offer in style and value.

Sales figures for the decade tell the story very clearly. LCBO Annual Reports for these periods show that total litres of Canadian wine sold for the year 1990 were 26,002,000 as compared to 45,476,000 for imports, or 36.4% in the LCBO, increasing to 52,952,000 for imports and decreasing to 25,795,000 litres, just 32.8% for Canadian in 1999. While the figures do vary somewhat year by year, the market share for imports by volume, which stood at 50% in 1983, would increase to over 66% by the end of the 1990's, confirming a trend that was of serious concern for the grape and wine industry.

In most wine producing regions, it is the local wine that commands the lion's share of the market, but this was not the case for Ontario at this time. Frenchmen preferred to drink French wine and Italians, Spaniards, and many others consumed much more of their own country's products than we did in Canada. Of course, we had a long tradition of making less than world class wine, but that notion was gradually fading and was less valid as an 'excuse' for our showing with each passing year. Our VQA wines easily complied with generally accepted standards of excellence and our international blends represented good value although there was the unfortunate perception that they were of lesser quality than VQA wines. Perhaps consumers continued to feel that Ontario was not positioned to produce the same fashionable style of wine as other New World areas like California, or Australia, or South America, and we would have to admit that 'big and fruity' was not what Ontario VQA was making. And we were still a young wine region, still experimenting with a variety of Vinifera grapes, and still trying to discover which grapes grew best in what places.

The wineries would continue to complain that it was simply a matter of product exposure with a lack of suitable sales channels. There was general agreement that the LCBO needed to provide more shelf space. More restaurants needed to offer Ontario wines. We needed private wine stores, or more winery retail stores, or wine for sale in convenience stores and grocery stores, or perhaps we could sell wine at farmers' markets. These were common practices in so many other countries but not in Ontario where the provincial government, used to controlling all distribution and sales, was reluctant to consider any dramatic change (except for Direct Delivery!) that might impact negatively on their revenue.

All in all, the 1990's was a time of remarkable growth and development, fueled by new investment, new regulations, and a new sense of pride with all wineries moving in the same direction and collaborating for the benefit of the industry in spite of the systemic problems facing it. As Linda Bramble has expressed it so well, "there was a creative glee that permeated everyone's collaboration in those days…a group of like-minded people who got along well and who enjoyed one another's company". Needing to defend their wineries and the industry at every turn, owners worked together as a team for the interests of everyone, whether it was fighting a serious court case that threatened the VQA when all members pitched in significant funds to help settle the matter or fighting for a more appropriate financial reckoning with government. The overall sense of camaraderie that evolved was indeed unique, a strange dynamic for such a competitive industry where you might expect self-interest to reign, and that served as a precursor of other greatness to come.

It also must be noted that much of the success would not have occurred without the leadership of a small group of individuals, our 'unsung heroes', representing all sizes of wineries, who stepped forward with their time, energy, and money, helping their own business by helping others. This co-operative spirit which served to solidify the concept of a wine industry even reached into government departments and the LCBO where some supportive individuals found a way on their own to provide a special consideration or effort for Ontario wineries.

Nowhere was this more evident than with what is often called "the wine press", the first wave of newspaper columnists, wine writers, and radio/tv commentators, who had emerged in the 1980's with a desire to inform consumers about wine, often educating and recommending at the same time, and helping to grow a wine culture in the province. Our wine industry was fortunate to have these people as friends, who saw our wine industry as a diamond-in-the-rough and took every opportunity to share its story in a favourable light. They also took as much interest in the fortunes of winemakers and the wineries as the wines themselves, visiting frequently and appearing at wine shows and tastings.

Although their field was the world of wine, they devoted a large part of their time to the Ontario scene, and their message had a powerful impact on consumers. From my experience I would have to acknowledge so many of them with sincere appreciation, including a large group from Toronto and area, Tony Aspler, Gord Stimmel, Konrad Ejbich, David Lawrason, Alex Eberspaecher, Frank Baldock, Dick Singer, Michael Vaughn, Dean Tudor, Margaret Swaine, Hirayr Berberoglu, Barbara and Margot Ritchie, and the frugal oenophile, Richard Best of Oakville, who are all indelibly etched in my memory sniffing or tasting a glass of wine – most of which they would spit! – while at the same time taking down notes. Dan Kislenko of the Hamilton Spectator was a tremendous help in my own development as was Peter Ward, wine columnist for the Ottawa Citizen, and Billy Munnelly from Stratford/Toronto. Hedonists to be sure, they fulfilled a leading role in championing the reputation of the Ontario Wine Industry.

For myself, the decade represented the pinnacle of my career, heading a team which took Stoney Ridge to the top of the awards list and myself as 'Winemaker of the Year' for 1997, as we evolved from a hobby to a commercial winery. It was certainly the busiest period of my life, a time when wine was my life, with wonderful, once-in-a-lifetime memories of customers and staff members who became friends, of friends like Larry and Lorraine Baatz and Don and Joan Morell who sacrificed their own time to help in our success, of the annual trips to the Toronto Wine and Cheese Show or the Ottawa Food and Wine Show, or Wineries Unlimited in Pennsylvania (a wonderful learning experience and trade show) and many other events, meeting the public while pouring our wines, of that memorable group industry trip to Bordeaux, including a stop at the famous Chateau Yquem, and of a great partnership that came and went so quickly.

How fortunate I was to have been a part of the evolving drama that was Ontario wine!

CHAPTER NINE

2000-2019: A tsunami of new millennium estate wineries!

"Everyone, it seems, wants to get into the wine business. This sentiment reminds me of something a hobby sailor once told me… 'The two happiest days in the life of a yacht owner are the day he buys the boat and the day he sells it'. This ultimate romantic fantasy (winemaking) is the most expensive mistress you'll ever service." Tony Aspler, "Tidings", 2006

"Who would dare predict the future of an industry as young as Ontario's wine industry? Four or five new wineries have opened in Niagara each year since 2000, and more are on the drawing boards." Rod Phillips, "Ontario Wine Country", 2005

Anyone who might have been worried about the health of the Ontario wine industry after its 'near death' experience of the early 1990's would have their concerns quashed once and for all with the unfolding of the new millennium and its exciting promise of a happy future for Ontario winemaking. Much of this was based on the continuing success of our VQA wines which, as of June 29, 2000, would now be regulated by an official provincial wine authority. The increase in production of VQA wines had been simply amazing, reaching one million bottles in 1994, one million cases by March 2002, and then doubling this amount by the end of the decade. Sales of icewines, with more and more wineries making them, had soared from 2000 cases in 1990 to over 21,000 cases by the early 2000's and over 1 million litres of production by 2006, generating healthy revenue for growers and producers. Likewise, VQA membership, which numbered 51 wineries in 2001, would almost quadruple by 2020, a reflection of the respect and trust that VQA had inspired for the industry.

It was no wonder then that an intense interest had developed in establishing new wineries, far surpassing any dream that might have been envisioned by Don Ziraldo and Karl Kaiser, I am sure, when they initiated the cottage industry in the mid 1970's. While the 'older' region of Niagara continued to lead the way in winery development, other parts of the province witnessed their own giddying growth, an unprecedented explosion of new grape wineries which would stimulate the creation of a brand new DVA for Prince Edward County and the blossoming of several 'emerging regions' with grape wineries popping up along the southern shores of Lake Huron and Georgian Bay, north of Toronto, as far east as Ottawa, and south to Norfolk County along Lake Erie.

As well, numerous fruit growers opened fruit wineries as an extension of their farm operations and this would lead to the development of an intriguing "craft" cider-making industry that would take the province by storm, with cider producers opening a business wherever apples were being grown in the province and at a rate that almost matched new grape wineries.

The wine industry was embracing a period of rapid change and nowhere was this more obvious than in defining the nature of a 'winery' itself. During the first century of Ontario winemaking, this was typically a business that bought its grapes from numerous growers rather than growing them itself. Growers delivered grapes to wineries for processing into a broad range of wines from ports and sherries to red, white, and rose styles, sparkling, and other 'concoctions'. With the arrival of the 'cottage' industry in the 1970's, while growers continued to grow grapes for the corporate wineries, the new wineries concerned themselves with growing most of their own raw material, a practice that became the rule in the 1990's when it was decreed that a new winery would have to be located on at least 5 acres of planted grapes and use those grapes in order to have a retail store on site.

With a shifting of the industry from impersonal corporate-size producers to very personal, boutique 'farm' operations, more wineries began to specialize in a select number of varieties and focus on a more limited range of products – and this eventually evolved to some wineries producing only VQA wines, or just a few Vinifera varieties, or only one product, icewine.

And, amidst all the excitement, another 'category' of winery emerged, described as a "virtual winery", that provided an opportunity for individuals to make wine in an already established winery without requiring the considerable investment involved in owning their own winery or even vineyards. Most joined VQAO although they could not have their own retail store and were obligated to sell through the 'partner' winery or on-line for home delivery. In some cases, an alcohol business that was not a winery at all, would obtain a wine manufacturer's licence and then have wine custom-made for it by an established winery, but would be able to sell the wine only to the LCBO or to licencees. It would even be possible for such a business to become a member of the VQAO and obtain VQA approval for the product.

Thus, as the first two decades of the new millennium would establish, the historical concept of a 'winery' was disappearing, with a much more open structure allowing for increased variety in every aspect of the business. Some might say that it had become "too easy" to enter the wine business and that too many new players were inexperienced or under-capitalized, as evidenced by the number of winery closures after 2000. Yet, with the rapidity of the industry's evolution in a most competitive business, the line between success and failure was quite fine indeed!

All in all, by the end of the second decade of the new millennium, the result of all the activity was no less than a tripling of the number of wineries - grape, fruit, and cider- staking their claims in Ontario wine country after the end of the century from tiny, rustic 'garagiste' or 'cult' artisans producing only a few hundred cases of wine that would often be very difficult to find, all the way to multi-million dollar, state-of-the-art corporate operations making thousands of cases of well-advertised brands. The Wine Country Travel Guide for 2020-2021 provides a listing and description for 129 VQA wineries complete with maps that make touring easy, although those oenophiles who are really adventurous can find other non-listed wineries which are also worthy of a visit (some smaller VQA members do not appear because of the cost and non-VQA wineries are not involved in the Guide). Seeking out some of the lesser-known wineries can be both fun and educational with the opportunity to make a real 'find' in the process!

While anyone might consider this winery activity a form of 'millenium madness', especially with an industry so often at the mercy of Mother Nature, the very number of serious new players indicated this was hardly the case. I am sure that most of them believed they could make a living in the wine business, although for some the priority was not money at all. After working elsewhere for a time and perhaps looking to pursue a new career, a few believed that the idea of becoming a vintner represented their 'true calling', or the fulfillment of a dream they had to make wine or even an item on their 'bucket list'. Many saw this as an appropriate 'family project' and an opportunity for a new lifestyle closer to nature! However, as Tony Aspler pointed out in an article for Wine Tidings, "The idea of owning a winery is the ultimate fantasy…But it is the most expensive mistress you'll ever service".

Indeed, as some would soon discover, while it was possible to make good wine in Ontario, it was also necessary to sell it and that would be a challenge for everyone given the continuing arrival of 'new kids on the block' and a difficult marketplace. Fortunately, momentum was on the side of the industry and thus the idea of dancing with Bacchus for most of these neophyte winery owners would prove both exhilerating and meaningful.

Making all this possible for grape wine producers was the continuing sustainability of vineyards planted in vines of the 'vitis vinifera' species which were now fueling the production of world-class wines in the province although at 42-44 degrees north latitude it was still considered to be a continental, cold-climate region that put the planting of such vines at risk. The Niagara Peninsula had long been known for its fruit production, however, as it was locked in by Lake Ontario on the north and the Niagara Escarpment on the south, which helped create a more moderate micro-climate that allowed fruit growing to be successful in spite of occasional severe winters or spring frosts or warming/freezing cycles that could damage buds or vines and ruin vintages. Obviously, those who decided to open a winery in Niagara, the largest planted area of all viticultural areas in Canada, were prepared to take the risk, believing the rewards were worth the challenge!

The same could be said for those opening wineries in the Lake Erie North Shore appellation, Ontario's most southern grape growing region with the longest growing season in the province and more sunshine hours and heat units than any other place in Canada. Here, vinifera vines have adapted well and generated significant winery development with stretches of vineyards found primarily along the shore of Lake Erie, the shallowest of the Great Lakes, which provides a moderating effect in temperatures that are needed for ripening quality fruit. Vineyard acreage is still much less than in Niagara and this is reflected in the number of VQA wineries, 14 compared to 99 for Niagara in 2018, and a significant difference in production with only 30,061 cases (9 litres) of VQA wine compared to Niagara's 2,319,643. Average VQA production in LENS per winery is just over 2000 cases while in Niagara that average soars to over 23,000.

It has often been noted that this region seems to fall below the radar of Ontario wine consumers, perhaps because of its distance from the GTA, although it is the home of two of our largest VQA wineries, Colio and Pelee Island, and it has become known as the source of some of our best red wines. But with land prices being more reasonable than in Niagara, investors have been taking more of an interest in south-western Ontario, and the number of wineries is continuing to rise.

Winery development in Prince Edward County, our northernmost region, located between Toronto and Ottawa along Lake Ontario, came later than the other DVA's but has provided a pleasant surprise for the wine industry in both number of wineries and quality of production. I recall travelling to 'The County' in the mid 1990's at the invitation of Larry Paterson (aka 'The Little Fat Wino) to talk to a small group of would-be grape growers who lived here and loved their region and believed in its potential for grape growing and winemaking where others might see only beaches, sand dunes, and miles and miles of boring, flat topography! I could sense that these people saw PEC as almost a paradise with a picturesque countryside and it was their dream to live on a vineyard and make wine. Although I shared their enthusiasm, with my own wine industry experience I was considerably more cautious and conservative in my thinking.

Considering the punitive winter temperatures and the relatively short growing season, I suggested that I envisioned little likelihood of success in growing Vinifera grapes at all and, with a short tourist season for winery visits and sales, I believed that opening a winery here was problematic. My final words were… "Do you really want to invest your time and money in such a risky and challenging venture?" The group was not at all dissuaded by my 'sermon' and many in attendance continued to forge ahead with their plans to plant Vinifera grapes, especially Chardonnay and Pinot Noir which they felt were ideally suited to the limestone soils of the region as well as some French Hybrids like Vidal and Baco Noir as a back-up.

Their passion, along with their stubbornness, won the day, and the results have been completely amazing. By 2007 the region had enough grapes planted to achieve status as a Designated Viticultural Area – no mean feat in such a short period of time – and growth has continued to be impressive. As of 2018 there were 40 wineries with 31 VQA members, more than double that of LENS, and production of VQA wine was almost equivalent at 29,411 cases, although average VQA production was only 950 cases per winery.

Indeed, most wineries remain quite artisanal in size and several rely on obtaining grapes from Niagara to make sufficient wine as this region can be very hostile to vines in winter. Most growers bury their vines for protection and that comes with considerable work and expense, indicating that these winery owners are very hardy souls who are in the game as a 'labour of love'. Few have been turned off by the suggestion, "Be careful! You might get what you wished for!".

Additional winery activity outside the DVA's and Prince Edward County at the beginning of the new millennium was for the most part in the hands of several fruit growers who believed there was a financial opportunity in establishing a winery that would make wine from the various fruits that they were already growing. The challenge of a 'cold climate' was not the same issue as with grape growers and thus fruit wineries began to appear in more northern locations where no winery had been before, from Guelph to Milton, to Caledon, to Bala, and north-east of Toronto to take advantage of the regulations which now allowed a fruit grower to make and sell wine on site. There was no rule obligating them to grow grapes, but they could still make up to 20% of their wine from grapes if they desired and both Cox Creek in Guelph and Scotch Block in Milton went ahead with small plantings of French Hybrids.

As fruit wineries did not qualify for VQA status and were often located off the beaten track, they truly existed in the shadow of grape wineries and suffered from a lack of expertise in marketing. Spearheaded by a trade officer with the Ministry of Agriculture in Guelph named Sharon Burke, the wineries decided in 1999 to form their own association, Fruit Wines of Ontario (FWO) with myself as Executive Director and, supported by some government funding, to create quality standards for fruit wines and change the perception of fruit wines in Ontario. By 2000, a national fruit wine organization was formed called Fruit Wines of Canada (FWC) which set about enrolling members from British Columbia to Newfoundland, including over twenty from Ontario with some grape wineries as well that were producing both grape and fruit wines (Stoney Ridge, Southbrook, Konzelmann, and Magnotta).

Within short order we had a fruit wine Quality Certified (QC) program, modeled on the VQA system, and had held the first ever All-Canada Fruit Wine Competition in Guelph. Although there was no dedicated section for fruit wines in the LCBO retail system, the first all-Ontario Q.C. fruit wines started to appear regularly in "Vintages" and Q.C. was off to an auspicious start, although due to VQA regulations our quality certified fruit wines could not even describe themselves as 'Product of Ontario' on the label. Still, this 'foot in the door' would lead to more credibility down the road when several 'cider' enthusiasts opened cideries and some VQA wineries joined in, initiating a trend that shows no sign of slowing! To-day, many Ontario ciders have become popular items in bars and restaurants across the province and are selling well in the LCBO system.

Whether it was the example of Prince Edward County, or a belief in the warming impact of climate change, or simply a desire to be in the winery business that some may find difficult to understand, numerous entrepreneurs began to open grape wineries far outside the boundaries of our three DVA's. Many of these were located 'up north' in relation to Niagara or the GTA, where the very idea of growing grapes usually aroused feelings ranging from skepticism to cynicism with most seasoned grape growers. Who could possibly believe that Vinifera grapes would survive the harsh winters of Meaford, or Grand Bend, or Collingwood, or Orangeville, but in recent years intrepid individuals have managed to find 'the formula' and opened a successful winery. Indeed, the numbers have increased so dramatically that it is now possible to speak of different areas as 'emerging regions', still lacking the total acreage of grapes required for a VQA designation but with enough wineries to catch everyone's attention.

Almost overlooked in the frenzy of winery development, is another new area from Peterboro to Ottawa – better known for its harsh winters and not what anyone would consider 'normal' grape growing terroir - where several small wineries have come into production. While some of these wineries are attempting to grow Vinifera grapes in challenging circumstances and burying vines for the winter, many are relying on more winter-hardy hybrid vines (like Marquette, La Crescente, and Frontenac), which were developed by a hybridizer named Elmer Swenson for use originally in Minnesota where winter temperatures can be brutal. Considerable interest in these vines was shown originally by wineries in Quebec and Nova Scotia as they had a better chance of surviving the cold winters there. Although consumers are not yet familiar with the names of these varieties and it will take some time for them to be considered for inclusion in the VQA listings (Marquette is the only one so far), they do make wines with abundant personality and will prove to be a source of interest in the future.

Another exciting region has developed in similar circumstances in what was traditionally tobacco country along the shores of Lake Erie further east than LENS in Norfolk County. Wineries in what is now called the South Coast are growing a mix of Vinifera, French Hybrid, and other cold climate hybrids and offering both VQA and non-VQA wines that have already started to appear in the LCBO. The challenges again will be to sustain vineyard growth and build consumer interest in yet another marginalized wine region. The same can be said for several wineries that have opened along the shore of Lake Huron and north of Toronto, stretching up to Hockley Valley outside Orangeville and Collingwood. While most of these wineries are targeting a local clientele, nearby restaurants, and tourists for the most part, several are producing some VQA wines that like their peers in the DVA's are of excellent quality and have already won awards in international competitions. Their achievements have been remarkable and continue to inspire others to follow their example.

As we approach the end of the second decade of the new millennium, the number of new wineries shows no sign of ending with over 200 Ontario wineries province wide. This activity has transformed our wine industry from half a dozen larger wineries in the early 1970's to a rich tapestry of cottage and estate wineries and changed the culture of the industry from an impersonal, corporate business mode where winery tourism was almost non-existent, to a more personal involvement with customers through wine clubs, on-site events and tastings of every description attracting millions of tourists and where visitors can actually meet and talk with the individuals who make the wine.

Where most wines used to be sold in the LCBO system, the sheer number of wineries has posed a challenge for the LCBO in providing new listings for wineries who wish to be represented here although the Vintages channel has made real progress in offering wines from all our regions. As a result, many of the wineries have never appeared in the LCBO and consumers who may wish to try these limited-edition wines must visit the wineries in person or take a chance and order them using the internet, a convenient retail 'tool' now, for home delivery.

With a customer-friendly wine industry and high-quality wines, this truly is the 'golden age' for Ontario winemaking leaving us astonished by everything we have seen since 2000: new grapes, new terroirs, organic and bio-dynamic grape growing and innovative wine styles like appassimento and 'orange' wine, an industry focused on 'sustainability', and above all... the number and diversity of new wineries!

Their owners all realized that this was an ideal time to join an industry which would give them numerous opportunities to be successful, one now achieving its potential of producing world class wines. At the same time, their commitment was demonstrating solid confidence in this industry and in its future.

Wineries that have arrived on the scene since 2000 and continue to operate in 2020 are listed below according to region. A separate list of wineries that have gone out of business since 1980 and are now 'ghost wineries' is provided in an appendix. I have made every effort to be as inclusive as possible with both lists but I apologize if I have overlooked a planned start-up or a winery that just did not materialize or that has gone out of business without my knowledge.

The Niagara Peninsula: The leading edge of the tsunami!

New millennium wineries east of the Welland Canal

- Arterra Wines (previously Brights, then Vincor)
- Between the Lines Winery
- Big Head Wines
- Byland Estate Winery
- Caroline Cellars
- Cattail Creek
- Colaneri Estate Winery
- De Simone Vineyards
- De Moura Family Wines
- Niagara College Teaching Winery
- Nomad at Hinterbrook Winery
- Palatine Hills Estate Winery
- Peller Estates Winery/Restaurant
- Perridiso Estate Winery
- Pond View Estate Winery
- Queenston Mile Vineyard

- Ferox Estate Winery
- 5 Rows Craft Wine/Lowrey E.
- Frogpond Farm Organic Winery
- Icellars Estate Winery
- Jackson Triggs Niagara Estate
- Lailey Winery
- Lakeview Wine Co./Diamond Est.
- Lundy Manor Wine Cellars
-Monastery Cellars
- Ravine Vineyard
- Reimer Vineyards
- Riverview Cellars Estate Winery
- Southbrook Organic Vineyards
- Stratus
- The Hare Wine Company
- The Ice House Winery
- Two Sisters Vineyards
- Wayne Gretzky Winery/Distillery

New Millenium wineries West of the Welland Canal

- Hamilton
- Central Valley Winery
- Puddicombe Wines/Cider
- Grimsby Region
- Leaning Post Wines
- Ridge Road Estate Winery

Beamsville: Escarpment to Lakeshore

- Angel's Gate Winery
- Atlantis Niagara Wines
- Bachelder Niagara
- Back 10 Cellars
- Cornerstone Estate Winery
- Fielding Estate Winery
- Hidden Bench Winery
- Kew Vineyards Estate Winery
- Legends Estate Winery
- London Born Winery (orig. Aure W.)
- Mountain Road Wine Company
- Peninsula Ridge Estate Winery
- Redstone Winery
- Rosewood Estate Winery/Meadery
- The Good Earth Vineyard/Winery
- The Organized Crime Winery
- Vieni Estates Wines & Spirits
- Villa Bacchus at Commisso

Vineland: Escarpment to Lakeshore

- Alvento Winery
- Cloudsley Cellars
- Domaine Queylus
- Featherstone Estate Winery
- Fogolar Wines
- Greenlane Estate Wine
- Megalomaniac (John Howard)
- Ridgepoint Wines
- Tawse Winery

Jordan: Escarpment to Lakeshore

- Calamus Estate Winery
- Flat Rock Cellars
- Cellaria Winery
- Di Profio Wines (now 180 E.W.)
- Dim Wine Company
- Harbour Estate Winery
- Honsberger Estate Winery
- Pearl Morissette Estate Winery
- Sixteen Mile Cellar
- Sue-Ann Staff Estate Winery
- The Farm Winery
- Westcott Vineyards

St. Catharines – Pelham

- Rockway Glen Winery
- 13th Street Winery

"Virtual" Wineries (operating through an established winery)

- Charles Baker (at Stratus)
- Fogolar (at Di Profio)
- Meldville (at Legends)
- Rennie (at Malivoire)
- Drea's Wine Co. (at Reif)
- Iroquois Shore (at Di Profio)
- Nyarai Cellars (at Coffin Ridge)
- 2027 Cellars (at Calamus)

Additional manufacturing licences:

- Fluid Assets, Generations/Union Wines, Paradise Grapevine, Stonebridge Vineyards, Triple Bogey Brewing

Lake Erie North Shore - Winery expansion in our southernmost appellation

- Aleksander Estate Winery
- Colchester Ridge Estate Winery/ CREW
- Cooper's Hawk Vineyards
- Dancing Swallows Vineyard
- Early Acres Estate Winery (Chatham)
- Erie Shore Vineyard
- Mastronardi Estate Winery
- Muscadere Vineyards
- North 42 Degrees Estate Winery
- Oxley Estate Winery
- Paglione Estate Winery
- Sanson Estate Winery
- Sprucewood Shores Winery
- Viewpoint Estate Winery
- Vivace Estate Winery
- Wagner Orchards/Winery

Prince Edward County - A new DVA for 2007 and a plethora of wineries!

- Amanda's Vineyards
- Black Prince Winery
- By Chadsey's Cairns Winery
- Casa Dea Winery (orig. Carmela W.)
- Del Gatto Estates
- Domaine Darius
- Exultet Estates Winery
- Half Moon Bay Vineyard/Winery
- Hillier Creek Estates
- Hubbs Creek
- Karlo Estates
- Lacey Estate Winery
- Lighthall Vineyards
- Morandin Wines
- Redtail Vineyards
- Sandbanks Estate Winery
- Sugarbush Vineyards
- Terra Estate Winery
- Bergeron Winery/Cidery
- Broken Stone Winery
- Cape Vineyards
- Closson Chase Winery
- Devil's Wishbone Winery
- Dragon's Reach Estate Vineyard
- Gravel Hill Vineyards
- Harwood Estate Vineyards
- Hinterland Wine Company
- Huff Estates
- Keint-he Winery/Vineyard
- Last House Vineyard
- Long Dog Vineyard & Winery
- Norman Hardie Wines Ltd.
- Rosehall Run Winery
- Stanners Vineyard
- TerraCello Winery
- The Grange of Prince Edward

- The Old Third Vineyard
- Three Dog Winery
- Traynor Family Vineyard
- Thirty-Three Vines Winery
- Trail Estate Winery
- Waupoos Estate Winery

Grape Wineries in the Five "Emerging Regions"

HS = Huron Shores GB = Georgian Bay NT = North of Toronto
L = Lake Erie, South Coast P.O. = Peterboro to Ottawa

- Alton Farms, Plympton-Wyoming, HS
- Cornerfield Wine Co., Bayfield, HS
- Dark Horse Estate, Grand Bend, HS
- Maelstrom Winery, Seaforth, HS
- 2nd Streetlight, Clinton, HS
- Schatz Winery, Zurich HS

- Coffin Ridge, Annan, GB
- Georgian Hills, Collingwood, GB
- Therianthropy (open 2021)
- The Creemore Hills, Creemore, GB
- The Roost Wine Co., Ravenna, GB

- Adamo Estate, Orangeville, NT
- Gallucci Winery, Stouffville, NT
- Willow Springs, Stouffville, NT
- Chesslawn Vineyard, Caledon, NT
- Holland Marsh, Newmarket, NT
- Windrush Estate, Palgrave, NT

- Bonnieheath Estate, Simcoe, L.
- Hounds of Erie, Clear Creek, L.
- Burning Kiln, Turkey Point, L
- Inasphere Wines, St. Williams, L.
- Rapscallion Wine Co., Port Dover, L. (Smoke & Gamble, Frisky Beaver)
- Villa Nova Estate, Simcoe, L.

- Domaine du Cervin, Chesterville, P. O.	- Domaine Perrault, Navan, P. O.
- Green Gables Oxford Station P.O	- Jabulani Winery, Richmond, P.O.
- KIN Vineyards, Carp, P.O.	- Rolling Grape, Bailieboro, P.O.
- Scheuermann, Westport, P.O.	- Smokey Ridge, Mountain, P.O.
- Vankleek Hill, Champlain, P.O.	- Villa Conti, Warkworth, P.O.

All-Ontario Fruit Wineries

- Algoma Highlands Fruit Winery	- Wawa
- Applewood Farm Winery	- Stouffville
- Bellamere Winery	- London
- Black Bear Farms of Ontario Estate Winery	- Kingsville
- Blueberry Hills Winery & Front Row Cellars	- Turkey Point
- Boreal Berry Farms & Winery	- St. Charles
- Carolinian Winery	- Thorndale (moved to Rush Creek Winery)
- Clafeld Fruit Winery and Cider House	- Picton
- Countryman's Farm Winery	- Prescott
- Downey's Estate Winery	- Caledon
- Gould's Apple Orchard & Fruit Winery	- Tottenham (closed)
- Kawartha Country Wines	- Buckhorn
- Moon Shadows Maple Winery	- Haliburton (closed)
- Munro Meadery	- Alvinston
- Muskoka Lakes Farm and Winery	- Bala
- Pine Farms Winery	- King City (closed)
- Strathmore Orchard & Winery	- Monkland (closed)
- Whittamore's Farm Winery	- Markham (closed)
- Wooden Bear L Winery	- Simcoe

CHAPTER TEN

A new millennium and the Wine Industry is "Poised for Greatness"!

"Although sales of VQA wines continued to grow in 2001, the rate of growth shows signs of flattening due to fierce international competition and marketing challenges." Len Pennachetti, VQAO Annual Report, March 2002

"Today...people at every level in the industry have come together ready to develop and adopt a focused strategy with the concerted, co-operative action needed to win a prosperous future for Ontario wines." "Poised for Greatness" – A Strategic Framework for the Ontario Wine Industry, November 2001.

"The primary challenge identified by Canadian winemakers is to increase their domestic market share...However, it would seem that Canadian vintners must explore export markets if they wish to reduce their vulnerability to the combination of a single customer (Liquor Boards) and intensifying domestic competition." Strategic Dilemmas of a Small Market Player, 2003.

The Competition for sales

With the arrival of the new millennium, everyone's eyes were turned to the future including all those involved in the Ontario Grape and Wine

Industry. On the surface, the industry appeared to be in good shape with the VQA now established in law and looking for growth in both sales and membership. Direct sales and delivery to restaurants were in place and 2001 would be remembered in our grape history as the first year that vinifera grape tonnage exceeded hybrid production, a significant milestone on the journey to achieve higher quality winemaking. Thanks to the financial support of the Ontario Government, recognizing the economic benefits of a thriving wine industry, growers had been able to make the transition to preferred grape varieties and many existing wineries had been able to expand their facilities and modernize.

But it was difficult to reconcile such 'good news' with other realities that continued to provide serious concern for a successful future. The industry presented a dual status with wineries on either side of a deep fracture. On one side were a small number of larger wineries that were legally able to produce 'international blends' with the ability to sell their wines in an independent retail network that numbered some 300 stores and on the other were all the other wineries, able to make only 100% domestic wine which they could sell in just a single store at the site of each winery. The fragmentation was an ongoing source of considerable friction in the industry that was making it difficult to operate as a united team in the fight for market share against imported wines which the industry had identified as its primary challenge.

Indeed, many wine critics and some of the small producers were maintaining that the blenders were misleading consumers with their packaging into buying what they thought were homegrown wines and were worried that these less expensive products were cannibalizing sales of VQA wines. Although sales varied somewhat each year and the VQA was still in its infancy, at this time non-VQA Ontario wines were outselling VQA in Ontario by 4 to 1 with some VQA producers having issues of profitability. The blenders insisted that these wines actually helped to prop up the industry as a home for some 50% of the harvest, a whopping 25,000 tonnes of Ontario grapes, while supporting a lot of jobs as a major part of their business (and they also made VQA wine). They were prepared to change the wording of their wine labels and would accept changes in the percentage of Ontario wine required in their blends that happened periodically, but they insisted that these wines were a legitimate part of the Ontario Wine Industry, and it was not right to censure them. Still, it was difficult to reconcile the success of these blended wines with sales of VQA wines which represented just 22% of all 'Ontario' wine sold in the province in 2002/3!

The issue of blended wines provided a true dilemma for everyone, winery owners, growers, and the Government, and it appeared that no one knew how to resolve this. A major question was, if steps were taken to restrict the production of 'international blends' in order to grow a purely local wine industry, would consumers switch to VQA wines or would this simply jeopardize the market share of the larger wineries with a potentially disastrous impact on the fortunes of grape growers?

This concern over domestic sales was heightened by an even more serious disturbing trend: over the years the market share of Ontario wines had continued to slide downwards in the face of aggressive competition from imported wines with Canada being one of the top destinations for exports from almost every wine-producing country in the world. Between 1990 and 2000, sales of imported wines in Ontario had increased by almost 75%, while domestic sales had risen by only 33% with imports now holding 65% of the total market. The smaller domestic share represented by our own wine producers is an anomaly on the world stage compared to other wine producing countries like France, Italy, Spain, and Australia who each own more than 85% of their respective home markets. As well, having a strong domestic base is considered a definite advantage in moving into export markets and this the Ontario industry simply did not have.

In the LCBO system at this time, faced with the competition of both imports and Ontario blended wines, VQA sales were approaching 10 million litres which represented just 9.72% of the total of 100 million litres of all wine sold in the province. Adding to these disappointing statistics, research had indicated that just one-third of Ontario consumers accounted for 75% of all wine consumption in the province, with only 14% of this group, 4.6% of consumers, regular buyers of Ontario wines. Agri-Food

Canada statistics would also show that there had been a decline in the domestic consumption of wine from 9.5 litres per capita to 8.8 litres from 1988 to 1999 while domestic production was increasing, meaning that competition was intensifying.

A new vision for the industry... "Poised for Greatness!"

All major industry stakeholders were aware of these shortcomings and agreed to meet starting in February 2000, to identify initiatives that would open the door to Ontario wine for more consumers, essentially by targeting the LCBO because it represented the primary wine market. The strategic plan that was developed by representatives from the WCO, the OGGMB, the LCBO, and four government Ministries was revolutionary, with a major focus on improving the overall environment and retail experience in the province's liquor stores in order to grow the provincial grape and wine industry. The LCBO, which previously had been somewhat reluctant to agree to fixed targets, finally agreed with the backing of CEO Andy Brandt to co-operate with the 'new' concept to support VQA fully, as it was realized that domestic wines returned far more value to the economy than imports (a survey by K.P.M.G. would show a benefit for the Ontario economy of $4 per litre sold as compared to 46 cents for imports). The changes would be simply 'good for business' and they became recognized as official government policy!

The work resulted in the release of a "vision" for the industry 18 months later on November 13, 2001 called "Poised for Greatness", unveiling goals to be achieved in 5 years and after a longer 20 year period, beginning April 1, 2003, which would be based on a partnership of the stakeholders. The target in 5 years was to achieve 50% market share for sales of Ontario wines in the province reaching $1.5 billion after 20 years with a massive 500% growth in exports, additional winery tourism, and vineyard expansion. This would include growing the VQA table wine market in Vintages by 170% in sales and the icewine market by 25%, as the industry aimed at using 90% of available grapes for VQA wines.

These aggressive goals represented the 'what' of the plan and it was now up to committees to delineate the 'how', the various innovative steps that would be taken to achieve the targets and to measure the success of each. Work began in June 2002, involving the LCBO, the Wine Council, and the Ministry of Consumer and Business Services, focusing on details of the 5 year plan. Four months later, on October 18, a list of 20 recommendations was presented to the Minister of Consumer Services. Hopefully, these would take the industry to a higher level, an industry that was now proving itself capable and ready.

"Greatness" was something never really defined by anyone but seemed to suggest a destination where plantings of vinifera grapes, winery development, wine sales, and employment, would be strikingly better than at present and provide for a prosperous future!

Beyond language referring to individual winery commitments to promotional plans and the need to co-operate on measurable goals, the major changes to be introduced centred on reaching more consumers through specific marketing advances in the LCBO for VQA wines. There would be an enhanced "Vintages Essentials" program and permanent VQA sections with permanent signage intended to create a wine country feeling and an Ontario wine "champion" from the Vintages staff as a customer resource, all to drive consumer interest in and awareness of fine Ontario wines.

As well, new options would be considered to support the Ontario wine section in all stores with expanded training for staff through a 'Wonderful Ontario Wine' (WOW) leader, and a series of pilots to test improved ways of shelving Ontario wines to appeal to customers. Smaller wineries would continue to benefit through the Craft Winery Program in 57 key LCBO stores, giving them an opportunity to establish their 'brand' if only in a small way. In addition, a new concept called the "Premier Wine Program" would attempt to expand the portfolio of higher-priced Ontario wines in the LCBO by finding ways to encourage wineries to provide their "better wines", usually smaller volumes of wines that generated higher profits for wineries when they sold them at their winery.

To deal with winery complaints about the challenges involved in selling to the LCBO, the provincial monopoly agreed to re-consider their supply chain policies for Ontario wineries "in keeping with the shopping needs of VQA consumers", encourage wineries to submit VQA wines to the LCBO by minimizing sales 'risks' (i.e. delistings), and maintain a depth of Ontario product offerings. Most importantly, the LCBO committed to increasing Ontario wine shelf space to an average of 35% in all retail stores province-wide with 'special treatment' for GTA stores to keep their shelf space to 4% above market share.

These were not huge gains for the industry but an important movement in the right direction. At the least, the commitments provided some optimism to drive changes in the spending habits of Ontario consumers with a sincere effort to make them better aware of the industry and educate them on VQA wines. The real challenge remained. Would more consumers 'buy' into the offerings and create a positive change in VQA wine sales?

When the results for year one of the strategic plan became available (April 1, 2003 to March 31, 2004), the industry would see a few positive developments compared to the previous year but generally little change. The number of VQA wineries had continued to increase, from 66 to 71, and sales of VQA wine to licencees were up by 13%, maintaining a healthy trend, while total sales by volume increased by 6.6%. This provided a 1.13% increase in market share although sales in the LCBO were virtually the same as the previous year and that was disappointing. At the same time, imported wine sales also increased over 5% leaving the Ontario industry no further ahead. Overall, the strategic plan was off to a less than dramatic start! It soon became clear that improvement would not happen overnight and that everyone's patience would be put to the test for another few years before all the work and effort and the impact of new developments would see real movement toward the projected targets.

The development of new wineries

To many, the year 1999 had felt like the successful end of the beginning of a more viable industry with the VQA's star rising and ready to shine its light of opportunity even more brightly, inspiring the proliferation of new wineries. Perhaps the actual impetus for this was the ability to sell and deliver VQA wine directly to restaurants or the burgeoning winery tourist activity or the hope provided by the "Poised for Greatness" strategy, that led numerous individuals to believe the time was right for them to take Bacchus by the hand and start their own winery.

In 2001, Ontario's two largest wineries, Andres and Vincor, led the way with impressive new wineries in Niagara-on-the-Lake, Peller Estates, a magnificent $20 million dollar winery with a world-class restaurant, and a stunning multi-million dollar winery for the Jackson-Triggs brand, as both intended to expand the high-end VQA part of their businesses. These two solid corporate players would enhance their positions just four years later adding wineries in the ultra-premium end of the business. Following a renovation of the Hillebrand winery, in 2005 John Peller of Andres bought Thirty Bench Winery, a tiny operation that had been producing highly esteemed Riesling, Chardonnay, and Cabernet based red wines from its prime vineyards located next to the renowned Lenko vineyard on the Beamsville Bench. The winery would go on to produce some of Ontario's most sought-after wines.

Not to be outdone, Don Triggs at Vincor had already undertaken a 50-50 joint venture with the Boisset family of Burgundy called Le Clos Jordanne, to develop exclusive Chardonnay and Pinot Noir wines from prized vineyards in Jordan which would be made by talented winemaker Thomas Bachelder and French consultant Pascal Marchand. Exciting plans for a Frank Gehry designed winery to follow were shelved, unfortunately, when Vincor was sold to Constellation Wines in 2006, and the entire brand itself was put on hold in 2012. Matching this sale, in 2006 the winery we knew so well as Andres (i.e. Baby Duck!), changed its name to Andrew Peller Ltd. in memory of the man who had founded the winery, signaling at the same time a renewed, more upscale vision for the business.

During the first half of the new decade, several wealthy entrepreneurs completed major investments in the industry including the Madronich family at Flat Rock, Norm Beal at Peninsula Ridge, Moray Tawse at Tawse

Winery, the Fielding Family at Fielding Estate Winery, David Feldberg at Stratus, John Howard at Megalomaniac (after selling his shares at Vineland Estates in 2004 to Fred de Gasperis), Harald Thiel at Hidden Bench, and Bill Redelmeier who moved his Southbrook Winery from Vaughan to a 30 hectare property in Niagara-on-the Lake to pursue his dreams and become Canada's first certified Organic and Biodynamic Winery. All these ventures became important names in the business, prepared to spare no expense in their pursuit of making high-quality VQA wines and they were not compromised by the need to make a quick dollar return.

Many other wineries were developed by people who were keen on making handcrafted, terroir-driven wines that would further solidify Ontario's recent artisanal trend, endeavours that would be personally, though not necessarily financially, rewarding. The perception was that they would make premium and ultra-premium wines for which they could charge a higher price. Such wineries opened all over the province in the first half of the decade including several in the Lake Erie North Shore DVA, the first grape winery in Prince Edward County called Waupoos Estates, our first organic winery, Frogpond Farm, started in Niagara by Jens Gemmrich and his wife Heike, and Canada's first 'teaching winery' at Niagara College with an initial class of 25 students in 2001. These and other grape wineries were accompanied by the first wave of fruit wine makers intent as well on establishing the quality of their wines made entirely from Ontario grown fruits other than grapes.

The task that all these start-ups faced if they were to remain in business was to prove that they could indeed make fine wines that were worth drinking and would sell. This could be quickly validated by wine writers, success in competitions, and by customer approval and word of mouth. Getting the news out might prove difficult for they were entering a competitive and crowded marketplace with most having little marketing expertise and experience in sales, a situation aggravated by a lack of domestic opportunities (restricted sales channels), and the need to compete with imported wines and Ontario 'blends' that were often perceived as better value and were widely available in the LCBO system.

Anyone entering the business had to appreciate that the five largest wineries were responsible for almost 90% of Ontario wine production with Vincor alone selling about 22% of all wine sold in Canada. Vincor, with sales of more than $376 million in 2001, and Andres with $139 million, combined accounted for about 75% of the Canadian wine sold in the LCBO. This left precious little room for the other wineries who, most of the time, ended up competing primarily with each other for any share of the market. At the same time, the capital-intensive nature of the wine business required that a winery have the resources to pay for their grapes, all fees, taxes, and operating expenses related to the winemaking, the bottling and packaging of its first wines, and then develop a market and be able to sell its first vintage as the second harvest would already be beckoning and additional capital would be required (by November!) to pay for the new vintage!

Having been there myself, I can attest to the stress of the wine business and how vulnerable even a good winery can be while attempting to develop credibility and handle the curse of any new business, ensuring adequate cash flow. In this challenging environment it is not surprising that several smaller wineries simply went out of business in short order (Trillium Hill, Grape Tree, Silver Peak, Nesher (Kosher), Cilento, Willow Heights, and Walker Hall) or were amalgamated by another business (Birchwood, Eastdell, Lakeview, and Thomas and Vaughn, all small wineries who merged with a sales agency named Diamond Estates headed by Murray Marshall, Murray Watson, and Andrew Green).

Some new winery owners would quickly realize that the wine business was more difficult than they had been led to believe and they began to question fees and mark-ups that they saw were unreasonable and to express their unhappiness at Wine Council meetings where complaining about the status quo seemed to be taken for granted. Indeed, this dissatisfaction in the industry was widespread and it would only become worse when Mother Nature provided an unpleasant 'surprise', as all Ontario grape growers and wineries would discover to their dismay.

Lady bug, lady bug, fly away home!

One day early in 2002, the owner-winemaker of Lakeview Cellars, Eddie Gurinskas, invited me over to taste a new white wine from the 2001 vintage. He had submitted it to the VQA tasting panel and it had been rejected, and as often happens with knowledgeable winemakers, he was confused and upset. After tasting the wine from tank, I was as puzzled as he was. Although the wine was still a little cloudy – he had submitted a filtered sample – it certainly seemed 'fault free' to me and all I could suggest was to re-submit it with the hope that the trained sensory panelists had simply 'made a mistake'!

In short order several other wineries had a similar experience with their 2001 wines, and it became clear that the industry had a serious problem. Most of the submitted wines, especially those made from Vinifera grapes, were being rejected because of an objectionable herbaceous character that was masking the varietal character of the wine – and no one was able to identify the cause. The Wine Council, The Grape Growers of Ontario, and the VQAO, although busy with the "Poised for Greatness" planning and with negotiations involving the European Union, immediately went to work on the new problem because of its potential disastrous impact on the industry. The research facilities at Brock University were approached to investigate the cause of the problem and to ascertain if there were any remedial actions that could be pursued to help with the tainted wines.

Everyone recalled that during the 2001 harvest swarms of lady bugs had descended on the vineyards after feasting on aphids in the soybean fields and then settled in the grape clusters when the soybeans were harvested. No one had given much thought to them as lady bugs had always been considered beneficial for aphid control and were commonly regarded as a symbol of good luck. Indeed, one cutting-edge winery, Malivoire, was using native lady bugs in their vineyards and had even named one wine "Ladybug Rose"! But the researchers discovered that these were Asian lady beetles, not the common indigenous ones, being the species 'Harmonia axyridis'. They had been imported by the U.S. Department of Agriculture from Asia on several occasions in the 1900's and released in places like California and Pennsylvania as a beneficial biological control agent for crops like apples, citrus, pecans, corn, and tobacco. Their activity in Ontario vineyards, taking shelter in the clusters and feeding on the sugars in damaged grapes, had proven to be an unfortunate, unintended consequence of this.

When disturbed or feeling stressed, these multi-coloured Asian Lady Beetles - they ranged in colour from creamy yellow to orange and red, with numerous blackish spots - excrete a yellow, odorous compound as a defensive mechanism against predators (known as 'reflex bleeding'). They had responded naturally as if attacked during grape harvesting and processing by 'bleeding' into the musts and juices prior to fermentation into wine. The compound was officially identified as 2 isopropyl-3-methoxypyrazene or IPMP for short, and it is unpleasant! It had left many wines affected with various levels of a musty, earthy taint, both in odor and flavour (LBT or Lady Bug Taint), which many people identified as asparagus or green pepper in nature with overtones of rancid peanut butter. It was determined that the average threshold for this was only 5 parts per trillion with talented tasters able to detect it at less than one part. Strangely, the threshold in Hybrid grapes was higher, some 25 ppt, and in Sauvignon Blanc grapes where methylanthranilate and other pyrazines seemed to help mask the character.

The good news was that there was no health hazard associated with the taint. The bad news was that the offensive presence did not degrade or disappear in the wine over time and that there were no effective remedies`to cure the illness. Millions of litres of Ontario wine had to be destroyed as the MALB infected wine was not able to be sold.

Wineries were devasted having to destroy the affected wine. They had paid for grapes that had produced wine they could not sell. Some wines made it to market and, unfortunately, the taint only became stronger in them, and they had to be recalled. Wine writers had picked up on the issue and, while sympathetic to the industry, kept the public informed about any winery releasing wine that was not up to par. In the end there was little acceptable Ontario wine to sell from what had been a good quality vintage and this shortfall was coming at a time when everyone was attempting to implement the "Poised for Greatness" strategies. Even worse, the reputation of the entire industry suffered, and many consumers refused to buy any 2001 Ontario wine.

The next question became one of how to deal with MALB in the future as it was realized only minute quantities of IPMP were required to wreak havoc and ruin a wine. Various insecticides were suggested to kill the lady bugs if they appeared, with the hope that they would fall out of a cluster and not be part of processing. Some wineries planned to use sorting tables to hand inspect their grapes but that would be a very costly solution most could ill afford. The use of an automatic shaker table, to literally shake the MALB out of the clusters and have them fall into a bin, was devised by some clever people, and eventually an electronic sorting machine would be created to eliminate the lady bugs. This was a problem that impacted on wineries of all sizes, with small wineries pushed financially to deal with it, and with large wineries needing to handle large volumes of incoming grapes where sorting was inappropriate. And growers were now pressured to deliver their grapes essentially MALB free…or face the possibility of rejection.

Forewarned is forearmed, and the industry fought on with even much greater care now taken for the quality of the raw material. Fortunately, there have been no other serious incidents with MALB since the surprise of 2001!

The industry lives with constant change, the new norm!

In other respects, expectations for the 2001 vintage were promising with grapes showing good concentration and complexity. Wineries purchased 41,267 tonnes of grapes from a harvest of 58,297 tonnes having no idea at this point of the challenge they would be facing from the ladybug crisis. Fortunately, the 2002 vintage was excellent and wineries were able to recover somewhat from the setback by purchasing 43,700 tonnes of grapes that were above average for sugar levels. However, the winter of 2002 would serve to remind everyone of the vulnerable nature of this business, confirming the fickle nature of our climate, with severe frost conditions that caused considerable damage to vineyards including the destruction of many vines. The resulting 2003 harvest was reduced drastically to 26,000 tonnes, a short crop situation that would see the government take action on behalf of the industry by amending the Wine Content and Labelling Act, 2000 (Ont. Reg. 659/2000) to address the shortfall of grapes.

In order to retain as much Ontario tonnage as possible for VQA wines, which still required 100% Ontario grape content, the WCLA was amended from requiring 30% Ontario content in blended products to just 10%, meaning a Cellared in Canada wine could consist of 90% imported material (Ont. Reg. 382/2003). The only stipulation was that the wine had to be packaged before February 1, 2005. VQA wineries could still concentrate on those wines while the 'blenders' were able to continue with their blends and not lose product offerings in the LCBO system.

Fortunately, the harvest for 2004 was better than average and wineries processed almost 48,000 tonnes of grapes with half of these Vinifera. This was good news for the wine industry but it would be short-lived. The winter of 2004-2005 was unusually cold and Ontario vineyards suffered badly once again. The resulting crop was the smallest in the modern era with only 8000 tonnes of Vinifera and 10,000 tonnes of Hybrids processed and this made it impossible to maintain needed production levels.

A "Memorandum of Understanding" was developed by industry partners creating a 3-year action plan to address this second short crop. The Regulations were again amended dealing with blended wines but this time to permit up to 99% imported material while reducing the required domestic component to as little as 1%, a step that would mitigate the effects of the grape shortage. All the wine produced would have to be bottled before February 1, 2007, when the minimum Ontario content would revert to 30% (Ont. Reg. 515/2005).

Such wines should have been sold bearing the name of the primary country of origin, but they were blends, after all, and thus they retained their "Cellared in Canada (CIC)" status. However, this time all Ontario wineries were allowed to use imported material in blends if desired, with a usage cap that would be calculated for each winery using a formula agreed to by the WCO and the GGO.

It was also agreed that grape prices would increase across all grape classes by 3% for 2006 and by 2% for 2007. Other clauses obligated the individual partners to agree to specific requirements to 'play fair', given the latitude of the agreement, to be transparent about the grape content of all wine manufactured in Ontario, and to keep good records! Winery owners new to the industry must have been wondering if they had underestimated the complexity of a wine industry that depended to such an extent on sensitive Vinifera grapes!

In spite of the turmoil in the industry with changed regulations and the grape supply, new wineries continued to open at an astounding rate with VQA membership growing from 44 in 2000 to 78 in 2005, a 77% increase! For Paul Speck, the first Chair of the Wine Council to come from a 'smaller' winery, and for Len Penachetti, Chair of the VQAO, it had been 5 years of extreme challenge and a tremendous amount of work in addition to running their own wineries, Henry of Pelham and Cave Springs. They had faced a difficult period head on with a supporting cast from the GGO and various government ministries, managing not only to maintain the status quo but to develop successfully other issues that would further the progress of all wineries.

September 16, 2003, for example, would see the finalization of an agreement on Wines and Spirits with the European Union ending two years of trade negotiations to allow VQA wines free access to European markets by reducing barriers to international trade, a step that would help change their almost exclusive reliance on the domestic market. At this time, Canada received over $600 million of wine from Europe while selling less than $500,000 in return. As part of the agreement to drop restrictions for wines that met the same standards as EU wines, the VQAO would provide an independent certification process for Ontario wineries exporting to Europe as required by the EU as a condition of access.

In addition, our wineries would be obligated to stop using the term "Champagne" on wine labels (along with 20 other generic wine names like 'Port' and 'Sauternes') which had been the source of an historic conflict between France and Canadian wineries dating back over 70 years. There had been court cases and lawsuits filed over the years (referred to as the 'Champagne Wars') as France and then the European Union attempted to force Canada to honour their trademarks and trade names, and this had resulted in restricting wine imports into the EU. Now, access for icewines and even table wines would be granted, and this would provide an opportunity to improve dramatically our feeble exporting record and expand our credibility internationally as a quality wine producing region.

At the same time, several new world wine producers including Canada, the United States, Australia, New Zealand, Chile, and Argentina, ratified the Mutual Acceptance Agreement which recognized and accepted the respective regulations governing winemaking practices in the participating countries. This was a major step in gaining international recognition for our VQA standards and wines and would streamline trade in wines between these countries.

The VQAO would celebrate numerous other advances during the initial years of the new decade with several important changes in regulations aimed at improving the marketing and quality of VQA wines. In 2003, after some serious consideration, screwcap closures were finally allowed on VQA wines along with organic labelling under specific conditions. The matter of a closure for wines had become complicated by a quality issue with corks in general that was a source of concern for winemakers. Some corks, but not all, were causing an offensive odour and taste in wine as a result of a chemical (tricholoranisole or TCA) generated in their manufacturing process. Unfortunately, it was not possible to predict at bottling if this 'taint' would show up later when the wine was uncorked, but in any case, dealing with unhappy consumers if the wine became tainted was the problem of the winery (and a costly one!). Screwcaps had improved their image a great deal since their introduction for use on inexpensive wines over two decades earlier, with the result that more and more winemakers were expressing a desire to use them even for their top VQA wines, including red wines. Considering that screwcaps had also improved so much in their manufacture and were being used with confidence throughout the world of wine, it was only logical for the VQA to grant acceptance for their use in Ontario. As with the burgeoning category of organic wines, as we shall see, the use of screwcaps had meant a shift in perception concerning wine quality, something the VQAO was determined to maintain for the benefit of Ontario wine consumers.

This was followed by an attempt to drive an improvement in overall Ontario winemaking by conducting an analysis of all VQA testing results that generated a 'report card' submitted to individual wineries to help them evaluate their own performance in relation to other wineries, followed by the creation of a 'Winemakers' Forum' which gave winemakers an opportunity to share best practices with each other.

Sub-appellations for the Niagara Peninsula

A major initiative came to fruition in the fall of 2005 after extensive research led by Brock University that helped identify 'unique' wine regions in Niagara based on climate, soil, and topography. 10 sub-appellations were established to help better identify the origin of a VQA wine, connecting the consumer with a more specific 'sense of place'. In the VQA Annual Report for 2008, the chair of the VQA, Greg Berti of Hillebrand/Trius, commented that this was an important development for the appellation system because "origin informs consumer choice". The existing Niagara Peninsula Appellation was sub-divided into the following ten sub-apps:

East of St. Catharines: Niagara River, Niagara Lakeshore, Four Mile Creek, St. David's Bench

West of St. Catharines: Beamsville Bench, Twenty Mile Bench, Short Hills Bench, Lakeshore, Creek Shores, and Vinemount Ridge.

Two additional regional sub-appellations rounded out the list, Niagara Escarpment and Niagara-on-the-Lake. In the new structure, wineries could label their wine as one of the sub-apps alone if all the grapes used in making the wine came from it, or as the more generic Niagara Peninsula appellation, or Niagara Peninsula plus a sub-app.

Although the creation of sub-appellations was considered a needed improvement for our VQA wines, not everyone agreed that the differences between some of the sub-apps were pronounced enough to justify creating so many and that this would only serve to confuse consumers who were still learning about VQA wines. However, furthering hi-lighting the origin of a particular wine, as studies in the U.S. had shown, showcasing the appellation status would add considerably to the value of the wine and thus allow for an increase in its price. This, then, was a marketing milestone for Ontario wines and it would bring added sophistication to the VQA brand at this early time in its own development.

Exorcising the Excise Tax: Beal's appeal!

From a historical perspective, you could forgive Ontario wineries for feeling that the Federal Government had never really appreciated the wine industry and its contribution to employment and the economic spin-offs generated by it in the province. Consider, for example, how badly it supported the industry at the beginning of the Free Trade negotiations, valuing it only as a source of millions of dollars of government revenue raised by the Federal Excise Tax. The industry believed that this tax was punitive and unfair because it put their wines at a competitive disadvantage in the marketplace. In the U.S., the Bureau of Alcohol, Tobacco, and Firearms provided an exemption for wineries on the first 500,000 litres of wine sold, but the Canadian government had steadfastly refused to change the tax regulation. At least, that was the case until a newcomer to the wine industry, businessman Norm Beal, founder of Peninsula Ridge in 2000, became Chair of the Wine Council in 2005.

One of his first tasks was to work with Executive Director Linda Franklin on the issue of excise-tax reform, a matter which the Canadian Vintners' Association (CVA) had been previously pursuing aided by Dean Allison, the Conservative MP for the West Lincoln riding. The new Conservative government headed by Stephen Harper, with Jim Flaherty as finance minister, seemed to be more receptive to a change in the tax and invited Norm to Ottawa to discuss the matter just prior to the arrival of a new budget. To the delight of the wine industry, the budget of May 2, 2006, introduced an excise exemption on the first 500,000 litres of 100% Canadian wine production annually, providing a maximum savings for a winery of $310,000, (although the rate from that point on and for all blended wines would increase from $0.5122 to $0.62 per litre to compensate for a 1 percent GST rate reduction).

However, the CVA did have some concerns with some exemption rules that impacted negatively on the corporate wineries. Companies with more than one winery could benefit from only one exemption for the entire corporation and would have to pay the increased tax amount on all their additional winery production, a truly inane position. After further discussion with the CVA, the government agreed to reconsider the new 'rules' and almost overnight surprisingly decided to eliminate completely the excise tax for 100 percent Canadian wine while removing the associated company ruling, effective July 1, 2006.

For all wineries this was significant tax-relief – a current savings of $0.62 on every litre of Canadian wine sold – and provided a lot of money for reinvesting in their businesses. Unfortunately, the European Union took exception to the ruling and decided to challenge it as an unfair trading practice. However, after a Canada-wide boycott of European wines was threatened, the EU relented, and the challenge ended in December 2007, leaving intact what was a very memorable and meaningful milestone on the industry's way to greatness.

Prodding the Provincial Government for additional needed support

Although occasionally maligned by some in the wine business, the Ontario government had proven itself to be a mainstay in its support of the industry and this was especially true for the first five years of the new Ontario Wine Strategy program (2003-2007). In 2004, the government provided $2 million for improved marketing and tourism activities and continued to collaborate with industry leaders from the Wine Council, the Grape Growers, and the VQAO on a regular basis. Yet, a long-standing issue for the industry had been the "pitiful margins" for a winery in selling to the LCBO which meant that many small wineries could not afford to sell in that channel. This also made it unprofitable for a winery to sell its 'best' wines, usually made in smaller volumes, to the LCBO. For the wineries, an improvement in the dollars they received (which at the time were less than 50% of the retail price), was a matter of survival. For the LCBO, mandated to generate revenue for the government, there was no desire to make any change.

Norm Beal and Linda Franklin led the Wine Council in discussions to find a way to change the mark-up dilemma that would not run counter to international trade agreements yet support the industry. Their work resulted in another major step upward for producers of 100% Ontario wine. In 2006, the Ontario Government announced what was called the VQA Wine Support Program intended to encourage the sale of VQA wines at the LCBO, increase the competitiveness of wineries, and encourage further innovation. The program, administered by the Ministry of Economic Development and Trade, would provide an annual grant based on sales of VQA table wines at the LCBO with a cap of 13,000 litres. The LCBO would calculate the sales after one year and provide a 30% rebate on the FOB price for each winery. The wineries had to 'justify' the grant, providing evidence that the money would be spent on activities meant to improve the business, for example on marketing activities, and they could not simply pocket the money as 'profit'. Significantly, blended wines were not eligible for the program.

"Twenty Bees" and a hive full of grape issues

For almost 60 years, since 1947 when the Ontario Grape Growers' Marketing Board was created (it changed its name to Grape Growers of Ontario or GGO in 2002), representatives from the wineries and the OGGMB have been obligated to negotiate the prices of grapes that the processors would pay with every grower receiving the same price for the same grapes. This regulated marketing environment had produced a confrontational "system" over the years with farmers always looking to increase prices and wineries looking to control their input costs. When labrusca grapes were the only game in town, the matter of the 'quality' of the grapes had been relatively unimportant as wineries could add considerable water and sugar to the grapes to stretch volume and increase alcohols (also known incredibly as 'amelioration'), leaving winemaking as a quantity issue. However, with the arrival of the French Hybrids and Vinifera grapes and the need to make wine that could compete on quality, wineries became more and more concerned with issues like ripeness, sugar, and acidity, and began to focus on the quality of the grapes. It was obvious that all grapes were not of the same quality and that the one-size fits all pricing was unfair, both to wineries and to growers who made a real effort to deliver top-quality material.

The marketing board 'system' did not take this into account, and as could be expected, the desire to establish quality as a factor in the purchase of grapes added another complex dimension to annual price negotiations. Wineries did pay more for French Hybrid and Vinifera grapes according to a pay schedule that placed different grapes in different categories, but once the minimum base prices were negotiated, contracts for the sale of grapes could not take place below this minimum base price and no individual pricing contracts were allowed between a buyer and seller. Annual negotiations were always difficult, taking on an adversarial relationship, with an arbitrator often brought in to provide a settlement (usually in the Growers favour!) and leaving both sides unsatisfied. With each passing year the dilemma seemed to become more problematic with growers unhappy when grapes of lesser quality were rejected by a winery or when they were left with surplus grapes that wineries were unable to buy while still importing material for their blends, and with wineries convinced they were paying too much for grapes, not all of which were top-quality. Both sides were convinced that the other was able to hold them 'hostage' and bad feelings were mutual.

In 2005 a group of disgruntled growers who had been selling to the corporate wineries took matters into their own hands and decided to start their own winery, believing this would cause havoc for wineries making Cellared in Canada wines while giving them a 'guaranteed' market for their grapes. The shareholders called themselves Niagara Vintners and they hired a man experienced in business development from the automotive industry named Helmut Klassen as CEO and to head up the Board of

Directors and build the $20 million dollar winery. According to Linda Bramble, the shareholders owned 4,400 acres of grapes, literally 25% of Niagara vineyards and were obligated to invest a minimum of $100,000 in the venture.

With experienced winemaker Rob Sommers on board and with Klassen providing skilled leadership, the operation formed a business plan with an eventual target of one million cases of VQA wine under the "20 Bees" name (there were 20 individuals involved), an ambitious undertaking for a start-up winery.

Everyone was impressed with the concept of producing inexpensive, good-value, table wines, especially the LCBO and they welcomed the Bees with listings even as the winery turned to a new winemaker, the talented Sue-Ann Staff, after Sommers left to join Hester Creek Winery in B.C. But other troubles arose in the hive almost from the outset resulting in the firing of Klassen on October 20, 2006, and causing legal issues over his dismissal. In 2006 the winery made over 3 million litres of wine from some 3,800 tonnes of grapes and found itself in a surplus position when the 2007 vintage came around. Suddenly, bills and suppliers were not being paid and some of the wine inventory mysteriously disappeared. Grower members never received any payment for their grapes in spite of the sales of wine and contracts for private labelling that the business had developed.

In only two years the business proved to be a complete failure and shareholders lost their entire investment, hundreds of thousands of dollars, in what proved to be an embarrassing fiasco for the industry. The business was purchased by Diamond Estates for just $17 million dollars, a bargain when the value of the building, the equipment, 3.6 million litres of bulk wine and 21,000 cases of bottled wine were considered, and almost overnight Diamond became Ontario's fifth largest winery.

The sad demise of Niagara Vintners would cause waves of concern in the wine industry at the same time as Niagara was reeling from other terrible news. The tender fruit and grape juice industries received word in 2007 that the Cadbury Schweppes plant in St. Catharines was closing, literally ending an era for the Niagara canning industry and removing a market that would drastically impact the livelihood of over 100 growers. While this did not directly involve those growing grapes for the wineries, it would mean that those affected would have to readjust the nature of their farming. With the passing of the Green Belt Act in 2005, a measure intended to preserve agricultural land in the Golden Horseshoe and GTA areas against loss and fragmentation through urban sprawl, farmers discovered that they were unable to sell their land for any other development, and many decided to switch crops and plant wine grapes – some 2000 acres!

For the grape and wine industry, however, still losing market share to imported wines, the idea of significantly increased grape production was concerning. Grape pricing was already a divisive issue in the industry and 2007 was the last year of a 3 year pricing agreement that would deliver a confirmed increase of 2% to growers who now were worried about the future. Ironically, 2007 marked the 60th anniversary of the Grape Growers of Ontario/GGO, and the 2007 vintage was considered the 'best ever'. And there was other goods news.

This same year witnessed the development of a new VQA Designated Viticultural Area, Prince Edward County, as several wineries had opened here since 2000 to take advantage of the numerous changes improving the fortunes of VQA producers. This coincided with the revitalization of horticultural research activities at the Vineland Research Station, with a $12.5 million investment in the Vineland Research and Innovation Centre by the Ontario Government, along with the creation of an Ontario Wine Secretariat and a Grape and Wine Research Foundation. And responding to the closure of Cadbury Schweppes, the government announced $3.8 million for an Ontario juice grape transition program to help growers switch their juice grapes to wine grapes and then a further $22.3 million came from the Federal Government to help the fruit industry adapt "to meet consumer demands".

Comparing the position of the grape and wine industry at the end of the first five years of the new Ontario Wine Strategy in 2007 to its start in 2003, one might have expected a marked improvement in its status given the number of significant developments in its favour during this time. For grape growers in 2007 this appeared to be the case, with the value of the grape crop, $75 million in 2007, the highest value ever, up almost $7 million from 2006, and a dramatic difference from the $26.5 million in 2003 when growers had to endure a 'short crop'.

Reflecting the changing nature of our vineyards, the grape vine census for this same period showed a continuing and expected drop in the number of "old" labrusca vines of 35%, a small increase of 1.3% in French Hybrids, and a significant increase in the number of Vinifera vines of 22.9%.

In winery purchases of the French Hybrids, Baco Noir proved to be the most popular red at 2596 tonnes, up from 1973 tonnes in 2003 and Vidal by far the most popular white at 8994 tonnes. Cabernet Franc at 5206 tonnes was the top red vinifera followed by Merlot at 4097, Cabernet Sauvignon at 3527, and Pinot Noir at 2078. Chardonnay topped the white vinifera purchases at 7858 tonnes followed by Riesling at 5123 and Sauvignon Blanc at 1391. For anyone once skeptical about growing Vinifera in Ontario, it was now more than obvious that this species would indeed be the future of our viticulture, notwithstanding the fragile nature of these vines.

Pursuing sales: not to advance is to recede!

Total wine sales, likewise, continued to increase annually, as LCBO management would proudly affirm, with advances in both imported wines and our domestic-international blended wines, with the only real disappointment in the VQA category.

Total Ontario sales:	2003	-	113,505,000 litres	2007	-	138,729,000 litres
Total Ontario wine:	2003	-	45,359,000 litres	2007	-	54,083,000 litres
Total Import wine:	2003	-	66,732,000 litres	2007	-	83,888,000 litres
Total VQA sales:	2003	-	10,109,000 litres	2007	-	9,127,000 litres

Total non-VQA sales:	2003	-	34,119,000 litres	2007	-	44,956,000 litres
% VQA of Ont. Wine:	2003	-	22.3%	2007	-	16.9%
% non VQA:	2003	-	75.2%	2007	-	83.1%
% Ontario wine:	2003	-	39.9%	2007	-	38.98%
% Imported wine:	2003	-	58.8%	2007	-	60.5%

Over the five years, all wine sales had increased in Ontario by 22.2% in volume. Ontario sales, VQA and non-VQA, advanced by 19.2% while imported sales increased by 25.7%. Anyone looking at these statistics from the LCBO and OGG Annual Reports would have to admit that our VQA wines had lost ground in the battle for market share even though their total retail value in 2007 had reached almost $220 million, up from $162 million, with sales to licencees up 75%. While there were slight variances from year to year in sales in different channels, unfortunately, the general trend was not our friend!

While the industry focus continued to be on increasing domestic market share, it did appear that our wines were still suffering from a historical consumer preference for imports which reflected a legacy of poorer quality wines that once characterized the industry. Even the arrival of top-quality VQA wines had not yet been enough to overcome this lingering perception and build the much-needed credibility to alter consumer tastes. The recent turmoil in the industry, from the ladybug problems to short crops, had not been helpful and the departure from the industry of valued leadership meant that it might take more time than expected to forge ahead.

Don Ziraldo and Don Triggs had both retired following the sale of Vincor to Constellation in 2006, and a valuable ally and supporter of the industry, Andy Brandt, who had been CEO of the LCBO since 1991, had joined them. As well, Linda Franklin, President of the Wine Council of Ontario, after 14 dedicated years as the "Queen of collaboration and consensus building" advancing the cause of all Ontario wineries, moved on to a senior position in government, leaving huge shoes to be filled by newcomer Hillary Dawson in 2007.

Although sales had flatlined somewhat, leaving us still "poised for greatness", the VQA industry was riding high in other ways with the removal of the excise tax, the development of sub-appellations, the agreement with the European Union, a new DVA and many winery start-ups, all of which represented opportunities for increased growth while creating the feeling that it was just a matter of time before the industry would be enjoying better success both at home and abroad, increasing both credibility and sales.

CHAPTER ELEVEN

"Owning our own market" - Do YOU VQA?

"If your main objective is to buy as cheaply as possible and still support the local wine industry, then you're likely forced to stick with CIC wines and there's sure to be lots of it although there is no 'sense of place' in a blended wine! If you want to support real Ontario wine and don't mind paying a bit more on occasion, then VQA is an easy choice." Richard Best, "The Frugal Oenophile", Winter, 2008

"The imports are fishing off our dock and eating our lunch." Jim Clark, President of Colio Wines.

"We look forward to sitting beside our grower community to help build the dynamic future of our industry and address barriers that have hindered the value and growth of our collective products." Winery and Grower Alliance of Ontario, Letter to the Farm Products Marketing Commission, November 23, 2009

In the grape and wine business, the word 'growth' can refer to many things with growth in sales usually the most critical, but you can also talk about growth in vineyard plantings or the growth in the number of wineries, or growth in market share of a particular segment. Wine sales in Ontario have shown consistent, overall annual growth, much to the delight of the wine industry and the LCBO, although the market share of the participants

(Imports, VQA, and non-VQA wines) has varied considerably from year to year.

The most obvious sign of growth for consumers by 2008 would have to be in the roster of 160 local wineries, including 102 VQA members, spreading throughout our three DVAs and into remote nooks and crannies of the province as if there were no limits to what the market could support. With all the new players in search of the optimal 'terroir' to fulfill their dreams, the game had become more sophisticated, with a corresponding growth in wine choice and quality, but more complicated as well with wine prices on the rise. With the increased competition, consumers might have expected some restraint in pricing but the costs of making wine, from the price of land and the grapes themselves to barrels, bottles, labels, and everything else, also increasing annually, made it difficult for anyone to hit the pause button.

That is, not until 2008.

To begin with, we must keep in mind the importance of the grape and wine industry to our province's economy. In 2008 it was estimated that this industry was 'worth' some $575 million to Ontario, employing 5,000 people, with every tonne of grapes sold contributing an average of $10,000. That is why the provincial government had always been so supportive of the industry, beginning with our grape growers whose grapes now represented 35% of all fruit grown commercially in Ontario with a farm-gate value of $75 million for the 2007 harvest. As well, our wineries had received considerable assistance to help them sustain their competitive ability and retain market share with Ontario wine now representing almost 40% of all wine sold in the province, some 6 million cases or just over 56 million litres.

But Ontario, like most places in the world in 2008, was about to feel the impact of the American sub-prime mortgage scandal that would bring with it a serious financial downturn and tough economic times worldwide. For the wine industry, the fear was that such a recession would result in a glut of grapes and drive down wine prices, especially the more expensive brands, and cause a decline in tourism which was becoming so important for the smaller local wineries. These concerns framed growing pains for the wine industry associated with what Hillary Dawson, President of the Wine Council, called its "awkward adolescence", a stage in its development where our 'reborn' industry was grappling with various rifts that collectively were hindering its growth.

For example, there was considerable and ongoing antagonism between producers of VQA wines and Cellared in Canada wines on several levels making for an unhealthy business environment, and an almost permanent adversarial relationship between the GGO and the WCO based on a collective bargaining process that many wineries wanted to dismantle and growers and government wanted to retain. All players continued to protest what they saw as outdated government regulations, both federal and provincial, that dictated the way wine was sold and an LCBO system that was obligated to respect international trade agreements, enduring constant criticism for not serving the domestic industry better. In spite of the efforts of the industry associations to effect change, so many of these issues seemed 'carved in stone' and were proving to be barriers to industry development. At the same time, virtually everyone was trying to find a way to deal with a long-standing consumer preference for imported wines (averaging 6 out of every 10 bottles sold) that left our industry constantly striving to overtake them and achieve a market share over 50%.

In truth, an analysis of the Ontario grape and wine industry would reveal a very conflicted business with a lack of respect among the stakeholders which made collaboration an ongoing challenge. It would take a monumental effort, if indeed this was possible, to generate a win-win-win scenario for growers, retailers, and government, all intent on achieving 'profit', while winning over the consumer at the same time. Considering the list of woes that simply would not go away, it was frankly amazing that the industry had performed as well as it had in such a short time. The new storm that was brewing would bring some of these matters to a head and the industry, once again, would be obligated to make a renewed effort at finding workable solutions.

In July, grape pricing negotiations began for the 2008 harvest with the ending of the previous agreement that had provided annual price increases over three exceptionally good growing years. Bill George, chairman for the Grape Growers, knew that this would be a 'challenging year' because of the economic downturn but the marketing board bargaining position was the same as always, to sell all the crop at prices satisfactory to the growers. Hillary Dawson, President of the Wine Council, was talking about supply exceeding demand this year due to increased plantings and many wineries still having full tanks with the suggestion that they were looking for significant price reductions in some varieties. George also realized that several growers had no contracts with wineries and that the Wine Council was determined to resist any increase in prices on behalf of its members. Some wineries were even talking about the need for a new, 'free market' pricing system that would allow private arrangements between growers and producers, and this represented a threat to the long-established marketing board system.

Thus, the stage was set for the traditional face-off of the two sides, which would see them travelling a road they had all been down many times before, each focused on their members' own best interests and seemingly unable to trust each other. By this time, someone should have realized that the price of grapes was linked to wine pricing and that growers and wineries had to co-operate for their mutual benefit. The equation appeared to be simple: without grape growers there would be little domestic wine and without wineries there would be no market for local grapes. The GGO and the WCO did understand that one side could not prosper without the other and that they were really members of the same team. After all, this was one industry, the 'grape and wine industry', but they were forced to be combatants by the 'system'.

By October, negotiations were at an impasse with a large harvest underway and a grape surplus, the nemesis of the GGO, looming. The GGO offered changes to the sugar schedules to reduce the price of low sugar grapes, but two rounds of negotiations were unsuccessful. An arbitrator, called in to settle the matter, ruled in favour of the GGO price offer but basically kept prices the same as the previous year, increasing the price of grapes in demand ever so slightly and holding the line or reducing the price of grapes in oversupply. Considering the market conditions, this appeared to be a fair compromise but the wineries still resented being locked into a process that was anything but collaborative, especially as almost 150 wineries were part of the 473 grower membership!

In the end, the vintage provided farm-gate revenue of $79.5 million, the highest ever, with almost 58,000 tonnes harvested (70% of which were now Vinifera grapes), but left almost 3000 tonnes of good grapes 'without a home'.

In what was labelled a "Stabilizing and Restructuring Strategy", the government quickly stepped in and agreed to a $4 million assistance plan to allow the GGO to purchase 2300 tonnes of uncontracted grapes from 79 distressed growers in late October. However, many were now asking why the large wineries were allowed to continue importing material for their blended wines, estimated to be the equivalent of some 40,000 tonnes, when Ontario grapes were left hanging on the vine, a simple and valid question which begged an answer. The response of the large wineries was that they already purchased 50% to 60% of the Ontario crop annually and sold most of the domestic wine but did not require these grapes. The issue was just one of many that were making a successful future for this industry such an enigma!

The government also insisted that this would be a "one time" bailout and that it was time for the two sides to resolve their problems once and for all. As a result, the GGO and the WCO scheduled meetings into 2009 to brainstorm innovative solutions and create a common vision and strategy for the future, building on the planning that had generated the "Poised for Greatness" document a few years earlier.

The Farm Products Marketing Commission continued to drive the process by assigning Dr. Frank Ingratta to facilitate meetings and negotiations on grape pricing and sugar schedules but, even with a beehive of activity, no agreements were reached until July 21 when grape prices were settled for the 2009 vintage. The result was an overall decrease by 8% in the price of grapes.

On August 14, the GGO and WCO released what was labelled a 'Transition Plan' reflecting the previous planning sessions that renewed their 'strategic vision' for the next 5 years until 2014. The hope was to respect all stakeholders needs and drive profitability across all aspects of the supply chain, from grower to retailer. Both sides agreed that the LCBO could do more to enhance the performance of Ontario wines in their stores including new sales targets in both General List and Vintages – a theme that was becoming commonplace – that would drive the plan to achieve growth in VQA sales at 15% per year and CIC sales at 6-8% for the next 10 years.

It also specified that the Wine Content and Labelling Act should be reviewed, along with the need for government to consider more options for retailing wine, and that the VQA support program which returned money to wineries for their sales in the LCBO should be continued. Other elements of the plan addressed contracts and pricing models for grapes to create a better balance with supply and demand and put the 'right varietals in the right wines at the right quality' in order to be competitive.

Just over two months later, on October 13, 2009, having reviewed all input into the matter, the Government unveiled their own plan "to strengthen the Ontario Grape and Wine Industry", with measures that would focus the entire industry on producing VQA wines which everyone agreed were the future of the industry. This would include allowing time for the grape growers to transition to those grapes needed by the wineries but it was also made clear that the government would not consider purchasing un-contracted grapes for the current vintage, and that the Farm Products Marketing Commission would continue to explore options "to modernize the system for marketing grapes". As well, the LCBO was directed to increase consumer access to VQA wines with clearer labelling and improved signage in their stores.

The Chair of the GGO, Bill George Jr., in a letter to his members on November 30, called this a "time of tremendous change and opportunity for the grape and wine industry" requiring the co-operation of all growers, processors, and the government. When funding was announced in late April 2010, VQA wineries were delighted to hear that the government would renew the Wine Support program for VQA wine sold in the LCBO system with a commitment of $6 million each year and an additional $3 million renewal of the marketing program for VQA wines (covering LCBO promotions, Wine Route maps, advertising and signage, and events like the annual Cuvee celebration and the Niagara Wine Festival). In addition, $3 million each year for 4 years was provided to help Ontario growers transition to needed grape varieties for high quality VQA wines. In total this came to $57 million to support VQA wines through 2014.

In order to fund the renewed VQA programs, the government set its sights on CIC wines sold in wineries' off-site retail store systems by levying a 10% markup increase on these blended wines. An analysis had shown that these stores sold approximately 90% CIC wines in this market having to pay only a 2% mark-up on them where the same wines in the LCBO incurred a 58% mark-up and $1.62/litre excise tax which produced far less revenue for the winery. In addition, there would be a short-term increase in the Ontario content required in the wines, to 40% from 30% (with a 25% minimum in any given bottle). Surprisingly, legislation would be introduced to eliminate the domestic content all-together by 2014 in order to free up more grapes for VQA wines. The producers of CIC wines were hit hard by these recommendations, being confused by what this last step would mean for them in 5 years and, naturally, quite upset to be sacrificing a lot of money in order to support VQA wines. Their reaction would be unprecedented!

The release of the government plan came when there was a real prospect of a surplus of more than 9,000 tonnes of grapes, with numerous growers unable to find buyers for their 2009 crop. One grower described the government plan as "like prescribing an aspirin for a patient desperately in need of by-pass surgery"! In the end the processors would buy just over 44,000 tonnes of grapes, down from 57,561 in 2008, with a decrease in farm-gate value of some $23 million. There had even been a significant decrease of 30% in import blending materials purchased by the larger wineries. But, in spite of all the talk and releasing of 'plans', the Ontario grape and wine industry was in turmoil.

The producers of CIC wines believed that they had been targeted by the government with a 10% 'surtax' that was to them both discriminatory and punitive. Their argument was based not only on the reality that CIC wines represented most of the Ontario wine sold in the province but also that foreign wines had escaped completely from the legislation with no new levy. The President of Vincor, Eric Morham, while indicating he would continue to fight Bill 218 which he predicted would cost this segment of the wine industry some $12 million annually, went so far as to suggest their company would have to revise all grape contracts in order to adapt to the changes in their requirements that price increases forced by the new tax would bring. He argued that "focusing specifically on CIC wines at wine retail stores is a direct attack on a specific segment of the industry that... keeps our industry strong".

His arguments, while valid, ignored the fact that the larger wineries were doing very well financially with this category in their store systems and with the LCBO while over 95% of Ontario wineries were denied the right to produce them or have more than one store in which to sell their VQA wines. As well, many people were voicing their indignation with the way the CIC wines were labelled, claiming they were 'hoodwinking' consumers into believing they were local products. John Peller, CEO of Andrew Peller Ltd, told CBC news at the time that "I think some of the critics are being a little unfair...these are wines consumers are really happy with for their taste and value". He added that his company's labelling was not misleading and they were not hiding the fact the wines were blends. Yet the government decided in the end to accept that these producers did have an advantage over most wineries that would allow it to justify using a small part of the revenue the CIC wines produced to help 'level the playing field'.

By the end of October, the major CIC producers, including Vincor, Peller, Colio, Diamond Estates, Magnotta, and Vinoteca, surprised the industry by announcing their departure from the Ontario Wine Council, creating a new association called The Winery and Grower Alliance of Ontario (Pelee Island joined but remained a member of the Wine Council). Within a year the membership of WGAO would include both small and large wineries who produced the lion's share of wine in Ontario including the majority of VQA wine, and several growers. For its part, the Wine Council of Ontario now represented most of the remaining wineries who were essentially smaller VQA producers.

Suddenly, the GGO now had two organizations representing processors, each with distinct needs, and no one was sure what impact this would have on the future of Ontario winemaking. But, in very short order, the GGO, WCO, and WGAO, were able to reach a 2 year agreement on grape pricing that was described as a win-win for both growers and wineries. For all white Hybrids and Viniferas there would be a 1% increase over the 2009 prices each year while these would remain the same for all red varieties. Four key grapes, Chardonnay, Riesling, Cabernet Franc, and Cabernet Sauvignon, were selected for a new pilot project called 'Plateau Pricing" that guaranteed a minimum price for these varieties ($1200 tonne for the whites and $1300 for the reds) with no tonnage restrictions, if their sugar level (Brix) was below an agreed number while maintaining higher prices for higher brix level grapes (starting at $1352 per tonne for whites, $1676 for Cab Franc and $1875 for Cab Sauvignon). This was indeed an optimistic start on re-aligning the industry, the result of all the discussions held between the stakeholders over the past year relating to the 'end use' of the grapes, that is for VQA or CIC products.

On July 19, 2010, just a week after grape prices were settled, the WGAO announced the signing of a high-profile Niagara business leader, Patrick Gedge, as CEO and President. Patrick had been the CEO of the Niagara Economic Development Corporation with a successful track record in international marketing, described by Chair Anthony Bristow as a "seasoned government relations professional". He would have an interesting job for sure operating alongside the Wine Council as WGAO members represented 90% of Ontario wine sold while processing over 70% of all contracted grapes.

With the first decade of the new century ending, it was now 35 years since Inniskillin opened the door on the boutique wine industry and 20 years since the introduction of our appellation system, the Vintners' Quality Alliance. In those 20 years Ontario vineyards had changed dramatically in their make-up, with the labrusca classes dwindling to less than 3000 tonnes in 2010 from 20,000 and vinifera classes producing over 32,000 tonnes, up from some 5,000. And, considering all the recent activity at a time of an economic downturn, the industry had good reason to be optimistic about the coming decade, one which hopefully would see the fulfillment of the "Poised for Greatness" vision.

The Grape Growers had been able to retain the marketing system which they believed was needed to sustain their livelihood, agreeing to the introduction of new developments in the pricing structure of grapes while continuing to work on aligning supply with demand and increasing the tonnage of VQA-appropriate grapes that would ensure a healthy future. There were now two provincial winery associations with each one focused on their major area of concern, the Wine Council on VQA wineries and the Winery and Grower Association on CIC producers.

In the past, the Wine Council had often proven to be a dysfunctional environment with small and large wineries having differing points of view, a source of friction in the industry that perhaps would now be reduced. Government had committed to supporting the VQA industry through a significant funding program intended to keep these wineries competitive and was determined to achieve harmony in the industry between grape growers and wineries. And there was hope that the LCBO would be making significant changes in their operations to help drive sales of Ontario wine in their store system.

Through the decade, sales of Ontario wine had reached 58,364,000 litres and imported wine 92,207,000, giving the domestic industry 38.7% of the market, a share which, unfortunately, was still decreasing. VQA sales, however, had nearly doubled during this same period and were now beginning to outpace non-VQA Ontario and imported wines, moving from a market share of 16.8% of all domestic wines in 2000 to a high of 23.7% for the 2009 sales year while maintaining a four year upward trend. And VQA membership continued to increase, now standing at 110 wineries. While this was encouraging, it is interesting to note that just 1 bottle of every 11 sold in Ontario was a VQA wine. At the same time, sales of blended CIC wines had been trending lower, down to 44.5 million litres or 30% of wine sold in Ontario.

"Owning our own market" at 50% or better of market share was proving to be a very elusive target!

CHAPTER TWELVE

Connecting with consumers in "Wine Country Ontario"

"Not because organic or biodynamic is definitively superior. Rather, it's because, as a cohort, these producers tend to be more rigorous and more committed to make genuinely fine wine." Matt Kramer, Wine Spectator, Nov. 15, 2009

"Sustainability isn't just about keeping things the way they are over time. It's about making things better." Angelo Pavan, co-owner/Winemaker, Cave Springs Winery, reported in Vintages Magazine, Sept. 14, 2019.

"Growing grapes and making wine in Ontario is not without its challenges and requires constant innovation, but it is always inspiring to see the resilience of spirit in our vines and in our people." Brian Schmidt, Winemaker, Vineland Estates, VQA Annual Report, Marsh 31, 2015.

Through the second decade of the new millennium, the grape and wine industry was energized by a positive, co-operative spirit among all stakeholders that was reflected by more amicable grape pricing agreements, a renewed Wine and Grape Strategy, a new Wine Marketing Association in 2015 (WMAO), and a pursuit of innovation and desire for 'sustainability' industry-wide that would result in achieving additional milestones in the ever-evolving plan for the future.

Although the industry had to accommodate considerable variation in quantity and quality of grapes from year to year, it had become more comfortable accepting the duality of our wine production, those wines which were now called "International Canadian Blends" (or ICB) and 100% Ontario wines, most of which enjoyed VQA status. Imported wines would continue to defy all attempts to reduce their dominant share of the market, in spite of the improved quality of our local wines, ongoing winery support from Government, and an industry that continued to grow its membership.

Yet, by 2019, grape growers had long established that Ontario could sustain numerous Vinifera varieties and these now represented over 60% of a normal harvest (68% in 2012!). The transformation in our vineyards from the older 'labrusca' varieties to the preferred varieties was indeed complete and both growers and winemakers had to be happy with the outcome. Through the decade, harvests had averaged 65,000 tonnes with 'short crops' near 50,000 tonnes occurring only in 2014 and 2015, and farm gate sales had reached a record of $115,000,000 in 2017 with an amazing crop of over 85,000 tonnes!

The Grape Growers of Ontario, which had certainly lived up to their mandate in driving our Vinifera future, trademarked a new marketing slogan that hi-lighted the changed grape landscape: "We grow the wines you love!" In Ontario, that translated into a harvest of over 50 different grape varieties, and this afforded wineries an opportunity to make and consumers to enjoy a cornucopia of distinctive wines. Producing such a varied portfolio makes our grape and wine industry special, if not somewhat unique in the world of wine where most regions distinguish themselves for a very small number of varieties. Burgundy, for example, has long been famed for its Pinot Noir and Chardonnay wines, and Bordeaux for Cabernet Sauvignon, Merlot, and Cabernet Franc. German wine regions are mainly known for their mastery of the Riesling grape. Other regions may grow several varieties but are principally recognized for two or three grapes that have put them on the radar of wine consumers, like Australia with Shiraz (Syrah) or New Zealand with Pinot Noir and Sauvignon Blanc.

In Ontario we have been successfully producing all these different varieties and several more.

To-day, wineries in three distinct appellations and others in 'emerging regions' are crafting VQA wines primarily from Vinifera varieties. VQA regulations list 79 different "vitis Vinifera" that are authorized to make a varietal wine but many of these are not yet grown in Ontario. Still, over the last 30 years, approximately 40 different Vinifera varietal names have appeared on an Ontario winery label, although in many cases only one or two wineries might have produced the wine. As a result, many consumers might never have had the chance to taste outstanding Ontario wines made from Kerner, Semillon, or Colombard, or even the more well-known Pinot Blanc or Viognier.

As well, 9 Hybrids may be used to make a varietal wine and another 15 Hybrids may be used in blends but are not permitted as varietals. Recently, a 'new' North American red Hybrid named Marquette was added to the list of 8 French Hybrids, the first of its type to receive VQA approval, and it appears that others may be accepted in the near future. Some wineries in colder areas of the province are experimenting with other North American Hybrids like Marquette, including Frontenac and L'Acadie Blanc, and finding that they are not only winter-hardy but also capable of making very promising wines.

Thus, the story of our young wine industry continues to unfold with wineries across the province making an amazing diversity of world-class wines from the considerable variety of grapes available and in a complete range of styles, literally creating a "something for everyone" scenario. We produce traditional red, white, and rose table wines, blends and varietals, including organic and biodynamic in nature, and several versions of 'dessert' wines, from late harvest to icewine, and even botrytis affected, an increasing number of sparkling wines made by the Charmat process (secondary fermentation in tank) and the 'traditional method' (secondary fermentation in the bottle) as well as the "pet nat" style (fermentation in bottle), fortified wines, nouveau wines, a growing number of 'orange' wines, and even 'vegan' wines!

Because we are considered to be a 'cool climate' wine region, it might be expected that the production of white grape varieties would exceed that of reds as in theory most reds require a longer growing season and more warmth to ripen them fully and our growing conditions normally make this challenging. Although each vintage brings a variation in tonnages of grapes produced, it is not surprising then that for 2018, with a processing crop of 63,251 tonnes, white Hybrids (17,677 tonnes) and white Viniferas (21,483 tonnes) totalled 62% of the harvest.

The French Hybrid Vidal grape continues to be the workhorse white in Ontario matching the combined production of the two leading white Viniferas, Chardonnay and Riesling. Baco Noir is far and away our leading red hybrid, producing slightly more tonnage than either Cabernet Franc or Merlot, the two 'top' red Viniferas. Other significant tonnage is generated annually by Pinot Gris/Grigio, Sauvignon Blanc, and Gewurztraminer in the white Vinifera category, and by Cabernet Sauvignon, Pinot Noir, Gamay, and Syrah (Shiraz), all red Vinifera. That makes a baker's dozen of different grapes that continue to provide most of the raw material for our wine industry.

While tonnage of each variety does vary from year to year causing changes in wine production, Chardonnay traditionally is our leading VQA Vinifera table wine by volume making 3 general 'styles' of wine, oaked, unoaked, and an aromatic clone known as Chardonnay Musque. In the March 2019 year end, it outdistanced runner-up Riesling 322,737 to 252,743 cases (9 litre) although both grapes are considered 'signature' Ontario varieties that have led the way in defining the Ontario white wine scene.

Pinot Gris/Grigio, our third most popular Vinifera, which has increased 400% in production to 221,155 cases since the year 2010, is also becoming a 'star' in the portfolio of many wineries while Sauvignon Blanc, a slow developer in consumer preference, is continuing to expand plantings and is now producing world-class wine. Gewurztraminer, which has been grown in Ontario for over 40 years, comes in fifth on the list of white Vinifera grapes, representing about 2.5% of total production. For some reason, whether consumers perceive it to be a 'sweet' wine or wish to avoid embarrassment in pronouncing the name, it has never achieved real success in Ontario as a varietal and to-day, with its spicy, fragrant personality, it tends to be used to advantage in proprietary blends or as a component in a Riesling-Traminer dual varietal.

The Vidal grape, our most widely planted white French Hybrid, is made as a varietal wine to-day by only a small number of wineries but has been used extensively in 'international blends' by the larger wineries as it is a less expensive grape than Vinifera whites but still has a wonderful character. One of its prime roles, of course, is for late-harvest wines and icewines, producing 72% of all icewines in 2018-2019. Riesling is considered to make a more elegant icewine that can live longer although it is more expensive, making just 12% of the total, while Cabernet Franc at 10% is the top production red icewine.

Red table wine production sees 4 varieties vying for top spot with Pinot Noir leading in 2019 at 142,176 cases, followed by Merlot, Baco Noir, and Cabernet Franc. While there are several impressive Pinot Noir wines being made by producers of all sizes, the grape itself has somehow avoided the acclaim in Ontario which it has achieved in New Zealand or Oregon. As a result, consumers are reluctant to stretch their budget on what they feel is good, but not great, red wine, although most local Pinot Noir wines are excellent value. Cabernet Franc, on the other hand, has produced some stunning varietal wines to date that have won major awards in competitions, while serving at the same time as a major component of Cabernet Franc – Merlot – Cabernet Sauvignon blends that are achieving considerable success on their own. Although Merlot and Cabernet Sauvignon are extremely sensitive grapes to grow with our challenging winters, they both produce very high-quality wine as a varietal and only await increased production from more wineries to become more appreciated.

Of all our red varieties, Baco Noir, though a French Hybrid and considered a second tier grape, has become synonymous with Ontario winemaking, enjoying a long and enviable run here as a less expensive yet enticing red wine that continues to surprise connaisseurs of Vinifera reds. Gamay Noir, like Gewurztraminer, tends to fly under the radar in the province although many in the industry feel it should be one of our leading varieties. It has a reputation for making a fruit forward, lighter-bodied red wine, that should produce well in our climate – and it does – but Gamay wines seem to be less popular with consumers in spite of the fact it makes a very appealing wine, sometimes as a fresh 'nouveau', and represents good value. Completing the list is Shiraz or Syrah, Ontario's most expensive grape at $2313 a tonne in 2018. The number of wineries associated with this variety is small but growing and they already have crafted some excellent wines, but they tend to sell at higher price points and this has limited their sales in competing with Australia, for example.

While some people believe that the industry should focus all its efforts on the 3 or 4 varieties that perform 'best' (already Chardonnay, Riesling, Cabernet Franc, and Merlot represent almost half of the grape varieties used here), growers are producing at least a dozen varieties that are making exceptional quality wines, and there is really no reason to question the diversity we enjoy. Over time, growers and wineries will discover that certain varieties do grow better in particular locations and adjust plantings accordingly, but with a significant number of different grapes, wineries can present interesting portfolios for all consumers, and this variety of grapes well serves an industry with so many boutique-size operations (148 of the 178 VQAO members in 2019 were considered 'small' wineries producing less than 100,000 cases of wine annually). If our industry did focus on a much smaller number of varieties, it would be at risk of any change in consumer taste as has happened in the past. To combat this, over the last few years many wineries have created wonderful domestic blends, usually from several different Vinifera grapes, both white and red wines, and there has been a growing interest in these for their quality and value.

In truth, the Ontario wine industry has continued to move forward this century as much as any other upcoming wine region, not only with its expanding diversity of grapes and sub-appellations, and innovative vineyard and winemaking practices, but also in emulating evolving wine trends and at the same time developing interesting 'new' wine styles. This has seen the industry blossom into a producer of exciting rose and sparkling wines that are worthy of international acclaim, appassimento and 'orange' wines made by winemakers who have been driven to explore and experiment beyond the tried and true, and an increasing number of organic and biodynamic wines.

Rose wines, as a sophisticated table wine category, have only come into their own in the last few years although pink-coloured wines have enjoyed popularity for some time. Inspired by a trendy, semi-sweet, rosey-pink wine made in California from the dark-blue Zinfandel grape which was being marketed as 'White Zinfandel', I made one of the first local 'blush' wines at Stoney Ridge Cellars in 1990 from a gentle pressing of Gamay grapes blended with a touch of Riesling, a fruity, appealing, off-dry refreshment wine which we called "Romance". We also sold a fortified wine called "Passion" at the time and my wife Charlotte was often heard telling a customer that you could find Romance and Passion at Stoney Ridge for just $20.00! Romance sold well, as much for its name as its quality, and became a mainstay at the winery, defying some connoisseurs who had predicted years earlier that blush wines were just a fad that would not endure.

But then a different style of Rose caught fire in the world of wine, a drier, more elegant table wine, sometimes made as a varietal but more often as a blend from different grapes. Local winemakers found that Gamay or Cabernet Franc or Pinot Noir were ideal for this style, fruit-driven and flavourful, yet suitable for use with meals. Some preferred to press these grapes lightly, bleeding off the free run juice for rose or to allow the must to ferment for a short period of time to capture more colour, while other winemakers blended red and white wines to create the flavour and colour they wanted. Thus, the colour of a rose varied from a pale grayish white to vivid pink, and all the way to a light red, made with little noticeable residual sugar and very stylish. Several Ontario wineries make this style of Rose to-day with production increasing to 4% of total table wines or over 1.1 million litres in 2018 (just 10 years ago no one kept statistics on roses) while continuing to expand the category with delightful Sparkling Rose wines!

The making of Sparkling wine has a long history in Ontario dating back to the end of the 19th century with production of "Canadian Champagne" and other sparkling wines from a variety of highly flavoured 'labrusca' grapes. Production increased through the 1900's when Ontario vintners followed both the traditional "methode champenoise" process of second fermentation in bottle to create the requisite effervescence, and the "Methode Charmat" with the second fermentation in a closed tank before bottling under pressure to retain the dissolved carbon dioxide.

The rights to this latter process had been purchased in 1928 by Dr. A. Sampson for his company, Canadian Wineries, and this helped the winery to make very fine "Champagnes" under the Chateau Gai brand. After the winery promoted the sale of its "Champagnes" in France, French Champagne producers sued Chateau Gai for damages and to curtail the use of the term "Champagne", in a court case which was held at Quebec in 1964. It took all of 10 years for the Court to decide but in the end the French won their case, although the Canadian government essentially ignored the result and the Ontario government continued to permit the use of the term.

In the 1970's, the LCBO still listed Canadian (and Australian, and American, as well as French) Champagne and even allowed a new winery to be called Podamer Champagne Company in 1974. The arrival of the VQA would properly bring an end to the use of the word 'Champagne' (and other wine terms like Port and Sherry) for such Ontario wines but did not stop the production of sparkling wines made by the traditional method, a category whose production began to increase dramatically with the availability of Vinifera grapes like Chardonnay and Pinot Noir, the basic grapes of French Champagne. In Ontario, these grapes are harvested earlier than normal, both to retain their lively acidity and to create lower alcohol wines that will undergo a second fermentation, producing wines that many now feel rival top-quality sparkling wines from France and other wine regions. In 2018-19, 136 different sparkling wines were approved by the VQA (including some amazing sparkling Icewine) totaling 123,226 cases of wine, a 6% increase over the previous year and up from just 27 sparkling wines in 2009-10 when only 19,487 cases were made. The industry is clearly taking advantage of our appropriate soils and climate to produce a range of sparkling wines which consumers are now buying as a more affordable alternative to French Champagne and as the use of sparkling wine with meals is increasing, with no end to the trend in sight!

When he was working as a diplomat for the Ontario government in Italy during the 1990's, Len Crispino acquired a taste for Amarone, a full-bodied, distinctive red wine from the Veneto region in the north. This wine is made from grapes that are harvested and then left to dry slowly on racks in a well-ventilated area until a certain 'target' is achieved (e.g. an elevated sugar level). The process is referred to as the 'appassimento' technique (from the Italian verb 'appassire' meaning to dehydrate), a way of concentrating the sugars by dehydrating the grapes. At the same time, the flavours and aromas of the grapes are intensified as they undergo further biochemical activity and this produces a wine with higher alcohol, more body from additional glycerol, with intriguing tastes of earth, leather, cloves, and raisins.

Len and his wife Marisa returned to Ontario and decided to enter the grape and wine business in 2000 to make wines following the Italian appassimento style of winemaking in Niagara. Another winery, Magnotta, was planning to make a red wine at this time using the same technique with winemaker Peter Rotar hoping to achieve high quality in what would become their flagship wine, 'Enotrium'. But the Crispino's were very much pioneers as well as they planned to produce all their portfolio using appassimento. They opened their winery, The Foreign Affair, in 2008, in part of a building which used to house the former Horticultural Research Institute in Vineland, an appropriate location for introducing their innovative wines made by the talented Andrzej Lipinski.

Although some doubted the validity of the technique, citing the intensive labour involved in dealing with hand harvested and hand sorted grapes and the risk of spoilage and higher volatile acidity levels from rot developing in the grapes, others could see real benefits in it. At a time when red wine consumption was outdistancing red wine production, the technique had the potential to mitigate risks from a less optimal, cool or wet fall season in Ontario, improving the quality of marginal grapes and sustaining the production of acceptable red table wine. At the same time, it might enable wineries to make outstanding, full-bodied, 'reserve' red wines in a year when the grapes themselves were already healthy, helping to build credibility for an industry that lacked a reputation for great red wines. In spite of the year-to-year weather volatility in Ontario, the idea of further developing flavours in red grapes and creating a new and unique style for the local market seemed a winner!

Before long, the Cool Climate Institute at Brock became involved in a 4 year project to research various aspects of the process and to assess the impact on wine quality, testing various methods of drying grapes including kiln drying, greenhouse drying, barn drying (traditional style), a drying chamber, and extended hang-time on the vine (natural). Results indicated that kiln drying was the most rapid in raising the brix level by 3 degrees, only 3 days, and that the natural treatment was the slowest, requiring 30 days of prolonged hang-time. In addition, each treatment showed differences in the resulting wines in both their chemical and sensory profiles.

Now armed with a clearer understanding of the process and the product, other winemakers soon realized that they could make full appassimento style wines or partial, back-blending a certain percentage of such wine with another to enhance quality, build more character, add a 'sweeter' taste, or to increase alcohol, producing top-quality wines which sold at higher price points. Some used the enriched skins of an appassimento fermentation to make a 'recioto' or 'ripasso' style of wine, following traditional Italian practices, enhancing a basic wine by leaving it in contact for some time with the appassimento lees. Lipinski went on to develop this style for other wineries in time, working at Colaneri Winery to produce not only red but white and dessert wines made in part with the appassimento technique, earning an impressive reputation for both the winery and himself, and inspiring a number of wineries to develop and grow this signature wine style.

In 2018, after successfully establishing their 'amarone dream' in Ontario and proving themselves to be leading-edge winemakers after only 10 years in the business, the Crispino's were persuaded to sell their winery to Corby's for just over $6 million, satisfied that this well-known distilling company would expand on their achievement. True to its mandate, the VQAO has revised the 'Vin de Cure' category, which provided for wines made from 100% dried grapes, to include the appassimento style, lowering the minimum brix requirement after drying to 27 degrees brix and accepting a drier, higher alcohol style wine. In addition, tasting and lab requirements were changed to permit a slightly higher volatile acidity level in the wine that is typical of the style.

To-day, with the appassimento technique, it is possible to make a table wine using some component of dried grapes blended in as long as the resulting alcohol is under 15% or a Vin de Cure that is over 15%, a class that has averaged just over 20 VQAO approvals each vintage for the last three years. Wineries across the province are picking up on the style, most from Niagara including Big Head, Kew, Ridgepoint, Cave Spring, Reif, Rennie, Ridgepoint, Arterra, as well as Foreign Affair, but there are producers outside the DVA's as well, including Adamo in Hockley Valley and Burning Kiln on Lake Erie. Most continue to use Cabernet Franc, Cabernet Sauvignon, and Merlot for their wines. Pillitteri Winery wanted to reproduce the style as authentically as possible and went to the trouble of planting the classic Italian grapes, Corvina, Rondinella, and Molinara in their vineyard, to make 'Fruttaio', a complex and concentrated version that retails for almost $100!

Well-known Toronto wine expert Konrad Ejbich recently held a tasting of 30 of these wines from vintages between 2013 and 2016 and found most of them to be still very 'youthful, tight, and closed', with disjointed aromas and flavours, higher volatile acidity, and what he called ' alcoholic disharmony', his unique way of saying that the wines needed more time to mature or at least serious aeration. In the article he wrote after the tasting, entitled "When Grapes Wither", he provided the following advice to appreciate better this style of wine: "Open, taste, decant, serve to-morrow"! Thank you for the dry-grape humour, Konrad. ("Quench', Food and Drink Magazine, September, 2019)

Everyone knows that wine comes in many colours, various shades of 'white' from green to golden, a red spectrum that ranges from purple-tinged to 'noir', myriad hues of pink, and also more specifically 'vin jaune' and 'vin gris', and the oxidized browns of sherry. More recently another colour has become fashionable in the wine world, orange (some use the term 'amber'), a word used since the early 2000's to describe a 'new/old' style of wine, again from Italy, called 'vino bianco macerato', where white grapes are fermented with the skins using the same technique as for red wine fermentation, producing colour from pigments in the skin but also impacting the aromatics, the flavour and the wine's texture from the prolonged skin contact (which may last for months, and even years). The wine, which is made in terracotta amphora often buried in the ground for temperature control, will be 'naturally' quite different from other white wines, sometimes cloudy if made unfined and unfiltered and bottled on the lees, with flavours of honey, beeswax, nuts, dried herbs, citrus, and earth, depending on the length of skin contact. The entire nature of orange wines is considerably different from white wines made from pressed juice only which typically results in wines that are clean, fresh, fruity, and without sediment, a testament to their pristine modern winemaking. This emphasizes the clarity, stability, and fault free nature of the wine and not the interesting complexity of completely natural, skin fermented whites.

In the distant past of winemaking, it seems to have been normal to ferment white grapes with their skins and even stems for an extended period of time in egg-shaped, clay fermenters (to-day these are called qvevris). This was a common practice in Georgia in the Caucasus where skin-fermented white wines have been made for thousands of years. Over time, the technique spread to other places, one of which was northeastern Italy, although here it had almost been erased from history due to advances in fermentation science dictating 'no skin contact for white grapes', and had been essentially dormant for decades. That was until two winemakers from the village of Oslavia in Friuli Collio, Josko Gravner and Stanko Radikon, re-introduced the technique in the late 1990's.

This skin contact with varying lengths of maceration and degrees of oxygenation accounts for the additional wine colour, golden-yellow, to orange, to ochre from pigments in the skins, and provides additional tannin and other phenolics which alter the taste but help preserve the wine from oxidation. Since the skins are the most flavour-rich component in the winemaking, many producers prefer organically or biodynamically grown grapes as being of better potential, and usually an aromatic variety. In the beginning, the wines of Gravner and Radikon, obviously unusual, were scorned and ridiculed by critics and other winemakers who could not understand why they were turning their back on modern winemaking, but slowly their efforts stimulated experimentation and a growing interest in their winemaking. Today, as these wines from numerous producers have become more widely available, they have become more accepted, admired, and even venerated by sommeliers, critics, and wine drinkers, including many in Ontario.

Before interest developed locally in this 'new' technique, some winemakers in Ontario had experimented with minimal skin contact on varieties like Chardonnay in the hopes of deriving more 'character' from their grapes. I recall making a Gewurztraminer at Stoney Ridge in 1991 which I left on the skins and tried to ferment as cool as possible in order to heighten the aromatics. The floral spiceness of the grape did survive the treatment, but tannin from the skins left the wine with a bitter, unpleasant taste, and I decided to forget the idea in future. This excess of tannin is what concerns most winemakers to-day and consequently they do watch the length of skin contact very carefully and often apply a modicum of 'modern' winemaking to the task, like fining or filtration.

Ann Sperling, a true winemaking 'guru' in Ontario where she has worked and consulted for many leading wineries, was one of the first local winemakers to develop an interest in making orange wines. "I wanted to take our terroir a step further by making a completely natural wine… a method that allows me to use no additives at all, while creating a complex wine that can age" ("Food and Drink", Autumn, 2019). As head winemaker for Southbrook Winery in Niagara-on-the-Lake, an organic and biodynamic winery that is Demeter certified, she was using the Vidal grape to produce a full-blown orange wine that she wanted to have accepted as a VQA product. Other winemakers, including Brian Schmidt at Vineland Estates, who had made his first orange wine in 2016 from the aromatic Chardonnay Musque grape, leant their support, hoping to create a new VQA category, pointing out that VQA wines produce 34% more revenue for the winery than non-VQA.

With so much interest in orange wines, it did not take long for Laurie Macdonald, Executive Director of VQAO, to initiate the process for VQA acceptance by creating a panel to research the style and establish its merit, although the 'rules' for production/labelling had to be created from scratch as no similar regulations existed anywhere else. As of July 1, 2017 VQAO had a brand-new wine category for skin fermented white and pink grapes and Ann Sperling commented: "It's wonderful! At least it broadens the spectrum of what VQA represents." Such a wine could be made from any hybrid or vinifera approved variety if fermented 100% with skins, for a minimum of 10 days, as long as the alcohol level was not less than 7% nor more than 14.9%. Normal VQA turbidity requirements for such a wine would not apply if it was bottled with lees (unfiltered). Surprisingly, in the first year of approvals there were 14 wines accepted as skin-fermented, orange wines and since that time there have been another 11 from the 2018 vintage with more coming along.

These wines very much reflect the individual philosophy of each winemaker with some macerating their wine for the minimum 10 days and others experimenting with much longer contact time following the 'original' Georgian/ Italian style. Some wines have been left long on their lees, some filtered, as experimenting from low tech to high tech continues with different grape varieties. Considering the nature of the style and its relative novelty in Ontario, the wines have met with a mixed response from consumers who are struck by their higher price as much as anything, but they are also intrigued and willing to sample the wines once they know more about their making. Yet, it seems to me that this is a wine for careful sampling from all the producers at this point as it is quite different from established white wines and the character of some may not be to everyone's taste. Nevertheless, the LCBO has shown interest in the category following consumer queries and recently a few trendy restaurants from Ottawa to Niagara-on-the-Lake have added them to their wine lists with some offering several different orange wines from many wine regions - including Ontario!

Skin fermented whites may or may not become accepted by most winemakers as an appropriate technique, and consumers may or may not find that this style produces quality wines they can enjoy, but for now, with a growing number of wineries in over 30 wine regions around the world experimenting with the process, it is fair to ask – "could orange be the new white"?

Over the last few decades, while so much energy was being devoted to developing creative fermentation philosophies and 'new' wine styles, our grape and wine industry, always at the mercy of the weather, has been obligated to show a heightened concern for the climatic assaults now occurring with more frequency and more severity that are impacting on the business. Wine regions world-wide have experienced severe drought, or wildfires, or hail, and general climate volatility that has produced short crops, or no crops, and is threatening the nature of grape growing.

The severity of climate change has not yet impacted Ontario as much as other wine regions which have already seen a shift in their growing season. In parts of France, warmer winters have meant an earlier spring and a much earlier harvest, causing issues for winemakers. In our region we have experienced warm spring spells followed by an unfortunate sudden frost that kills buds on sensitive vinifera vines and decimates the crop. In the future we could still see a dramatic change in the kind of grapes we will produce, with a warmer climate making it possible to grow certain varieties we cannot grow now or making it challenging to grow some that are considered to be true 'cool-climate' varieties. Wine styles may be forced to change, or grape growing may spread beyond its traditional 'terroirs', as is now happening in our 'emerging wine regions'. Climate warming has already cast a shadow on the production of our famous icewine, gradually reducing the number of days suitable for harvesting properly frozen grapes and putting extra pressure on growers and wineries.

Because winemaking is rooted in the cycles of nature, an increasing number of individuals in the industry believe it must now be more concerned about such issues as climate change and taking care of the planet. Not only must we do a better job of growing grapes and making wine but we must consider our production methods at the same time for their overall impact on the environment. This has brought considerable interest in growing grapes and making wines organically and biodynamically and in a manner commonly referred to as 'sustainable'. It is certainly a fair question to ask how these 'philosophies' are playing out in Ontario to-day and what they mean for our wine industry's future.

While mitigating the impact of climate change is a major issue, it is beyond the ability of our wine industry to manage by itself other than for gathering data and researching ways to adapt by seeking new grape regions, more suitable grapes, and innovative wine styles. Other specific industry practices that have come to be a serious concern to-day can be controlled, including soil enrichment and vine disease management with synthetic chemicals to deal with weeds, fungal attacks, insects, and pests, as well as water and energy usage in the vineyard and the winery and a growing deployment of chemical additives in winemaking. This concern would result in what is now called 'organic farming', viticulture based on respecting nature and eliminating negative ecological impacts. Accompanying this was the belief that following a similar protocol in the winery using organically farmed grapes, a conscientious winemaker would be able to make wine more naturally, with the potential for exceptional quality...organic wine!

For almost the entire 'history' of converting grapes into wine, all grape growing and winemaking could be considered 'organic' by nature, during the thousands of years when it was not possible to treat grapes with chemical or synthetic products and when there was little 'technology' applied to the winemaking process. Grapes were harvested by hand and crushed by foot, followed by 'wild' yeast fermentations with only minimal intervention by winemakers from that point on. It is understandable that such wine could be described as 'natural' – the wine literally made itself – but from a modern point of view somewhat 'raw', often leaving the health and stability of the product at risk.

With advances in scientific knowledge and the need to deal with the grape crisis in Europe in the late 19th century, the nature of grape growing began to change with growers acquiring the ability to fight fungal and bacterial threats with "chemicals". Content with saving vineyards around the world and producing 'better' grapes, man seems to have given little thought at the time to the consequences from using products that would in time be considered dangerous to himself and the environment. At the same time, technological achievements changed the nature of winemaking, allowing for the use of innovative equipment and methods and the introduction of additives from cultured yeasts to inorganic products, along with a more 'hands-on' approach from winemakers, all of which became accepted for better controlling risks in the name of quality winemaking.

Eventually there would come a push-back to this from a small number of individuals concerned that the modern fungicide sprays, herbicides, and chemical fertilizers were truly hazardous, totally unsafe for vineyards, groundwater, wildlife, anyone working or living on or near a farm, as well as consumers. Even the use of copper compounds, although such an effective weapon against downy mildew, and sulphur dioxide for its bacterial control in winemaking, were deemed to be necessary evils at best that should be reduced, if not eliminated over time.

In spite of a developing interest in this alternative approach in the 1990's, growing grapes organically in Ontario was thought to be impossible, considering the long history of failed vineyards in eastern North America prior to the introduction of modern technology. With Vinifera grapes finally gaining a foothold in our difficult humid climate, it was considered foolhardy not to use the available materials to deal with threats which could make growing grapes economically unsustainable. And wineries were not yet willing to pay more for the few 'organic' grapes available as there was no real demand for organic wine at the time. But things would change!

In 1996, Jens Gemmrich and Heike Koch bought a ten acre farm in Niagara-on-the-Lake that had once grown fruit trees and planted grape vines that they intended to nurture using only safe and sustainable practices. To be considered an 'organic' vineyard, they would have to establish that their farm had operated for three years in accordance with the principles of organic farming, preserving its ecological integrity, before they were able to apply for certification. 5 years later they produced their first vintage using only sustainable practices, becoming Canada's first organically certified winery in the process, with certification from Pro-Cert Organic, to-day one of five certifying bodies in the province. They are the only winery in Ontario to-day that produces their entire portfolio of wines organically. To-day, the name Frog Pond Farm Organic Winery, is well-respected as a dedicated steward of their land and water resources, relying on 100% 'green' energy, and producing premium VQA wines.

While other winemakers might have agreed with Jens on his eco-approach to winemaking and the concept of working in harmony with nature, the idea of complicating the process by adding additional risk and expense still proved to be a deterrent for most wineries for following in his shoes. Very high-quality, organic wines were becoming available in the LCBO system from other wine regions and they were receiving rave reviews, but it would take a few more years before other wineries in Ontario willingly embraced ecologically-conscious farming and winemaking. Three that have added their names to the list of organic growers include Malivoire, an innovative, gravity-focused winery that is well-known for its Lady Bug Rose (indigenous ladybugs are used to clean up aphids in the vineyard), Hidden Bench, with three organic vineyards on the Beamsville Bench that have been farmed organically since 2010 (Locus Lane, Rosomel, and Felseck), and Kew Winery that since 2013 has made an organic Riesling from grapes grown on the Young Vineyard.

With organic wine beginning to attract a dedicated following in the 2000's, the first of another wave of individuals who believed strongly in allowing 'terroir' to tell a wine's story, developed vineyards and a winery where they planned to work with nature even more closely. Their efforts, while respecting the prohibitions and fundamentals of organics, went one or two steps further, following a system that the LCBO Vintages magazine would describe as "organic plus" and "organic on steroids", or, as the wine industry has come to recognize it, "biodynamic", a term based on Greek words for 'life and energy'. In Ontario since 2008, five wineries have been certified "biodynamic" including Southbrook, Tawse, Stratus, Ravine, and Redstone, all dedicated to following farming techniques that were pioneered in Europe in the early twentieth century.

In the early 1920's, a German/Austrian named Rudolf Steiner (1861-1925), a multi-faceted intellectual, mystic, scientist, economist and philosopher, had developed a system to be applied to agriculture which he had been warning was in trouble due to the widespread use of chemical fertilizers and pesticides. He was asked by a group of farmers who had noted a decline in the health of their soil, plants, and animals since using 'chemicals' on their farms, for some insight into their problems. His 'help', delivered in the form of a series of lectures not long before his death, represented a unique approach to agriculture based on his belief that the physical world and the spiritual world are interrelated.

For Steiner, a farm was a living organism with an immune system that needed to be maintained in a biodynamic way as he defined it, not destroyed by chemicals. The farm should be considered a self-sufficient, closed-loop eco-system where everything needed is grown, produced, or lives in an integrated fashion. Man, animals, insects, and crops, everything inhabiting that space, must exist to-gether in harmony to maintain the vitality and integrity of the property.

Natural composts and cover crops would enrich the soil, not synthetic fertilizers, and chemical pesticides and insecticides would be banned, replaced by 'friendly', natural techniques of controlling issues, using helpful insects and animals as part of the solution. Beyond respecting the farm's natural resources, biodynamics required that certain operations be conducted in tune with cycles of the moon, stars, and planets to achieve the optimum timing. As well, growers would make their own homeopathic preparations from materials found on site, compost mixtures and 'teas', based on Steiner's original eight suggestions, which they would spray at specific times, reflecting a cosmic influence in their application. One of these involved packing cow horns with manure and burying them among the vines to funnel the energy of nature into the soil. The horns would be dug up and the contents mixed with water for spraying on the vines.

For many farmers, Steiner's approach would transform their practice of agriculture, although others believed his system was unscientific and derided it as 'witchcraft'. Yet, a few wineries in Europe did embrace biodynamics with its life/energy practices as being best for their particular 'terroir' and applied the same passion and dedication in their winemaking. Most of them insisted on minimal intervention in the process itself, hand-harvesting, 'gentle' treatment of grapes, juice, and wine using basket pressing and gravity flow as an alternative to more aggressive technology, with little or no filtration, no synthetic chemicals in the winery, only natural additives, and a very restricted use of Sulphur dioxide as an anti-bacterial agent in the wine (sulphites could be legally added up to a maximum of 30 ppm 'free' and 100 ppm 'total', or not at all, in organic winemaking).

Some of these practices were 'old school', others controversial, risking the health and ageability of the wine and leaving some winemakers to question if there really was an improvement in wine quality that would justify the extra effort required and added expense. Certainly, admirers of biodynamic wines believed they tasted 'better', a word in wine circles that is sometimes hard to define, and in wine competitions they performed extremely well, winning numerous awards and establishing fine reputations for all concerned. As a result, many who were originally rather skeptical about 'natural' winemaking, changed their mind, agreeing that as far as quality is concerned, wines labelled 'biodynamic' were as good as, if not 'better', than any wine produced by 'modern means'.

At the beginning of the new millennium, there were no certified biodynamic growers/wineries in Ontario, but with the "green movement" growing ever more influential, there was a good chance that someone with the courage and the insight and the means, would take the needed leap of faith and pioneer the philosophy for our wine industry.

When Bill Redelmeier sold his family farm in north Toronto where his award-winning winery, Southbrook, was located, he could have easily retired to spend the future drinking his yummy 'Framboise' fruit wine on some sunny island. But he had a passion to pursue, one that he could now afford, and that was to create a vineyard and winery like no one had done in Ontario before, not just organic but biodynamic as well. Bill and his wife Marilyn bought a 65 acre site in Niagara's Four Mile Creek sub-appellation and proceeded to build what can only be described as a dream winery, designed by acclaimed designer Jack Diamond. Opened in 2008, the winery obtained a prized LEED gold certification for the socially responsible nature of its buildings, grounds, and activities, while receiving the honour of becoming Canada's first Demeter certified Organic and Biodynamic operation (named for the Greek goddess of agriculture, Demeter certifies wineries world-wide).

Bill is truly one of the industry's unsung heroes, one of the founders of the Fruit Wines of Ontario Association, an original director of Fruit Wines of Canada, a tireless traveler 'across the pond' to promote Ontario VQA wines, both his own and others, and a visionary, always busy innovating and improving his winery, even personally delivering his wines to customers, and fortunate to have hired two outstanding winemakers along the way, Derek Barnett and Ann Sperling who have produced numerous awards with the entire range of their portfolio, from fruit wines to biodynamic wines, and now orange wine.

When Paul Pender, one of my top students in the Niagara College Winemaking Program, was hired by Moray Tawse to be the new winemaker for Tawse Winery in Vineland, he could not have been more fortunate for Tawse was a wealthy investment banker who planned to spare no expense in creating a leading-edge winery, providing the graduate with a wonderful winemaking opportunity. Moray first accumulated several properties on the Beamsville Bench which he proceeded to certify organically and biodynamically following Southbrook's lead. Pender was provided with a marvelous array of grapes, a 6 level gravity-flow winery, complete with a geothermal system for renewable energy, a wetland/pond for filtering and reusing winery water and the inspiration to go biodynamic using a lunar calendar to direct the timing of operations.

From the beginning the wines were stunning, allowing the winery to wine "Winery of the Year" four times in the Canadian Wine Awards, 2010,11,12, and 2016, an absolutely (bio) dynamic achievement! On top of that, Paul was named "Winemaker of the Year" in 2011 at the Ontario Wine Awards. In the meantime, Moray Tawse purchased another property that he named Redstone because of its red clay terroir and that was certified organic and biodynamic in 2013. Like its elder brother winery, it too has gone on to win "Winery of the Year" in the Canadian Wine Awards, leaving the name "Tawse" firmly established as one of the wine world's leading producers for Chardonnay, Pinot Noir, Cabernet Franc, and Riesling – right here in Ontario!

Currently, Ravine Vineyards and Stratus Winery, round out the list of certified biodynamic wineries. Stratus, which is owned by David Feldberg, CEO of Teknion Corporation, was the first building in Canada and the first winery worldwide to achieve the Leadership in Energy and Environmental Design (LEED) certification for its stunning Niagara-on-the-Lake facility. A geothermal system with 25 wells dug 250 feet into the ground provides all the heating and cooling for the winery, and like Tawse Winery, Stratus is a 100 percent gravity flow system that ensures gentle handling of the wine. With J-L Groulx as winemaker, this winery produces what Tony Aspler has called "some of the best wines made in Canada", a tribute to the effort and dedication of all involved.

Ravine Vineyard was founded in 2006 on a property in Niagara where grapes were originally planted in 1864, 3 years before Confederation. Today there are just over 30 acres of seven vinifera varieties being farmed organically and biodynamically, producing highly sought-after wines. The winery is also known for its retail store and hospitality centre located in a building that dates back two hundred years, the William Woodruff House, which was moved piece by piece from its original location in Port Hope. In only a few years, Ravine has become acclaimed for what is a leading tourist facility where you can enjoy outstanding VQA wines and a wonderful restaurant/bakery.

As we approach the 100th anniversary of his death, Rudolf Steiner's eco-centric approach to farming, transforming the practice of agriculture, has become successfully established world-wide, achieving a well-deserved respect he did not enjoy while alive. His system, which was pioneered in the United States in the 1980's, has been adopted by thousands of farms across North America along with a movement known as 'Community Supported Agriculture'. People began to use the word 'sustainable' in reference to responsible farming practices, a term that over the years has by extension been applied to include almost every other aspect of the business.

With organic and biodynamic farming and winemaking becoming a reality in Ontario, and consumers understanding that they were not a trade-off for quality, the Wine Council of Ontario led the way in creating a self-auditing environmental charter for the entire industry called Sustainable Winemaking Ontario in 2007. With 32 members, the original program focused on all aspects of wine production including managing water and soil and synthetic pesticides and non-organic chemicals in the vineyard, and controlling wastewater and air quality, and conserving energy, in short, environmental sustainability which would leave things as good as or better than at the start.

This concept quickly evolved into the notion of accepting accountability for both the environmental and the social impacts of the overall business, its activities, and relationships with its employees and the community, to ensure social health and welfare and at the same time a financially profitable business. Employee health, safety, and compensation received proper consideration as did the concerns of neighbours and the community over issues from noise to exposure to chemicals. Sustainability, literally, touches on everything that is related to the winemaking.

In Ontario, sustainability is an ongoing program aimed at maintaining responsible practices with continuous improvement, doing the right thing for planet Earth from the vineyard to the bottle, and now into the supply chain as well where retailers have their own sustainability issues. Everyone is becoming concerned with meeting their present day needs successfully without compromising the ability of future generations to meet theirs. It has snow-balled with peer and market pressure, as wineries concerned for their reputation seek to develop a good marketing story about their values and culture by doing the right thing for planet Earth! Indeed, as sustainability expert Bob Willard has said, "don't think about sustainability as a problem to be solved. It is, rather, a solution to the other problems businesses have". (Hamilton Spectator, November 8, 2019)

To-day, statistics indicate than 50% of consumers actually take 'green factors' into account when making a purchase, 66% will pay more for sustainable wines, and 73% would change their consumption habits to reduce their impact on the environment.

Once just a buzz word, sustainability and its commitment to a better future, is not going away. And why? Wine quality is constantly improving, and everyone can enjoy a glass or two while at the same time reducing their carbon footprint!

As I reflect on all the developments over the last few decades and consider where the wine industry is now, only one word comes to mind… "WOW" – that is, Wonderful Ontario Wine! The industry may be small when compared to other world wine regions (producing only "a drop in the bucket" according to one winery owner), but consumers have no reason to look beyond Ontario to find a great wine at a very reasonable cost from amazing wineries that offer something for every taste and every use at a level of unprecedented quality.

It is no wonder that we can now talk in real terms about achieving the "greatness" that was sought just twenty years ago.

CHAPTER THIRTEEN

Excellence in the making: Defining "greatness" in 2020

"It has thankfully come to the point in the industry's evolution that promoting local wine can be done confidently, with overall quality much improved, if not universally improved (which hinges more on individual wineries and winemakers rather than the places the wines come from)." David Lawrason, Wine Align, September 13, 2019

"The rise of Ontario wine matters because wine is an expression of culture, a reflection of people and places, of shared beliefs and attitudes." John Szabo, "Spectacular Wineries of Ontario" (Foreword), 2012.

"We no longer need the approval of the rest of the world to tell us our wines are good!" Len Pennachetti, President, Cave Springs Winery (recipient of the Order of Canada, 2021).

As the second decade of the twenty-first century comes to a close, there is no longer any doubt that the Ontario Grape and Wine Industry has successfully transformed itself from its often-maligned port and sherry past, when Concord was 'King of the vineyard', to its modern, respected identity. At more than one point in this transformation, the survival of the industry itself was in question, but after an odyssey that has taken it through challenging, sometimes perilous economic and political circumstances, it has reached world-class status and is now accepted as the peer of any "new World" wine region, producing high-quality wines that speak for themselves. Indeed, the very process of 'surviving' has made it appropriate now to talk of the "greatness" which was hoped for when the "Poised for Greatness" vision was first unveiled some twenty years ago.

The journey has witnessed consistent improvement in our vineyards now producing a diverse range of Hybrid and Vinifera grapes, the foundation of our renewed winemaking. This has inspired exceptional growth in the number of new wineries and the arrival of the VQAO, a strong and transparent regulated appellation system that has built credibility for our wines while inspiring consumer confidence. Given the awards, achievements, and the milestones reached along the way, Ontario wine drinkers have every reason to be proud of the industry's evolution. With its fine wine quality, a reflection of our winemakers' talents and skills, Ontario wine is truly here to stay!

Fifty years ago, when public interest in quality wine was hardly overwhelming, who would ever have thought that such success would be possible for our small wine region with no venerable winemaking tradition? Yet, in spite of this success, even to-day there are wine drinkers who still consider Ontario wine as a paradox and refuse to acknowledge our hard-won "greatness". They may feel this way because we lack an accepted classification system that establishes a hierarchy of renowned terroirs/wineries or since we do not yet produce acclaimed 'icon' wines that inspire wine enthusiasts with scores of 95 points or more in publications like the "Wine Spectator". They might also say that our industry is not capable of producing wines that will age for decades in a connoisseur's cellar or that it does not put appropriate emphasis on vintage ratings or is simply too young to qualify for "greatness".

I will agree that some wines require time in a bottle to mature or require more complex winemaking practices (e.g. champagne) or may be of exceptional quality in a given vintage and as a result are deservedly more expensive than others, but it doesn't concern me at all that no Ontario winery is producing any table wine of such an elite status that people will be asked to pay $3000 a bottle, as they would for a 2017 Chateau Le

Pin, or even the hundreds of dollars to buy certain wines from esteemed vineyards in Napa or Burgundy, for example. It is simply appalling to ask such high prices compared to other wines and it is ludicrous that some winery owners feel their 'terroir' is so entitled that this somehow justifies charging so much for their wines. Yet, there are people who can afford and willingly buy them, defying common sense in their pursuit of the world's 'best' wines.

As a winemaker, I have always chuckled at those people who insist on asking how long a wine will last or when should it be opened – as if anyone knows for sure! These are not questions that need to be asked for most Ontario wines which are made to be enjoyed 'young'. Certainly, the wine trade and the wine media are concerned with these issues and other minutiae of winemaking, sometimes for self-serving reasons, but they are irrelevant for defining the "greatness" our wine industry has achieved.

For just over a century since the industry's birth in the 1860's, '100% Ontario' wines represented well over 50% of our wine market at a time when 'fine' was simply not a word anyone would use to describe any of them. But, from the 1970's on, imported wines had taken over and had steadily increased their market share to over 60%, mainly because of the growing demand for decent table wines. By the time the new millennium arrived, the Ontario industry was at last producing a significant range of table wines itself and it decided that it was time to end the dominance of the imports. The "Poised for Greatness" vision set as a priority the achieving of 50% market share for Ontario wines, that is the VQA wines with then barely 10% of the overall market. The Ontario 'international blends' (ICB) far outsold VQA wines and this too was a source of unhappiness for some wineries and consumers as, strictly speaking, these were not "Ontario" wines, but essentially the wine industry saw the imports as their primary concern.

It would be a challenge to increase sales to 50% market share even combining both blended and VQA wines but to assert that VQA wines would ever own the market was and remains to this day an unrealistic target. Given the strong sales that ICB wines enjoy, it is unlikely that VQA will ever be able to overtake the ever-popular and less expensive blends, no matter how strongly the wineries advocate for authentic, local wines and a 100% Ontario wine culture – not without a significant change in our winemaking regulations! Helping VQA by weakening the ICB category, although there are valid concerns about the privileges ICB producers have, would only bring further division in the industry.

The dominance of imported wines continues to be a festering sore that has become an annual lament by the Craft Winery Association, i.e. we aren't doing enough to alter the status quo in support of small wineries, and a reason to try whatever seems feasible to increase VQA market share. Thus, the constant attempt to acquire more shelf space in LCBO outlets, improved presence in the Vintages sections, additional markets for retailing these wines, and to reduce taxes and fees. Such efforts have proven worthwhile over time in helping wineries, but the imported category remains a formidable competitor. It is huge compared to our tiny industry, representing many countries with long-established and well-known wine regions offering diverse, ever-improving wines, strongly entrenched brands, and icon wines. Many of these are viewed by some consumers as 'superior' in quality or better value than our local wines or simply 'different', providing a different taste profile, while offering some wines from local indigenous grapes that we do not make. Incredibly, some would say that the LCBO still does not provide enough choice in imported wines! Clearly, many wine consumers like them and prefer to taste the world more often than tasting local. They will continue to buy them for whatever reason, even though they also enjoy VQA wines.

It goes without saying that true "greatness" in reference to Ontario wines is much more than the market share desired by our visionary stakeholders.

If we stop considering those elusive market share targets as our 'Achilles' heel' and consider actual wine sales over the last decade, the growing success of our wine industry is undeniable. The following chart shows the change in sales for all categories from 2009 to the present and indicates that both VQA and ICB sales have significantly outpaced imported wine sales with VQA sales now growing faster than ICB, while the all-Ontario wine market share versus imports has moved from 39% to 43% during this same period, an indication that the gap may finally be shrinking!

Statistics are taken from LCBO and VQA annual reports - in 1000's of litres

Category:	2009 sales	2019 sales	Growth
VQA	12,142	19,800	63%
ICB	45,353	67,110	48%
IMPORTS	89,409	112,754	26.2%
Other provs.	689	601	minus 12.7%
VQA export	1,243	2,376	91%

A cursory examination of VQA sales over the last two decades taken from VQAO Annual Reports gives another glimpse into this segment of the Ontario market's overall success. From 2001 until March 31, 2020, VQA sales in total increased significantly from $144,755,723 to $459,282,088 with the greatest volume growth coming in licencee sales from just under 1 million litres in 2001 to over 4 million litres by 2019, a clear indication that Ontario wines have finally become popular in our restaurants. Growth was also impressive in the LCBO system with sales reaching 9,778,211 litres up from 3,454,158. Surprisingly, given the increase in the number of wineries and the strong impact of tourism, sales at winery retail stores increased the least, from 2,591,260 litres in 2001 to just over 6 million by 2020.

Still, these are impressive statistics, and they reflect a considerable amount of support from a government that was wise enough to back a winner knowing that increasing wine industry success would inevitably result in more tax revenue, additional jobs, and other beneficial financial spin-offs. For example, the government renewed the Ontario Wine and Grape Strategy (a $75 million dollar package) for five years commencing in 2015-2016, continuing to enhance the sale of VQA wine in the LCBO system and expanding on grape and wine research and improvement projects. This program followed on other reforms affecting the wine industry that were announced by the AGCO in September 2014. To address a long-standing source of friction involving the 'blending' of wine in Ontario, a provision was included for wineries established after 1993 to be able to blend Ontario and imported product with the restriction that the wine could only be sold through the LCBO or delivered directly to licencees.

At the same time, in 2015 Ontario Premier Kathleen Wynne surprised wineries by approving sales of Ontario wine at farmers' markets across the province in a two- year pilot program. This was a sales channel that fruit wine producers had been pursuing unsuccessfully with government for almost 15 years as a logical extension for them of their already existing fruit and vegetable sales at farmers' markets. Unfortunately, those wineries were shut out of the farm markets when the Government, ignoring complaints of blatant discrimination from the Fruit Winery Association, authorized the sale of VQA wines only. In the first year, with 100 markets and 67 wineries involved, sales of VQA wines were over 60,000 litres with a value of almost a million and a half dollars, an excellent beginning considering some of the restrictions put on the wineries. The move was welcomed by most of the smaller wineries who were quick to take advantage of the opportunity.

Two years later, when a review of this sales channel was held, fruit wineries were finally allowed to participate along with VQA wines.

Work reviewing the retail distribution of wine was continued by the Premier's Advisory Council on Government Assets in 2015 under the leadership of Ed Clark, former CEO of the TD Bank, that would soon see wine (and beer) sold in a limited number of grocery stores, thus removing a roadblock to increasing access to market that the wine industry had complained about for many years.

When Doug Ford's Conservatives came to power in 2018, they pledged to further "modernize alcohol sales by expanding sales to more grocery stores, as well as convenience and big box stores". While this news was welcomed by some segments of the alcohol business and consumer advocates as it represented the culmination of efforts to rid the business of a century-old Prohibition mentality, there is no doubt that it was controversial. The unfortunate 'Buck a beer' pledge by Premier Ford did hi-light a fear by many that the government was ignoring health reports that the wider availability of alcohol would only increase problems like drunk driving and violence and individual physical issues including heart disease and depression. Clearly the government wanted to help the beer and wine industries and satisfy consumers by making the purchase of alcohol more convenient, but the move was bound to fly in the face of many other people who were more concerned with the increasing access to alcohol in our society.

In the end, the Conservative Government approved several changes to regulations under the Liquor Licence Act to enhance consumer choice and convenience and reduce the administrative burden on businesses while the AGCO amended its policies to reflect these changes beginning May 6, 2019. This regulatory modernization allowed wineries with a "By the Glass" sales licence to provide a wine serving in any size desired and service could now begin as early as 9 a.m. every day of the week. Advertising guidelines for licensees and manufacturers were made less restrictive, allowing them to use such terms as "cheap drinks" and "happy hour" for pricing and promotions. These represented enhanced opportunities for the beverage alcohol industry after years of denying what some considered basic common sense.

With sales soaring to new heights, anyone looking into the wine business would have expected the financial state of the industry to be healthy, but a performance study led by the VQAO and Deloitte that was initiated in 2015 to support the reporting commitments of the renewed Wine and Grape Strategy, provided some surprising metrics. The survey covered active wineries and grape growers, 99 wineries described as 'vertically integrated' (with grape growing capabilities), 7 wineries not involved in growing grapes, and 42 independent growers, a meaningful representation of the industry with 95% of Ontario wine production involved. Wineries were divided into 5 categories reflecting their sales, over $10 million (8), $5 - $10 million (6), $2 - $5 million (16), $ .5 - $2 million (36), and under $.5 million (40). The average wine production ranged from 13,434 litres in the last category where 50% of the wineries had been in business less than 5 years to 887,292 litres in the over $10 million sales category where all wineries had been in operation for at least 20 years.

The report which came out in March 2016, provided considerable insight into numerous financial, operational, and business aspects of the wine industry including statistics on winery assets and accounts payable, liabilities and accounts receivable, inventory, employment, and profitability, but some of the most interesting information concerned actual sales and expenses associated with each category of winery.

The bottom line was surprising: only 28% of the wineries in the under $.5 million category were shown as profitable with that percentage increasing to 58% for the other four categories, and this in spite of annually increasing sales! Having so many advantages over the smaller wineries including the ability to sell blended wines, and with more economies of scale, all of those in the top sales category were the most profitable (average 14.5% profit) while many of the wineries selling less than $2 million were unprofitable, with the under $.5 million category showing an average operating loss of 41.1%! The larger the winery, with the ability to sell more wine in the LCBO system and with greater sales to other provinces and to the export market, the better was the chance to show a profit. This was true even though the average sales price per litre for an over $10 million winery was only $5.84 (mainly non-VQA wines) compared to $15.88 for the smallest category (mainly VQA wines).

The survey confirmed what the industry already knew that smaller wineries do face challenges in becoming established in what is a very competitive market, finding it a perpetual struggle to build sales. Many are too small to take advantage of the LCBO or establish any export business. Some, with only a short time in the industry, could still be categorized as 'start-ups' dealing with the costs of becoming established or with cash flow issues, or learning that their location was not as dynamic as Niagara-on-the-Lake, for example. However, with the information now at their disposal, wineries could benchmark their performance with peers and hopefully identify ways to improve their profitability. It was also evident from the results that achieving overnight success in the wine business is not easy and that anyone starting a winery in Ontario must be in the game 'for the long haul'.

This industry performance study was repeated each year until 2019, allowing data to be gathered to assess the financial state of the industry annually and helping to inform decisions on future industry activity. The results from the last year show similar overall growth trends as previous years although the make-up of the participants did change slightly each year as did the consumer and business landscape. For 2019 there were 181 businesses involved, 94 vertically integrated wineries, 12 others which did not grow grapes, and 75 independent growers. The wineries represented 96% of Ontario wine production and 28% of all grapes grown in the province.

Over the five years of the survey, the good news was that the profitability of some wineries had improved, up to 36% (from 28%) of wineries in the under $.5 million sales and up to 70% (from 58%) of all other wineries. Average profit for wineries in the first category was still disappointing at minus 20.6% but all other categories showed positive results with the over $10 million category at an average 17.5% profit. Obviously, these statistics were music to the ears of the wine industry, reflecting record sales, even if not all players were enjoying the dance!

In an industry with over 200 wineries that continues to experience profound and often rapid changes, it might be expected that any snapshot of the members on any given day would be different from the next photo taken as new wineries open and other wineries transform in different ways, from changing their name or moving to a new location, or selling to a new owner or, unfortunately, going out of business. Stonechurch Winery on the lakeshore in Niagara, for example, became Small Talk Vineyards and Shiny Apple Cider Company, and Aure Winery on the escarpment above Beamsville was re-incarnated as London Born Winery, while Hillebrand under the Peller Family ownership adopted the name 'Trius' from that very successful line of high-end wines, and Twenty Bees signaled a change in the image of the winery by bringing back the name 'Lakeview' from one of the small premium wineries it had acquired.

Some winery owners took advantage of the opportunity to sell their business to buyers eager to become involved in the evolving industry. David and Donna Lailey, after a long and successful involvement in both the grape and wine business, sold their thriving winery in Niagara-on-the-Lake, to an eager foreign buyer, leaving winemaker Derek Barnett to establish his own 'virtual' winery named Meldville at Legend's Estate Winery. Alvento Winery in Vineland put itself on the market and was sold in short order while Coyote's Run was sold, re-opened, and then sold again to a major player in the marijuana business who closed the winery. After the unfortunate passing of Lionel Rancourt just one year after opening his winery, Vignoble Rancourt was purchased by German-trained winemaker Fabian Reis and his wife Stephanie who renamed it 'Ferox', the name of their previous virtual winery. And the Mike Weir Winery, which had taken over the former EastDell site in Beamsville, simply closed while facing an uncertain future after some financial issues forced the business to be put up for sale. In 2020 it was purchased by real estate developers and a catering company with plans to reopen after hiring well-known Jeff Innes as winemaker.

For some, the time was right to sell, or perhaps retirement was catching up to them, while for others someone simply came along with an offer that was too good to refuse and that involved both small and large operations. One major acquisition produced considerable excitement when Constellation Brands, which had itself acquired Vincor in 2006, sold the business to the Ontario Teachers' Pension Plan in 2016 for $1.03 billion, putting the winery back in the hands of Canadians! The Niagara Falls winery was renamed 'Arterra' and it promised "to build the brands that people love" (the business already produced 7 of the 20 top brands in Canada!).

Constellation had closed Le Clos Jordan, its ultra-premium winery in Jordan, in 2012 after just a short time in operation, but Arterra decided to bring back the wines, using the same grape source on the 20 mile Bench and the same winemaker, Thomas Bachelder, who had in the meantime started his own winery. The first wines from the reborn Le Clos, a 2017 Chardonnay and Pinot Noir, were released late in 2019 to considerable acclaim. These wines, and a new premium line of Arterra wines made by the talented Marco Piccoli, their winemaker at Jackson-Triggs Winery, represented a major step-up in quality for the business which seemed eager to compete head-on with long time 'rival' Peller Estates in producing some of Ontario's finest VQA wines.

Although followers of Ontario wines are aware of the ebb and flow of wineries, such developments are seldom noted by the general public whose familiarity with local wines is often limited to their availability at the LCBO, whether a VQA or ICB wine. Nor would it have been important to most consumers that the Wine Council of Ontario, the industry's long-time organizational body, decided to change its name in 2018 to the Craft Wineries of Ontario to reflect better their mandate of working with VQA wine producers. Likewise, few people outside the industry would have been concerned when the Winery and Grower Association was formed by the larger wineries to foster blended wines or even realize that as of 2020 it is now known as the Wine Growers' Organization. And how many consumers have noted changes in the rules which occur periodically with VQA wines, including the refreshed VQA logo which appeared in September 2019?

Fifty years ago, when almost all Ontario wine was based on labrusca grapes, one wine became an overnight success, a refreshment wine named Baby Duck, made by Andres Wines, a winery only recently established in the province. You could even argue that it was the industry's first 'block-buster' although an unusual one, achieving notoriety for its grapey, sweet, pop-like character rather than fame for exceptional quality, but it made Andres a great deal of money while inspiring the other corporate wineries at the time to emulate the style.

During those same days in the 1970's, another group of winemakers, in a remarkable leap of faith, decided to move in a completely different direction, away from labrusca grapes and all the concoctions they had generated during the previous century. Their first wines were revolutionary and exciting, and it would not be long before cottage winemaking was taking center stage. The industry was, in fact, starting over again, aware that it was only a tiny player in the world of wine with no presumption of "greatness" at all, although there was indeed a feeling in the air that it had the potential to achieve 'great' things!

Only a few years later at the beginning of a new millenium and having survived tremendous turmoil in the previous two decades, our wine industry would issue a vision for the year 2020 named "Poised for Greatness", which amounted to a promise of a marvelous future for all concerned, and it was an eye-opener! Industry stakeholders, the growers, the wineries, their associations, the LCBO, VQAO, and the Government, believing that Ontario was now ready to be considered a serious player in the world of wine, declared their commitment to achieving what they called "greatness", with expectations that Ontario wines would be accepted and enjoyed by more and more consumers. Should the industry's star continue to rise, this would confirm that our wines were of high quality, crafted by an industry with an enviable reputation of which we could all be proud.

Although defining 'greatness' may be a controversial matter in itself, today there is general agreement that Ontario wineries are producing an amazing variety of wines of outstanding quality. A consumer shopping in the LCBO faces an embarrassment of riches in the Ontario sections and is truly challenged to select one winery's offering over another! A number of 'celebrities', impressed by the reputation of the industry, have worked with different wineries, lending their name to high-quality brands – think "Cuddy by Tawse" and "The Tragically Hip" wines made by Stoney Ridge. Wine writers are lavish in their praise of Ontario VQA wines and our winemakers and wineries. A visit to an Ontario winery today is proof of this, not only in the wines to be tasted but in the effusive 'spirit' that seems to pervade the winery environment where visitors happily make their purchase before continuing to another winery to enjoy the same experience all over again. Authoritative wine publications like The Wine Spectator now report favourably on Ontario products, confirming the reality that our wines are the equal of others from around the world. And numerous wineries continue to win major awards in national and international wine competitions.

As a new decade begins, we are blessed with wines from a tremendous variety of wineries, from tiny, family operated farm ventures to spectacular, large-scale facilities who have turned what was once thought to be a disadvantage to growing premium grapes – our cold climate – into a thriving, fine wine industry. These passionate winery owners, the many dedicated grape growers, and numerous other people related in some way to the wine industry from suppliers to government, are collectively responsible for the industry soaring to new heights. These people are not miracle workers, but they are extraordinary and the real reason why it is appropriate to talk about the "greatness" that our grape and wine industry has achieved by bringing pleasure to so many lives.

Today, the wine world is welcoming and drinking Ontario wines as evidenced by the increasing volume of VQA wine that is now being exported compared to only a few years ago when exporting was simply not an industry priority. In 2018, for example, according to the VQA 2019 Annual Report, 31 wineries applied for export certificates required by the European Union involving 277 wines, and in 2019 there were 1968 certificates issued in total for all export markets. Ontario wines of origin are recognized as being distinctive and sought after, bold and creative, reflecting consistent and exceptional quality and a dedication to excellence, all convincing proof that the industry has indeed exceeded expectations!

Nowhere is this more apparent than with the people responsible for crafting the wines themselves, our winemakers, many of whom have been identified as "super-stars" by the LCBO and acknowledged as "Winemaker of the Year" (see Appendices) or recognized by wine judges for their achievements in various competitions. To-day, many winemakers have become the face of the winery where they work, well-known by consumers who have their 'favourites' and are very loyal to their wines. Prior to the 1970's, consumers rarely attached themselves to a winery in this way and it was not until Paul Bosc began to appear on television for Chateau Gai that consumers started to identify winemakers by name. Younger consumers to-day may not recognize the names of our pioneering winemakers from the 1970's and early 1980's, including Karl Kaiser, Joe Pohorly, Ewald Reif, Carlo Negri, Rudi Mueller, Joseph Zimmerman, Karl Podamer, Ernst Fischer, and Paul Bosc, but their work inspired other individuals to open wineries in the 1980's creating a solid base for the 'greatness' that was now developing. The arrival of these new 'boutiques' allowed visitors to meet and talk with the people making the wines and get to know them, adding to the wonderful experience of touring wineries.

Traditionally, it had been the custom to refer to winemakers as "himself" as this was a field populated predominantly by males. Perhaps this was due to the perception that winemaking was too physical a job for women, but a winemaker was normally considered a man, historically referred to as a chemist. The first female winemaker that I recall meeting was Mira Ananicz, a Polish chemist who was hired as assistant winemaker at Chateau Gai in 1973 and went on to make superb wines with Bright's Wines as their Chief Winemaker, but it was not until the 1990's that the gender inequality was ended, and female winemakers began to make their presence felt in the industry. Although there were several women working as winemakers, two who rose to prominence were Ann Sperling, who carried on a family tradition that began with grapes and wine in the Okanagan Valley, becoming the winemaker at Cilento Winery and then consulting winemaker for several other Ontario wineries, and Deborah Paskus who also forged innovative new paths working at several wineries in Niagara and Prince Edward County.

With the opening of the educational programs at Brock University and Niagara College, many women were able to explore various aspects of the wine business and some soon became standout winemakers, welcomed by a rapidly growing industry. To-day there is an ever-increasing number of female winemakers spread all over the province at some thirty wineries, and they are just as proficient at winning awards as their male counterparts. Four have been selected so far as "Winemaker of the Year" including the talented Emma Garner at Thirty Bench, Sue-Ann Staff who operates her own winery, Marlize Beyers at Hidden Bench Winery who is working with certified organic vineyards and Anne Sperling, now a trailblazer at Southbrook Vineyards in the production of organic and biodynamic wines.

Ontario's cadre of winemakers is as varied as the nature of the wineries themselves. Some are 'imports' who have continued their winning ways at wineries in all of Ontario's wine regions while the majority can be called 'homegrown talent', with their skills sharpened as amateur winemakers in some cases or as graduates of our educational programs at Brock University and Niagara College. Others have simply learned through hands-on winery experience after following an interest to work in the wine industry.

To-day, about 20% of industry winemakers are owner-operators, acting both as President and winemaker, a dual role that is extremely demanding, while the rest would be considered employees or consultants. As winemakers, some have worked at more than one winery looking to broaden their experience or further their career, while others have been associated with the same winery for many years. It would be hard to think of Cave Springs without Angelo Pavan who has been winemaker since their opening in 1986 or Alan and Brian Schmidt at Vineland Estates who have provided consistent, high-quality winemaking there for 35 years or Ron Giesbrecht, who was responsible for putting Henry of Pelham Winery on the map over a 25 year period and now teaches at Niagara College while operating a brand-new small winery called Wending Home. A small number serve as winemaker for two wineries including Dave Johnson (Featherstone owner and Back 10 Cellars), and Ilya Senchuk (Leaning Post owner and Good Earth Winery), while Andrezej Lipinski (Big Head Winery) and Thomas Bachelder (Bachelder Wines) have helped several wineries to establish their reputation while polishing their own identity and establishing successful wineries.

Over the last five decades, our winemakers have indeed been fortunate to have at their disposal a wide range of the same grapes that are grown in all wine regions world-wide to-day, grapes like Chardonnay, for example, possibly our best-performing white table wine grape, or Pinot Noir, which is also capable of making some fine red table wine. These, and other Hybrid and Vinifera grapes, in the hands of skilled winemakers, have propelled our wine industry to the greatness we now enjoy. Winemakers during the time of our native wine industry had only 'labrusca' grapes to make their wines, and although few people have ever commented on this, they did a remarkable job in creating successful products at the time from those grapes.

The 'labruscas', like Concord and Catawba, often required considerable manipulation in the winemaking process including the addition of generous amounts of water and sugar to balance the 'must' and reduce 'foxy' flavours, or heating wines and fortifying them by adding alcohol, resulting in wines that were serviceable and for the most part successful but certainly not 'great' from a modern point of view. As a result, when we talk about the beginning of the "greatness" achieved by our current wine industry, it is usually traced back only to the 1970's and the introduction of table wines made from the 'new' French Hybrid and Vinifera grapes.

During the 1980's, wines from many of the 'new wave' wineries began to impress consumers who were no longer interested in traditional Ontario ports and sherries. And as more small wineries like Vineland Estates, Konzleman, Stoney Ridge, Cave Springs, and Henry of Pelham started up, crafting the likes of Riesling, Chardonnay, Merlot, Vidal, and Baco Noir, the wine media happily spread the good news. There was no doubt that these wines represented a significant improvement over historic table wines as winemakers began to implement innovative techniques like micro-oxygenation on red wines and temperature-controlled fermentations for whites while experimenting with cultured yeasts, French and American small oak barrels, and new processing and fermentation equipment. So much seemed to be transforming so fast that no one had time to notice the advances in reputation taking place.

Ironically, at the very time the quality of our wines was starting to be appreciated, the industry ran into headwinds generated by talk of "Free Trade" and the threat it posed to wineries and growers. However, after surviving the initial setback that new agreements caused, the fortunes of the craft winemakers began to soar once again, inspiring an eye-popping increase in the number of new wineries throughout the 1990's. A massive change in our vineyards, with thousands of acres of 'old' varieties simply pulled out for replacement by Vinifera vines was underway, while at the same time some of the Hybrid and Vinifera vines planted in the 60's and 70's had come into their own and were sought by the wineries as 'old vines' to craft reserve quality wines.

Although there was a new confidence in the air as wineries established their own winning track records, there were still sceptics who refused to believe that Ontario wines were 'as good as' wines from more established regions. One individual, more than anyone else in my experience, was determined to prove that our wines could stand up to any competition, and he set out to prove it. Larry Paterson, an employee with the LCBO in the Peterborough area, had followed the development of our wine industry and used his knowledge to spot-light Ontario wines in his store with shelf-talkers of his own making, going so far as to invite local winemakers to come up to Lakefield and meet customers in his store on a weekend.

His efforts snowballed into holding tastings at his home, aided by his supportive wife Barb, with imports and Ontario wines presented to a group of friends and people in the wine media for a mixed 'blind' tasting. Everyone would rate the wines tasted and Larry would track the results, presenting them to the group at the end of the tasting. He took great delight when an Ontario wine won, especially when the winemaker was also present. I participated in numerous such tastings in the 1990's and I am pleased to say that invariably Ontario would come out as the winner, establishing exactly what Larry was trying to prove. On one occasion he organized a tasting of red wines for dignitaries in Ottawa and the format was the same, a selection of well-respected imports purchased at the LCBO and local wines chosen by Larry, in a blind tasting. To the amazement of many, Ontario wines captured the day, being preferred to some expensive Bordeaux chateaux, and Larry was in his glory, showing more than a few sceptics that the 'proof was in the pudding'! Few people realized that he put on many of these tastings at his own expense. Unfortunately, the LCBO did not take too kindly to his efforts, after some importers began to complain, and Larry received a not-too subtle reprimand from his superiors.

That did not stop Larry. Another of his pet projects was a public tasting event he helped organized in Buckhorn, north of Lakefield, called the Great Canadian Wine and Cheese Show. This was an all-day Saturday tasting event that attracted a huge crowd of locals and cottagers in the area who came to sample the offerings of the many wineries that Larry had talked into participating, and it ran successfully for several years. In his 'spare time', he busied himself trying to convince wineries in Quebec and Nova Scotia to plant hybrid vines like Frontenac, Landot, and Landal as they were quite winter-hardy and made good wine. And Larry knew good wine, becoming himself an award-winning, accomplished amateur winemaker.

As a final achievement, he organized the first true 'craft' winery organization for smaller wineries which he called the Ontario Viticultural Association (OVA) because he believed so strongly in what they were doing and thought they were working at a disadvantage in the industry. He then managed to talk me into helping him produce information documents and arrange meetings for members to share their concerns about the industry and work to-gether to resolve them. I was simply amazed at his energy and his work ethic and these did not go unnoticed as he attracted a loyal following of Ontario winemakers and wine writers, many of whom were invited to his home for fishing excursions north of Peterborough.

Larry was known affectionately to all as "The Little Fat Wino" (though neither fat nor a wino!), a true evangelist and unique hero of Ontario winemaking who demonstrated time and time again that Ontario makes wine every bit as 'good' as any other region in the world of wine. Sadly, after a sudden illness, he passed away on November 29, 2010 at 57 years of age, leaving his family, friends, fish, and fermentations far too soon. Larry's contributions to Ontario winemaking were significant, and they will ensure that his memory will be treasured for a long time.

Larry would have been delighted to watch the progress of the wine industry over the last decade as the greatness for our wines that he believed in has become reality. Twenty years ago, the industry saw itself as ready or poised for greatness, knowing that in only thirty years it had transitioned itself from a native grape based to a Hybrid and Vinifera based wine producer and that this offered the potential to achieve a reputation for quality wines once never thought possible. The industry has moved on from 'poised' as the wines continue to excel as unique and superb expressions of Ontario wine, validated by a respected appellation system, authentic wines of origin that reflect our own region's personality and identity.

The story of Ontario wines is not a myth about becoming the 'best' or the 'greatest' in the wine world but an odyssey of finding success and soaring to new heights after a long and determined effort to achieve greatness.

CHAPTER FOURTEEN

Bacchus to the future!

"The wine world can change faster than you think...2018 was beset with trade wars, and more climate-change-driven chaotic weather events which made some wine regions winners, some losers. 2019 promises similar contrasts, surprises, and the continuation of some of last year's trends." Elin McCoy, Bloomberg, reported in the "Hamilton Spectator", January 19, 2019.

"The problem with history is that it's in the past. What comes next is much more interesting. At least to us. VQA Wines of Ontario is making what's next in wine. So, if that means breaking rules, defying conventions, expectations, forging our own style...Then that's what we'll do." VQA Wine Manifesto in "Wine Country Ontario Travel Guide", 2020-2021

"Even in good times the wine business in Ontario is not very profitable... most winery owners are willing to put up with this in the hopes that next year will be better!" Bill Redelmeier, owner Southbrook Winery, September 30, 2020

"Throughout the COVID-19 crisis, people have continued to enjoy wine, and one lesson wine teaches us is that time marches on, and one vintage will surely be followed by another." Wine Spectator, Editorial, July-August 2020

It is 2020, the beginning of a new year and a new decade for an industry whose history began just over 150 years ago in the years immediately preceding Confederation. To be more accurate, Ontario has witnessed two wine industries over time, the original one which survived a century of dependence on a small number of 'labrusca' grape varieties, and the new industry based on the preferred hybrid and vinifera grapes that have replaced the 'old' varieties over the last half century. Closer examination would reveal that our current industry itself leads a double life, the one identified with 100% local wines, mainly VQA, and the other producing wines blended from local and imported material, now referred to as ICB or International-Canadian Blends. Although many bemoan this duality, the success of our current industry is due to the existence of both 'brands', the one affording reputation and respect, the other financial resilience.

Our winemaking has evolved from a somewhat disrespected past to the brilliance of our present-day "world-class" status, a rather recent phenomenon that gained traction only over the last few decades with the momentum driven by our VQA producers who have made the province a hotbed for crowd-pleasing wines. The result is an industry that in 2019 contributed 18,000 jobs in the province and a total economic benefit of more than $4 billion annually including winery tourism that alone generated $850 million while attracting over 2 million visitors!

Yet, as many involved in the industry will attest, winemaking in Ontario is indeed "no easy art". It is expensive to start a winery and expensive to maintain and the owner must have expertise in grape growing, winemaking, marketing and sales, and in the world of government relations and regulations. And while winemaking itself is not 'rocket science', it still requires a deft touch on the part of a skilled winemaker to achieve consistent, high-quality wine, wine after wine, year after year, that will appeal to ever more discerning consumers. It is a complex craft that annually faces myriad challenges and the winemaking team must be totally focused from vineyard to the bottle.

However, as we have seen, winery activity has truly intensified in Ontario during the last three decades with numerous individuals joining in the dance and taking VQA membership in 2020 to the 180 level, with some of the new players seemingly oblivious to the ongoing risks and threats with which they must contend. Given such a reality, this is amazing, for you would have thought that many current winery owners would have been much less eager to take the plunge if they had 'done their homework'. That this has not been the case suggests that the 'mystique' of winemaking is very intriguing, and that the sound of music inviting one to dance with Bacchus, an enticing siren's serenade, for some is impossible to resist!

Ontario wine consumers, content to buy and drink their wine, for the most part seem unaware of the perils of our wine industry, so vulnerable to the whims of nature, government, and man, and have been happy simply to watch and enjoy the show.

More than ever as we consider the industry's future, we are being reminded that this is both a grape and a wine industry although the grape growers and the wineries over the years have had their confrontations – essentially over the pricing of grapes – which has required government intervention to calm the waters. Yet, the saying is true that as go the wineries so go the growers. To-day, both partners share a concern over the uncertainty of 'climate change' in the coming years and how it may impact the growing of grapes in both established appellations like Niagara and the newer emerging regions. The Intergovernmental Panel on Climate Change has warned that over the next decade, if the current trend continues, the world is on track to warm by more than 1.5 C, and that, according to the National Academy of Sciences, would result in the loss of almost half of the regions that grow wine grapes to-day.

With climate warming, for example, there could be excessive precipitation, which can lead to damaging vine diseases, or hot temperatures that would 'burn' grapes and result in poor sugar-acid ratios. Ontario might lose its identity as a 'cool-climate' zone known for superb Chardonnay and Riesling wines, while losing our cool, and find that we can now make red wines of a character never anticipated before, leaving Ontario as the new home of great Cabernet Sauvignon wines; or it might turn out that other vinifera varieties will find a suitable home in places where it is now a challenge to grow them. Yet, most worrisome is the potential negative impact of climate warming on our production of icewine!

Climate change could require grape growers, once again, to re-structure their vineyards, uprooting vines and replanting with 'new' varieties as they have been obligated to do in the past, at considerable cost to themselves and with a significant impact on wine production as well. Growers and wineries will be 'locked' into changes with the hope that consumers will be willing to accept wines from different, and possibly unfamiliar varieties like Marquette and Zibibbo!

Being aware of the issues, both the Federal and the Provincial governments joined to create a $2 million support program in early 2020 (the Marketing and Vineyard Improvement Program or MVIP) aimed at assisting growers to implement new technologies and equipment for improving grape quality. It follows up on another Federal $11 million funding for the Canadian Grapevine Certification Network research cluster to secure domestically certified pathogen-free grapevines and analyze growing practices that are better for the environment.

Whether you consider our vineyards to be our pride and joy or a constant risk, it is true that both grape growers and wineries have to contend with disparities in our annual grape production that make life difficult for both partners who literally live by the tonne. Over the last five years according to GGO statistics, the Ontario harvest has varied from a low of 53,252 tonnes in 2015 (valued at $63 million) to 70, 851 in 2016, then a record 87,567 tonnes in 2017, back to 64,773 in 2018 and then up to 81,115 in 2019 (valued at $109 million). Such variability presents a special challenge to an industry that depends on satisfying consumer demands with some form of consistency in production while maintaining its revenue streams as well.

However, even with the constant changes in annual production, certain trends have become clear over these years. Growth in both vinifera reds and whites is continuing to outdistance the French hybrids although Baco Noir is still our second most widely planted red grape, just behind Cabernet Franc which is our top red variety at 5955 tonnes in 2019, while

Vidal continues to lead all white grape production, followed by the viniferas Riesling and Chardonnay. Growth of the new hybrid Frontenac continues to surprise in the reds, up to 903 tonnes last year, while Sauvignon Blanc and Pinot Gris show the most dramatic growth in whites as they each head to 4,000 tonnes. Last year overall, white hybrid production exceeded red, 22,295 tonnes to 7,965 and white vinifera outpaced red vinifera 29,842 tonnes to 20,406.

Still, after 50 years of growth in production of vinifera vines in Ontario, it is difficult to pinpoint our 'signature' grape, that variety which will become the standard bearer for the industry in the future, with some advocating for Chardonnay, others for Riesling, and others for Cabernet Franc. These 3 varieties along with Merlot currently comprise almost 50% of our grape production, but that statistic could be irrelevant 10 years from now. In total production, according to the 2020 VQA Annual Report, Chardonnay continues to lead the way in whites at 13% of all grapes followed by the red grapes Cabernet Franc and Merlot, each at 11% and then Riesling at 10%. Most of this production ends up in 'single varietal table wines' with Chardonnay again on top at almost 256,000 cases but with Pinot Gris (9% of grapes) not far behind at just over 240,000 cases. Pinot Noir (6% of grapes) is the top single varietal red wine at 146,004 cases with Merlot close behind at 126,579 cases. A lot of Cabernet Franc is used in red blends and it seems less popular as a varietal at only 84,525 cases.

From my own experience as a winemaker and consumer of Ontario wines, I believe a great deal of our future success will depend on Chardonnay, the very first vinifera grape made as a commercial wine in our province in the 1950's, and the one which to me seems best suited for our climate and limestone terroirs. Chardonnay has won many awards for a wide range of Ontario wineries in international competitions since the 1980's with these wines offering a unique take on the grape in the wine world representative of its 'cool climate' status. They can be both delicate and powerful, substantially oaked or not at all, fragrant with fruit or subtle and elegant, but with wonderful depth, length, and complexity and the ability to 'age' well in the bottle. And Chardonnay almost alone of our grapes has been capable of making wines priced over $50 which still represent good value, indicative of its potential for producing a true 'icon' Ontario wine.

Perhaps this focus on Chardonnay can be traced to an Ontario wine tasting in May of 2010 in London, England appropriately labelled the "Seriously Cool" Chardonnay tasting that inspired some of our winemakers, led by Thomas Bachelder, a top Chardonnay producer, to create and launch the International Cool Climate Chardonnay Celebration (now known as i4C) in 2011. This incredible annual international event (not a competition!) is now held during the third weekend of July and brings world-class Chardonnay wines, international visitors, and the eyes of the world to Ontario. For the immediate future, Riesling, Pinot Gris, Pinot Noir, and other successful varieties remain in the shadows cast by Chardonnay, and although outstanding in their own right and skillfully made by many wineries, they and others will have to take a back seat to my favourite grape.

For most wines, aside from taxation, grapes comprise the major portion of the product's cost which makes grape pricing a very sensitive winery issue. For decades, the value of grapes has been decided through a process of negotiation between the growers' association (the GGO) and winery representatives, the Wine Council in years gone by and to-day by two associations, the Ontario Craft Winery Association and the Wine Growers of Ontario (the WGAO rebranded as WGO in July 2020), representing the larger wineries, farmers, retailers and tourism operators. It has always been a struggle to find a happy medium between what the growers desire as appropriate compensation for their crop and what wineries can afford to pay and still remain competitive.

Grapes are divided into different 'classes' with a price agreed upon for each one. Recently, there has been pressure from wineries to change this process (historically called a marketing board system involving grower-winery contracts) in the hopes of having a more 'open' system, but there is strong resistance from the GGO for such a change. To-day, the end result is that all wineries will pay essentially the same base price for their grapes (by variety). And grapes in more demand, like Pinot Grigio and Shiraz, will end up costing wineries the most. Some grapes can still be priced higher if they are higher in sugar (on the 'Brix' scale), or if a winery and grower work to-gether to reduce tonnage per acre with the grower compensated accordingly for premium grapes, or if a winery has a private agreement with a producer to pay a form of 'bonus' for grapes from a valued location.

Since juice/wine production per tonne varies considerably (red grapes fermented on their skins will provide more volume than white grapes pressed for juice, for example, and some grapes are 'juicier' than others), if we accept an 'average' figure of 700 litres per tonne of grapes, the base cost of the liquid in a bottle becomes clear based on 2019 harvest pricing (a 750 ml. bottle would cost ¾ of the per litre price).

The Vidal grape, the industry's workhorse white hybrid, at $674 per tonne, would cost approximately $.96 per litre, while Riesling ($1548), the leading white vinifera at 10,688 tonnes in 2019 would cost $2.21 with Chardonnay ($1580) at 9552 tonnes only slightly more at $2.26 per litre. Pinot Gris, the most expensive white vinifera to-day at $1808, would be $2.60.

The difference in cost between a hybrid and a vinifera white is similarly reflected in red wine grapes where Baco Noir at $964 would cost a winery $1.38 per litre compared to Cabernet Franc at $1830 with a cost of $2.61. Gamay, the least expensive red vinifera, would cost $2.00, Pinot Noir $3.03, Merlot and Cabernet Sauvignon $2.90 and Shiraz, our most expensive grape at $2396 per tonne, $3.42.

With these differences in price, it is understandable that vinifera wines should be more expensive than hybrids and reds more expensive than white. This does not explain why a Riesling made at one winery will retail for $14.95 and at another for $29.95 when they are both fine VQA wines. Certainly, part of the 'mystique' of wine lies in the variation of prices that a consumer can pay for a bottle and sometimes that is justified by additional production costs and sometimes by the reputation of the producer and awards won in competitions.

Wine is still a very traditional product in this modern world of high technology in spite of the mystery of its pricing, but it is so much more than just a 'commodity' whether it comes corked, with a screwcap or other synthetic closure, or in a bottle, box, bag or can! With a beverage that provides a record of history, or a wonderful range of experiences from the cultural and intellectual to the sensual, it is natural for beauty to lie in the eyes of the label beholder, who may simply want a particular bottle of wine at that moment in time and is prepared to pay whatever price is asked.

No wonder that many look to the future with considerable optimism in spite of the challenges inherent in the wine business. Recent studies have indicated that the global alcoholic beverages market is continuing to grow with sales expected to reach $1,684 billion over the next 5 years, a market which is being driven by a young adult demographic with a surge in disposable income, and a rise in consumer demand for premium and super premium products.

As wine prices continue to rise, it is understandable that some of our wineries are pushing the envelope on pricing, creating 'Reserve' or 'Platinum' series wines that imply their quality is elevated and a higher price is justified. The wines may reflect 'older vines' or a very restricted production (e.g. from a reduced tonnage per acre) or 'better' grapes with higher sugars or from a vineyard whose reputation for superior grapes has become acknowledged in the industry. A growing number of our wineries that are highly esteemed by the wine media, with significant awards in competitions or producing otherwise highly rated wines, have earned a kind of 'seal of approval' enabling them to convince consumers that their wines merit a premium price. Thus, well-known, very successful wineries like Tawse or Two Sisters or Thirty Bench or Bachelder, and others, have many wines in the $40 to $70 range, while premium craft winery Kacaba, on the Bench in Vineland, has found a niche selling older, much-awarded library wines at over $100 a bottle.

But these are 'limited production', award-winning wines, not the 'bread and butter' wines that are being made in larger volumes to generate economies of scale in what is an extremely competitive industry. To-day, that competition comes from many directions including the ICB wines, an ever-increasing number of imported wines, then from the major brewers and distillers and the burgeoning 'craft' brewers, distillers, and cideries.

And why not add Sake and Seltzers to the list? This is why those in the wine business are so concerned about developing 'free' inter-provincial markets while urging the government to stop 'importing' domestic wines (a needed bureaucratic change which would reduce their price), and achieving more guaranteed shelf space in the LCBO, both General List and Vintages, for VQA wines, or improving access to consumers with more retail outlets and private wine stores, because, at the end of the day, wineries have to be able to sell their wine! And most wineries are very sensitive to the resistance of consumers to buy local wines that appear to be more expensive than the competition.

Still, prices for all wines continue to increase and this requires everyday consumers to scrutinize LCBO shelves for wines they feel deliver the 'value' they seek. Our local wineries are responding with evolving standards and ever- improving quality, attempting to keep the VQA identity relevant and engage with consumers. It is interesting to note that total wines sales in Ontario for 2019 were down 1.8% over the previous year while VQA sales were up by 2.3% over 2018, a significant statistic compared to the 1.4% drop in sales of non-VQA wines and 2.6% in imported wines. And reaching almost 20 million litres last year, VQA sales show a 20% increase over the last 5 years with a rise to 9.9% of the market although all 'Ontario' wines still own only 43.4% of the total market (non-VQA wines have 33.51% and imported wines 56.6% market share). But Ontario consumers continue to drink a lot of wine, for the second year in a row just over 200 million litres!

Statistics like these bode well for the industry's future, but other black clouds have seemingly appeared out of the blue this year to threaten what is an impressive record of success. The industry was taken aback by the recent challenge from Australia of several provincial and federal regulations that Australia cited as being discriminatory trade barriers but which have helped promote the sale of our local wine. Recently Australian wines have been losing market share world-wide resulting in the Australian government attacking Canada, a suitable target because wine sales here are controlled by provincial governments that must respect the international trading system. This was in spite of the fact Australia is the fourth largest supplier of imported wines to Canada, outselling 100% Canadian VQA wine (even in Ontario!) which, unfortunately, has become the victim of their attack.

Early in 2018, the Australian government filed a protest with the World Trade Organization (WTO) citing examples of Canadian practices they believed were inconsistent with the GATT 1994 agreement including the differential tax rates now in place and especially the federal excise duty exemption on 100% Canadian grown fruit that our wineries enjoy, as well as restrictions on grocery store licenses and the operation of wine boutiques in grocery stores. Not surprisingly, other countries wanted to join in the discussions in order not to be left out of the potential benefits for their own wine sales.

On July 27th this year, our International Trade Minister, Mary Ng, announced that Canada had reached a "partial agreement" with Australia after serious negotiations with the Trudeau government. Canada was forced to backdown and Australia's arguments prevailed resulting in the elimination of all tariffs on Australian wine exports to Canada. Various restrictions on Australian wine sales in British Columbia, which had been a major reason for the challenge, will now be ended, providing Australian wines with additional shelf space there.

This agreement has now set a precedent that other wine-producing provinces, including Ontario, will have to follow. Commenting that our government is 'commited to the rules-based world trading system', as part of the trade dispute settlement, the Federal Government has agreed to reimpose by June 30, 2022 the federal excise duty on 100% Canadian wines, repealing the exemption that the Steven Harper Conservatives established in 2006.

This is shocking news for all provincial wine industries as wineries that have come into existence over the last 15 years have never had to pay excise tax and will soon have to add that into the price of their wine. The British Columbia Wine Institute has estimated that the cost of a case of local wine would rise by about $6 unless the Trudeau government can somehow find a replacement program for the exemption which had been wonderful motivation for the development of new wineries.

Australia was delighted by the outcome, declaring rather hypocritically that it did not want to impede the development of local wine industries, but is still pursuing the matter with the WTO so that their producers can stand tall on that infamous "level playing field". And this at a time when you cannot find a bottle of Ontario table wine for sale in Australia! It is sad that our wine industry finds itself in this situation only because all alcohol sales in Canada are considered a function of provincial liquor boards controlled by governments that must respect the WTO. As Bill Redelmeier, owner of Southbrook Winery, declared in a recent blog, "If the WTO were to tell Tesco, Walmart, or Costco that they had to give Australian wine more shelf space, they would be told to get stuffed"! Privatization, anyone?

And as I write what is next to my final chapter on the evolution of Ontario winemaking, we all have been overwhelmed by a virus now known as COVID-19, the source of a deadly pandemic that continues to paralyze almost every aspect of our lives. For the wine business, which is positioned at the intersection of many related sectors including agriculture, hospitality and tourism, and various sales channels, it has posed a threat which recalls the pessimism generated 30 years ago with the signing of the notorious 'Free Trade' agreement which many believed would throw our wine industry into a death spiral.

Beginning in March 2020, the hospitality industry and tourism came to a grinding halt and wineries watched as their on-site retail sales disappeared with the first lock-down along with sales of wine to restaurants, at farmers' markets, at duty free stores, and to the export market. As well, the virus closed the door on all public events where wine tastings might occur, including the LCBO tasting panels, and all wine competitions. In short, COVID-19 disrupted the continuum needed to move wine inventory just as the 2019 vintage wines were starting to be bottled. If there was to be an ongoing drop in wine sales, the industry could face devastating financial damage, especially the smaller wineries who depend so much on sales at their winery store. And in addition, a glut of wine unsold would certainly put a damper on the purchase of grapes when the 2020 vintage inevitably comes along. A significant tonnage of grapes unsold this fall would be disastrous for growers.

Wineries of all sizes have seen their revenue streams dry up while at the same time agricultural and winemaking costs have remained constant. Grapevines must be tied and pruned by a significant workforce while winery staff tend to the wines in tank and barrel, activities that put a financial demand on the winery at a time when dwindling sales have stopped generating necessary dollars. Dan Sullivan, proprietor and winemaker of Rosehall Run Winery in Prince Edward County, reflecting the reality of most family-operated wineries, admitted that winery tourism is "the most significant profit centre for our winery" while adding "We're extremely concerned that the longer this drags on, the tougher it's going to be not just for us, but for everybody".

Fortunately, consumers have still been able to purchase alcohol, including wine, from LCBO retail stores and grocery stores with both retailers showing 25-30% higher sales. LCBO sales have been a boon for the larger wineries with their portfolio of both blended and VQA wines and this has helped counter signs of a slowing of overall sales growth that appeared in 2019. As well, restaurants have been allowed to 'retail' wine by the bottle when they prepare meals for pick-up at their door or for home delivery, a new sales channel for all wines now confirmed as permanent by the Ford government. And the pandemic has helped accelerate the movement toward digital wine sales as consumers move from on-site to on-line purchases. Many wineries are offering special prices and free shipping for internet orders which is virtually their sole channel for sales if they do not have LCBO presence, although this has been at considerable cost to them. And not all wineries are yet well-known or able to 'get their message' out to consumers, especially wineries who have only been in business a short while. But there are some who are now selling more wine on-line than they were at their retail outlet before and this appears to be a trend that is not going away.

As July 2021 comes to an end, we are seeing a slow return to more 'normal' times and at some point the worst will be behind us, although no one can really say when that will be or what the lasting impact of the damage will be. Certainly, with tourism and direct delivery to licencees, there will not be a speedy return to normal ways and for many wineries this is making their future somewhat uncertain even as we move forward with cautious optimism.

At about the same time that the corona virus was beginning to change our life in March, the 5th annual Deloitte "Ontario Wine and Grape Industry Performance Study" was made public. This is a comprehensive, benchmarking survey of the present state of the industry, that is from July to December 2019, with participating wineries covering 90% of all wine made in the province and 17% of the grapes grown (97 wineries with vineyards, 13 wineries without vineyards, and 72 independent grape growers).

The data has been consistent over the five years of the research although the number of participants has varied slightly and this would make direct comparisons difficult. However, the results continue to show an industry with numerous challenges, some of them 'perennial', and with a main one being the LCBO's domination of all things alcoholic and the consequences of that.

It is astounding to read that only 45% of wineries selling under $5 million of wine annually and 88% selling over $5 million are PROFITABLE, and this includes those wineries selling over $10 million who are ALL profitable! This is an industry of mainly small players and the sad reality is that small wineries are having a very difficult time turning a profit. Wineries that sell ICB wines, which tend to be the larger wineries, are the most likely to be profitable. Although small wineries sell more wine on site than larger wineries by percentage of sales (averaging 75% of sales) and are more likely to sell at farmers' markets, these wineries sell virtually no wine in the export channel and have smaller sales to the LCBO (averaging only 6% of their sales). Reliance on the LCBO as a sales channel increased with winery size, with larger wineries selling almost 39% of their wine through the LCBO (both blends and VQA). Wineries in the smallest category, with sales under $.5 million, sold almost all their wine in Ontario with only a small volume sold to other provinces in spite of Canada-wide demand.

Wineries in the larger categories exported more to other countries than they "exported" within Canada essentially because many Canadians outside the province can't legally get their hands on their wine as some provinces still forbid individual consumers from ordering shipments of wine produced in other provinces. And people who try, risk being fined! In spite of years of industry complaints about the challenges of inter-provincial retailing of wine, governments through provincial liquor boards insist on obstructing this channel, with the result that consumers across Canada simply have a difficult time sourcing "Canadian" wine! As Le Vieux Pin winemaker Severine Pinte put it, "It's easier to send wine to China"!

In line with this is the dilemma of selling wine to the LCBO, damned if you do and damned if you don't, with margins so low and rules so stringent that many wineries simply avoid the LCBO all-together. Moreover, last year, LCBO sales accounted for a lower percentage of total Ontario wine sales across all segments, with the smallest category showing the greatest decline in sales.

Obviously, the LCBO is set up to deal in larger volumes of wine that sell through quickly, large brands that are well-promoted by larger wineries, not small lots of more expensive Ontario wine, an indication that with the LCBO size does matter! To be fair, over the last three decades the LCBO has attempted to assist smaller Ontario producers who have shown a desire to sell in this market, with programs aimed specifically at wineries who do not meet the normal criteria relating to volume and promotional support. Wineries have been allowed to deliver directly to stores within their local area, more effort was devoted to introducing wineries to the system, and a far broader range of wineries were at last accepted into the Vintages' channel. But, with so many wineries vying for such limited shelf space and the reality of making little profit even if the wines do sell, the LCBO environment is still not a welcome market for many in the wine industry.

Yet, some wineries have found success with their products in the LCBO system, whether General List or Vintages, because consumers have enjoyed and continue to buy their wines and wineries that sell well are willingly 'invited back' by the LCBO. Over the years wineries like Henry of Pelham, Cave Springs, and Konzelmann have become favourites in the stores and consumers are always looking forward to the next wine from Featherstone or Flat Rock. The Vintages' catalogue, which appears usually every two weeks, is a well-produced marketing tool that always features an Ontario winery and provides interesting information on the range of new products coming to the shelves. Although Ontario wines are always represented here, the underlying reality is that they are overwhelmed by so many imported wines as the LCBO attempts to offer the world of wines in a very limited retail space.

Another catalogue that appears from time to time, entitled the "Classics Collection", while interesting to read, promotes very limited quantities of wines deemed to be 'Classic' by the LCBO, that is "an exciting assortment of the best, most iconic, most collectible wines" at prices that require a bank loan. While many are indeed 'icons', classified growths, aged ports, and the like, it is just inappropriate to describe them as 'the best'. After all, how can anyone justify using the word 'best' when it comes to wine, a term that cannot be defined objectively. They may be 'fine' wines and certainly do represent products that are otherwise very difficult to obtain, but if you desire any you will have to pay royally for the rarity. For the most part, they are very expensive, often in the hundreds of dollars, a ludicrous price to pay for any wine, no matter how 'stellar'. Ontario is usually represented by only one or two producers – the July, 2021 collection has one out of the 133 wines available and none for August – which seems to indicate that our wines are not yet classic or 'legendary' enough to merit the over-pricing involved. Frankly, this is a service for those wealthy customers who have the money to fuel LCBO coffers and who eagerly snap them up with no need to be concerned about 'value'. Such is the inane mythology of superiority in wine that all these "curated selections" sell out in a hurry. sell

Ironically, many local winery owners are facing a challenging future where their survival is at risk even though no one doubts any longer that we can make great wine in Ontario! Fortunately, surviving is something that the industry has done well over time, even when the wines produced were not highly regarded. With roots dating back to the mid nineteenth century, Ontario wineries have proven to be resilient time and time again, twisting and turning in the face of numerous perils and stumbling blocks, surviving Prohibition and the ensuing Depression, two World Wars, a wholesale transformation of Ontario viticulture, the menace of Free Trade and intense, ongoing competition.

Overcoming these challenges while at the same time searching for greatness has indeed made for a unique and fascinating odyssey in the world of wine, a long transformation from Concord concoctions to iconic icewines and vintage vinifera that now amaze the wine world. And along the way the industry has achieved significant milestones, giving birth to two esteemed research and educational programs at Niagara College and Brock University and a successful appellation system, the VQA, based on a revolution in Ontario viticulture that has inspired the production of world-class hybrid and vinifera wines.

Unlike the epic of Odysseus, the story of Ontario winemaking is not yet complete, and no final destination has been reached. Wineries always have new and daunting surprises to deal with, hopefully not always as serious as COVID with its unprecedented challenges, must work with a Liquor Control system that does not satisfy the needs of many, and live in a tax environment that continues to change at the whim of governments. And just as organic, biodynamic, and sustainability were beginning to offer the promise of additional greatness, the grape and wine industry is facing changing market dynamics after the global pandemic and the uncertainty of global warming with potentially serious consequences for everyone.

The Ontario wine industry has proven itself as capable as any other in both adapting to and expanding on new trends and this has helped to keep it relevant. For example, our wineries now produce a truly exciting range of rose wines made from several different grape varieties and using different techniques. The sparkling wine category continues to evolve after the same fashion with clever names to label wines that cannot legally be called 'Champagne'. And there are an amazing number of excellent white blends, with so many wineries creating their own version from any number of varieties, attempting to find the aroma and tasting profile that will win over the media and consumers alike.

Several wineries produce intriguing 'orange' wines while others are now experimenting with the latest 'fad', a wine 'beverage' made by adding water and sugar and flavourings to left over grape pomace for a refermentation. This process, once called "a second run", produces an inexpensive form of wine called "Piquette" that for centuries was made by poor farm workers who could not afford the real thing. To-day, wineries are looking for a wine product to compete with the unbelievably broad range of spritzers and seltzers that have taken the market by storm – and this is it, according to sales! However, the products reaching the market are all over the map in taste and style and they will not be for everybody. With all the added water, VQA status is out of the question but with great wineries like Tawse and Leaning Post now making Piquette, you may be intrigued enough to give this emerging category a try.

Somehow our wine industry has always risen to the challenge, taking on each new vintage when it arrives with the same loving concern as with any newborn; and knowing the passion, the ingenuity, and positive spirit of our winemakers, I am convinced they will continue to be successful and not only survive but even thrive, with all wineries enjoying the dance with Bacchus.

I very much look forward to what promises to be a wonderful future!

CHAPTER FIFTEEN

TERROIR - Wine is made in the vineyard!

"It's a naïve domestic burgundy without any breeding, but I think you'll be amused by its presumption." James Thurber, 1944

"For an industry that rambles on endlessly about 'sense of place', the effects of a climate landscape shifting under every vintner's feet is nothing short of an existential threat." John Szabo, "Wine Align", August 2021

"No one knows how to make a grape, a vineyard, or a wine naturally express a mineral terroir." Kevin Begos, "Tasting the Past", p. 182

"Can there be any other business (wine) where there's so much bullshit!" Carole Meredith, Scientist, U.C. Davis

"Terroir is a shibboleth that establishes an in-group in a world unto itself (the wine world). This isn't wine appreciation...it is more like wine snobbery." Mark Matthews, "Terroir and other myths of winegrowing", p. 205

During the 1990's, Stoney Ridge Cellars was described by one wine writer as "the small winery that makes the big wines" and we did win more than our share of awards in wine competitions, both local and international. You could say because I made so many different wines and entered many competitions that I had a better chance of winning, or perhaps it was just good luck. Certainly, we never bottled a wine of which I was not proud.

The reputation of Stoney Ridge helped ensure a loyal consumer following and some consideration from the wine media which established myself as one of Niagara's many talented winemakers. At that time the winemakers were the 'stars' of the grape and wine industry and we were just scratching the surface on the important role of grape growers.

But how fortunate I was to work with grapes from growers on what were considered excellent vineyards located on the Grimsby-Beamsville-Vineland Bench. And, surely Bill Lenko, Marv Krilick, Mike Plekan, Don Eastman, and Murray Puddicombe, all experienced and dedicated grape growers, deserved some of the credit for our success because of the work they did in their vineyards. Early in my winemaking career I knew very little about growing grapes, trellis systems or spraying and fertilizing, and I depended greatly on the grower's word when it came to harvesting. They all grew wonderful French Hybrid and Vinifera grapes that were always in demand from wineries since their locations were considered superior to many others in Niagara for their natural air and water drainage. Beyond that, the idea of the special value of a specific site was still in its infancy. But I did believe that good grapes, raised by growers who made real efforts to achieve top quality in their vineyards, were giving me a leg up on the competition! I believe it is fair to say that we were the first Ontario winery to put the grower's name or vineyard name on our wine labels in recognition of their contribution to our winemaking! And it was at this time that we began to hear the line "Wine is made in the vineyard", a compliment to Ontario grape growers to be sure but really a valid confirmation of the importance of grape character in the winemaking process.

Of course, every other winery won awards as well using the same varieties of grapes as myself, an indication that the 'new preferred varieties', and the role of the grower were key factors in turning the entire wine industry in a winning direction. And soon the actual location of the vineyard became a matter of concern. In Ontario by the 1980's this still had not yet received attention as a factor in grape quality, perhaps as a result of our vinous 'history'. When Bright's Wines received their first shipment of French Hybrids and a few Vinifera vines after World War Two, little attention was given to the suitability of the site where they were planted. When Bright's discovered that they were able to grow Chardonnay successfully, additional vines were imported but again the focus was on improving their overall vineyard plantings by just getting additional vines in the ground and not matching any variety to a specific site. And then it became a matter of convincing other growers to pull out their American Hybrids and replant with French Hybrids and Vinifera, all in the same location as before with little concern for the nature of the site.

The lack of familiarity with these vines and the not knowing whether a specific variety was suitable for growing in Ontario or not, or perhaps the belief that had developed after the phylloxera crisis that there were only a few exceptional grape varieties in the world, the so-called French 'noble' vines, resulted in only a handful of different vines being planted here for some time, those already being promoted. Who could fault Paul Bosc, then, for planting Chardonnay, Pinot Noir, and Gamay, all grapes with which he was familiar, or German winemaker Herman Weiss, who planted his own clone of Riesling on the bench in Vineland? Others, quick to follow their lead in the 1970's, planted the same classic varieties. You might say that in the end this was a fortunate development as these varieties were able to grow successfully in Ontario's 'cool climate'.

The same pattern was taking shape in other developing world wine regions, the planting only of vines considered 'the best' for winemaking, with the result that by 2010, less than a dozen different French grape varieties comprised 67% of vineyard acreage in the New World. In Ontario, even with the lack of diversity in Vinifera plantings, by 1980 the first solid step had been taken in creating the potential for a fine wine industry with new plantings of Riesling, Chardonnay, Merlot, Gamay, and Gewurztraminer. Soon, other varieties like Pinot Gris, Sauvignon Blanc, Cabernet Sauvignon, Cabernet Franc, and Syrah began to appear on Ontario wine labels as growers gained experience and harkened to the requests of wineries, adding them to the list of Vinifera plantings. Still, the focus was on the grape variety itself with much less concern for the location of the vineyard.

It was believed that the French Hybrids made a wine superior to the American Hybrids, at least for table use (e.g. Baco Noir or Marechal Foch compared to Concord, or Vidal Blanc versus Elvira or Niagara), and that Viniferas were more suitable for quality wine than French Hybrids – the French themselves banned these Hybrids for table wine use in the 1950's – but it would take a while for growers and winemakers to appreciate that 'place of origin' of the grapes also mattered.

In the world of wine to-day, it is accepted that specific sites can be more suitable for certain grape varieties than others and we seem to take it for granted that some regions and vineyards contribute more to wine quality than others. Indeed, as anyone knows who has wanted to buy Cabernet Sauvignon wines from numerous producers in Napa Valley or Bordeaux, vineyard location can make a tremendous difference in reputation (and in both demand for a wine and wine pricing), although we may not be able to explain HOW the place contributes to this We tend to assume that superior wines from a certain location are supposed to have a specific character, a distinctive taste derived from local growing conditions, the soil and the environment, that elevates them above others. However, seldom is science called upon to support this. Consumers willingly pay what wineries are asking as if it is expected and justified by the appropriate Appellation, and this reinforces the belief that the right grape is growing in the right location for making superior wine. From here it is just a small step to elevating certain wines to luxury or even legendary status. Thus, the wine world lives with 'First Growths' and 'Grands Crus' and a hierarchy of other trophy wines that are accepted intuitively or without question as extraordinary as a result of the place where they are grown. Unfortunately, many of these wines have become so expensive that most wine consumers will never be able to put that claim to the test.

Yet it does seem bizarre in the competitive world of wine that they are seldom entered in wine competitions where their 'quality' can be judged on an equal footing with wines from around the world. That role is usually performed by the all-knowing wine media with ratings that always seem to hit the high 90's!

It is easy to be cynical about this and blame industry or marketing hype because it might seem difficult to believe that one wine can be so much 'better' than another made from the same grape in the same area or even other parts of the world. Yet, the famous 'Judgment of Paris' event in 1976 illustrated clearly that exceptional wines made from the same varieties could indeed come from different countries of origin, in this case from somewhere other than France.

Still, someone must believe there is a significant difference which can be justified by the considerable difference in price! Wine enthusiasts will remind us that some European vineyards/wineries do have a much longer tradition of making wine and that this hands-on experience with their site is meaningful. On this basis, one might expect Ontario Chardonnay, for example, to show some differences in character to a Chardonnay from Burgundy where growers have had a much longer time to understand their vineyard. However, there must be something else at play other than history to account for the considerable difference in price between our own world-class Chardonnays and those esteemed white Burgundies that retail for hundreds of dollars!

Assuming a good clone of an appropriate vine has been planted, any grower will tell you that there are specific environmental factors that play a role in creating the character of the grapes. Issues to consider would include different micro-climates, weather (sunshine and rainfall), drainage, soil types and sub-soils, micro-organisms and soil fertility, and topography, for example. Their impact can be significant, increasing sugar levels and moderating acidity, contributing to ripeness and tannin development and rich fruit flavours. When a site becomes known for grapes that offer better winemaking potential on a regular basis, it acquires a reputation that is usually confirmed in both the perceived quality and the price of the resulting wine. This often means that such a wine shows a 'sense of place'.

The importance of site in relation to the quality of the resulting wine gave rise in France several centuries ago to the word "terroir", a term that over the last forty years has become ubiquitous in wine speak although it has never been 'legally' defined and can mean different things to different people. Related to the word "la terre" and derived from the Latin "terra" meaning "earth, land, or soil", its original use was in reference to the impact of the soil on plant growth and on resulting wine character. Unfortunately, despite increasing knowledge about how plants grow, many people to-day continue to believe that it is the soil primarily which is responsible for wine quality and still erroneously accept that wine flavours come directly from the soil!

As early as the 1500's, the word appeared in the expression "gout de terroir" or "taste of the soil", with a negative connotation in respect to wine flavour, suggesting a strong and unpleasant earthy taste derived from the soil itself. If you could taste the "terroir" in the wine, this usually meant that the wine had some disagreeable quality. Over most of this time, there was little actual science available to provide an objective analysis to help explain why some wines were considered better than others, and thus the assumption grew that it was the "terroir" (soil) that provided for wine quality rather than people or wine growing practices.

Wine being a traditional product, this notion endured for centuries, but more recently the wine world has come to understand that "terroir" should mean more than just the impact of soil on the wine. The change in usage seems to have coincided with the emergence of the Appellation system in France some time ago when the total environment was considered to contribute to the uniqueness of vineyard's grapes and "terroir" was used to define a specific geographical space. Then, following the "Judgement of Paris" according to Mark Matthews in his book "Terroir and Other Myths of Winegrowing", the word almost overnight saw a dramatic increase in usage, "worming its way into wine culture".

When the Appellation d'Origine system was created, "terroir" came to encapsulate everything 'natural' that contributed to the distinction of a vineyard plot, the total environment of a vineyard that was responsible for defining the status of a wine...and ultimately its value! "Terroir" implied everything that made each site unique and accounted for differences in wines from different vineyards without the need to list all the natural conditions which influenced the biology of the vine reacting with each other (and not just the soil). And by this time, the word had lost any pejorative connotation.

To-day, the word has been appropriated by grape and wine industries around the world to link a sense of place with the nature and taste of the wine, (e.g. the wine 'reveals' its terroir), with some authorities suggesting that the character of a wine can actually allow for identification of a specific site. Thus, many would accept the definition offered by Bruno Prats, owner of Chateau Cos d'Estournel in Bordeaux (2006) that "Terroir is all the natural conditions which influence the biology of the vine and the composition of the grape itself, a combination of an infinite number of factors, e.g. climate, soil, landscape, reacting to-gether with each other". Matt Kramer of the Wine Spectator has defined this even more succinctly, commenting: "Terroir is everything that contributes to the distinction of a vineyard plot." For a local take on this, I like the comment by long-time Toronto wine authority Dean Tudor who suggested to me that "Terroir means simply "of the region" in regards to climate, soil, grapes, etc. and is just a term that is used to invoke recognition when one tastes and re-tastes the same wines of that region. Defining "terroir" is certainly not revealing anything. You must experience it to enjoy it."

In Ontario, where our vinous experience is measured in decades and not centuries like some wine regions, real interest in the location of vineyard sites (sense of place) first blossomed with the arrival of the VQA and our initial 'appellations', but the guiding factor here was to establish 'authenticity' of grape origin and varietal integrity in resulting wines in order to legitimize Ontario wines for sale in world markets. Along with this came the notion of 'quality', an idea that was a real innovation for local wines which previously had no 'world-class' reputation. Thus, the VQA as an appellation system could be promoted as a way to build local consumer confidence as well, protecting them with production standards and regulations from poor wine. The wine label became a guarantee of authenticity, outlining the physical boundaries of the product, and suggesting as well that the wine was of high quality.

There is no question that the new system gave an important impetus to our grape and wine industry, helping to establish it as a successful world player, although some were concerned that the new appellations acted like a monopoly, allowing one group of producers (VQA) to maintain economic benefits from the advantage they now enjoyed while making it more difficult for other producers to benefit. The largest wineries making 'blended' wines (from local and import materials) had to live with the notion that these wines were less fine than VQA as they were made outside the new regulations; and VQA members were able to defend their territory with the backing of government regulations. Fruit wine producers as well discovered that they could not use the term "100% Ontario fruit" on their wine labels since that term was limited to Ontario grape wines and protected politically in support of VQA.

Within a few years, once the public had gained a good grasp of "VQA", the industry decided to establish 'sub-appellations', after an extensive study of the Niagara Region led by Tony Doyle of Brock University, taking into account unique influences on vineyards within an appellation, as in topography or distance to/from Lake Ontario or the Niagara Escarpment. There were some who believed that it was too early in the life of the VQA to move in this direction, and that stressing specific differences in the sub-appellations was simply a marketing ploy to benefit VQA wineries. However, Ontario wine consumers accepted the new terminology with little complaint.

To-day we are beginning to move forward even further by recognizing exceptional vineyards in Ontario as the foundation for higher quality wines with most of these located on the "Bench" at the base of the escarpment from Grimsby to Jordan. Heading the list would be Wismer's Foxcroft Vineyard and Vineland Estates in Vineland, the Lenko and Thirty Bench vineyards in Beamsville, and properties owned by Hidden Bench Winery. These merit a premium for the resulting quality of the grapes they produce but the resulting cost of these grapes still comes nowhere close to grape prices for recognized 'icon' properties in other regions. Fortunately, wines made by various wineries using these grapes, although more expensive than some would like, are a 'steal' compared to so-called world superstars. It is now up to consumers themselves to decide whether the idea of a vineyard having a special character is valid or merely a commercial invention!

While some saw the growing site as the dominant influence on wine, others were concerned that "terroir" alone was being used to account for a wine's unique qualities. Perhaps various farming practices should be considered as well, like the choice of rootstock or clone of the grape, use of pesticides and herbicides that impact on soil organisms, or the role of vine density, or trellising system, or leaf pulling to expose grapes to more sunshine, or green harvesting to reduce the cropping level or the use of different fertilizers. In other words, should the efforts of a grower to produce 'better' grapes be a part of "terroir"? Some winemakers also stressed that decisions were made during winemaking, from processing techniques to yeast selection, to the temperature and method of fermentation, to the use of additives and barrels, and many other options which could alter the expression of "terroir" in the wine.

Thus, the word came to mean different things to different people, the original meaning defined by the "Oxford Companion to Wine" as "the complete natural environment in which a particular wine is produced" to a more inclusive definition that integrated the grape, rootstock, vines, and all natural components with the human role in farming and winemaking. Perhaps all of this is a reflection of the subjective nature of wine with so many words simply resisting defining although they are used frequently by the wine industry, the wine media, and consumers, with the term "terroir" being an indispensable concept for the development of an 'appellation d'origine' system.

Before long, a related concept began to find expression in modern wine speak, that it was actually possible to taste the vineyard geology in the wine. In French, the official language of wine, it would appear as "le gout de terroir", that is tasting the character of the site in the wine, with the nature of the soil contributing to actual wine flavour. This is not the same as a Cabernet Sauvignon tasting of blackcurrants, or a Pinot Noir of raspberries or a Chardonnay of peaches or lemons or apples, which are flavours considered typical of a particular grape variety expressing themselves so nicely in the wine. Indeed, recent research has shown that grapes have abundant flavour producing genes which can generate a specific compound that is suggestive of another fruit or chocolate or one of numerous spices.

Those who accept the validity of tasting the soil in the wine would feel that it is indeed logical for Cabernet from Coonawara in Australia, one of the most distinctive "terroirs" in the wine world, to reflect its red iron-oxide, terra rosa soils in the wine and for other soils like limestone to provide a mineral note. This last concept has been well promoted in Ontario, for example, with the 2019-2020 Wine Country Travel Guide commenting... "Prince Edward County sits on a foundation of porous limestone and stony soil that create concentrated fruit with a uniquely crisp minerality and bright acidity". Does science really support this assertion? Is this 'unique' minerality so blatant that Chardonnay from PEC is more distinctive than comparable wines from Niagara or Lake Erie North Shore? Does this really generate a signature style for this region's wines that can be described as "un gout de terroir"? It is true that similar wines can hail from different places (people often confuse Pinot Noir from Burgundy and Oregon, for example), but science has never substantiated the idea that wine flavours have come directly from the soil. Whether fact or myth, wine writers around the world continue to lavish words on the flavours they assert they are tasting in a wine based on the location where the grapes are grown.

It is my experience that most consumers of VQA wines would have a difficult time in a blind tasting identifying the regional location of an Ontario vineyard using the nature of the soil as the criteria. Others have been more sceptical, finding this a romantic notion which makes for a powerful marketing tool. Some have come right out and declared that this is just scientifically impossible. There is no solid evidence that heavy pesticide use in a vineyard leads to a significant concentration of harmful chemicals in wine in spite of other negative consequences for a vineyard. Likewise, according to Kevin Begos, "Science has established that a wine does not pick up minerals from the ground" (p. 191). Will we ever know for sure? And should we let this issue interfere with our enjoyment of any given wine?

No matter which way you turn and almost at every state of the process, wine seems to generate a fair bit of controversy, but one thing is certain, with the evolution in wine science and technology combined with man's efforts, wine has never tasted better. Wine drinkers are concerned about the taste of their wine, but for the most part they are not really concerned about where that taste came from, leaving most decisions up to the name of the grape and the producer of the wine.

At one time in Ontario, long before "terroir" became a commonly used term, growing grapes was a quantity over quality business while clever winemakers would manipulate their musts with water and sugar to produce several different styles of wines from a small number of labrusca grape varieties. Rating a vintage on a 100 point scale, an exercise found useful to-day by publications like the 'Wine Spectator' and some wine critics, was irrelevant then as the only real vintage concern was the variation in the total amount of the crop from year to year (which could be significant). The important issue with soil was under draining, not soil vitality, as it was believed that it's 'good for the vines to struggle' and force their roots downwards to seek out nourishment. Vineyard location did not really matter as labrusca grapes seemed very forgiving, being able to tolerate conditions and prosper wherever they were planted.

The wines suited the times until times changed after World War Two and then it became almost a national sport to criticize them as being somewhat less in quality to imported wines. Gradually that criticism changed, and now, with such a high quality in most wines which have also become virtually fault-free, a wine critic has become someone who can claim the ability to distinguish between a 92 and a 95 point wine while asserting that it is not only possible but appropriate to evaluate wines in this way. Yet, invariably, high scores are associated with highly esteemed "terroirs"!

Whether this is a sign of sophistication or sophistry, rating wines with numerical systems or 'stars' has become accepted by many consumers who seek guidance in making their purchase from such a plethora of wines available to-day. But is this necessary? Certainly, both viticulture and viniculture in Ontario have never been more quality oriented and technically controlled. Vineyards are computerized to aid in maintaining them and harvest dates are assisted by satellites to inform the winemaker's decision after he has examined everything from the colour of seeds in the berries (wait on green seeds, go on brown!) to berry flavour and phenolic ripeness. Winemakers have access to amazing equipment to help them pursue top quality at every step of the winemaking process, whether it is culling poor quality grapes at processing with electronic sorters, or selecting different pressure programs in pressing grapes, or controlling fermentation temperatures with a flick of a dial on their glycol chilling system (as opposed to using blocks of ice as in the 'good, old days'), as winemaking has evolved from pursuing high alcohol levels to to-day's pursuit of fine flavours.

Once, a winemaker was known as a 'chemist', a term no longer used although a knowledge of chemistry is useful in achieving healthy, stable wines. Now, some winemakers prefer to be called 'non-interventionists' as they allow a wine to be made as naturally as possible without the winemaker attempting to sculpt or alter the wine's intrinsic character. Trading off risk in order to allow the "terroir" to shine through, they may insist on 'wild yeast' fermentations and a reduced use of additives like sulphur dioxide, or enzymes, or tannins. Of course, wine was made 'naturally' for several thousand years before our day when no cultured yeasts were available nor appropriate additives to allow the winemaker some ability to achieve a healthy wine – and the questionable quality of wine during this long period of time had to be accepted. Fortunately, advancing the cause of natural or 'raw' winemaking to-day with knowledge and skill, winemakers no longer produce such wine.

On the other hand, an 'interventionist' would be a vintner who has a vision of the wine he wishes to produce, a feeling for what he wants the wine to exhibit, that may involve considering options and acting on them using technology or additives or some form of manipulation hoping to achieve the highest quality possible. Since he has the ability to direct and control the process that makes wine, why would he want to leave this to chance? Taking advantage of modern technology, this winemaker truly believes he can craft the best wine possible by applying known science to the art of converting premium grapes into a carefully fermented beverage.

Winemaking is truly about considering the many choices available at each step of the process whether you are a terroirist or naturalist or interventionist and choosing the path which will lead to a sound and stable product. It is not about which winemaker will make the better wine but whether the wine successfully reflects his beliefs and intentions as an 'artisan'. One winemaker might better capture the typicity of a specific grape by stressing 'wild yeasts' while another might prefer to use a specific cultured yeast to deliver a desired effect or new oak aging in preference to neutral barrels for added complexity, but both can craft top-quality products, simply different in character.

And then there are winemakers who produce 'industrial', high-volume wines, blends and big brands, while achieving consistency from year to year. They may have to forgo being described as a terroirist or a naturalist although their wines may still be very good. To generate top quality at this scale for a corporate entity is an achievement in itself, and I am sure that they are very happy to be called 'the winemaker' without further elaboration.

So, is wine made in the vineyard? Is soil the main factor in producing fine wine grapes or did that manure spread down the rows by the grower play a part? And let's not forget the winemaker, no matter his role in the process.

In the end we are left with a bottle of wine and a glass to be filled, perhaps five glasses to the bottle. The wine in the glass could be one of a thousand choices to-day costing as little as $1.50 per glass up to $200 per glass or even more depending on how prestigious that wine is. Inexpensive wines may not offer whatever it is that icon wines have (a list of these attributes might include 'opulence', or 'intensity', or 'elegance', or 'flamboyance', or perhaps 'ageability' for those who like a mature wine), but no matter the price, almost any wine purchased to-day is going to be good or few will buy it. While some may be more concerned than others about the validity of "terroir" or biodynamic wines or high scores or high price, or matching the perfect wine to the right food, we should not forget that wine is just a drink, a glass of pleasure to be enjoyed as Paul Lukacs comments in "Inventing Wine" p. 314, "And when all is said and done, pleasure in all its various forms…remains the only reason why anyone has ever cared about wine at all."

So, caveat emptor. Let's open a bottle of Konzelmann Pinot Blanc or Kacaba Unoaked Chardonnay, or Vineland Estates Semi-Dry Riesling, or almost any other Ontario wine, and expect to be pleased.

APPENDIX A

Defining wine: A taxing matter!

"Wine is a beverage containing more than 0.5% but not more than 22.9% of absolute alcohol by volume that is produced by the alcoholic fermentation of an agricultural product, a plant, or a plant product, other than grain." Canadian Excise Act, 2001

"Ontario" wine is

(a) Wine produced in Ontario from grapes, cherries, apples, or other fruits grown in Ontario, the concentrated juice of those fruits or other agricultural products containing sugar or starch and includes Ontario wine to which is added herbs, water, honey, sugar, or the distillate of Ontario wine or cereal grains grown in Ontario, or

(b) wine produced by the alcoholic fermentation of Ontario honey with or without the addition of caramel, natural botanical flavours, or the distillate of Ontario honey wine, or

(c) wine produced from a combination of (i) apples grown in Ontario or the concentrated juice thereof to which is added herbs, water, honey, sugar, or the distillate of Ontario wine or cereal grains grown in Ontario and (ii) the concentrated juice of apples grown outside of Ontario."

"Wine is water – plus a miracle." Tom Harpur, "The Spirituality of Wine", p. 155

"Wine maketh merry but money answereth all things." Ecclesiastes

When I was teaching the 'Introduction to Winemaking' course at Niagara College in the early 2000's, I decided to begin the first class in September with an exercise that would serve as an icebreaker and provide an opportunity for the students to show what they knew about 'wine', rather than assail them with a pedantic lecture on the subject. Everyone was asked to jot down a completion for the statement "Wine is..." and I would use their responses to stimulate a conversation.

I did point out that the topic was wine as we know it today, a beverage that can stand alone and is worth using for itself, to be enjoyed at almost any time and on any occasion, although civilized man has been making wine for perhaps eight or ten millennia with other uses in mind. For most of this time wine was revered as a 'gift from the gods' since our early ancestors had never been able to understand the mystical process that created it and had concluded that the gods had to be responsible for bringing such a beneficial beverage to mankind.

There is ample evidence that 'ancient wine' was quite a different beverage than what we drink to-day even though the process itself - fermentation – remains the same. Early drinkers used numerous unusual additives to help preserve their wine and mask oxidative and acetic faults, concocting a drink that probably would have been unpalatable for a modern drinker. Indeed, as Paul Lukacs says in "Inventing Wine" (p. 9) "Ancient wine, the drink itself as well as its role in society, serves as modern wine's precursor, not its progenitor". Unfortunately, while fascinating, the subject would not be the concern of our winemaking program.

The students gave some excellent answers, weighted heavily to the physical and sensual reality of the beverage. And the discussion revealed that they knew the names of many grapes and local wineries, enough to run through the alphabet with both. Perhaps the most enthusiastic suggestion came from a student who said simply "Wine is for drinking", not a bad idea! Certainly, from the range of ideas presented, it was obvious that trying to define 'wine' is a complex and challenging matter and we were just scratching the surface. It was also obvious that the students were more than ready to enter the magical world of fermentation!

No matter how you prefer to define wine, in terms sacred or profane, our governments for decades have seen it in somewhat of a different light, considering it foremost as a product associated with 'sin' and that, of course, because of its alcohol content. Considering that man has had a millennia-long love affair with wine as a sacred and beneficial product (whether punishing anyone's palate or not), this might seem paradoxical. However, as a result and because alcohol, both a stimulant and a depressant, can have mind-altering effects and a darker side, we have been obligated to accept that it requires regulating by government and licenses, control of sales through minimum 'floor pricing' (wine cannot sell below this price point as a means of discouraging over-drinking), and the use of taxation which increases the price and thereby slows down sales and the consumption of the 'sinful' ingredient in the product. This financial demand, which contributes billions of dollars to government revenue annually, is still called a "sin tax", although it may take other forms variously known as fees, levies, mark-ups, or charges.

Most consumers in Ontario pay little regard to the taxation of their alcoholic beverages, primarily because the government has buried the taxes in the shelf price of the product, the one price paid at time of purchase. As well, alcohol is one of the very few products sold including the 13% HST where normally this tax is added on top of the retail price. Thus, consumers do not see the numerous taxes involved in the pricing structure and have no idea of the amount of tax they are actually paying when they make their purchase, a clever, if not devious way to conceal how much governments are really raking in!

Both the number of taxes and the fact they accumulate in a tax-on-tax scenario have a tremendous impact on the final price which, as we shall see, bears little resemblance to the 'net' price charged by the producer. But the government's mandate is to raise revenue for itself and this seems to justify its activity (it raised from Ontario wine sales alone almost $800 million in federal and provincial taxes and LCBO mark-ups in 2015 and this amount has increased each year), retailing in attractive stores that are meant to encourage sales while at the same time working to safeguard public health and welfare against the excessive use of alcohol!

In our province, the Liquor Control Board (LCBO) has been the main protagonist in the alcohol business for almost 100 years, ever since it was created by the government at the end of Prohibition in 1927 as a Crown Corporation to control the production, importation, distribution, and sales of alcohol in Ontario. Although it introduced its own new retail store to sell both local and imported products at that time, one of its main functions was to clean up the local wine industry, 'encouraging' poor quality producers to shut down or sell their business while agreeing to accept for sale only quality products in the new system.

It also obligated wineries to pay proper prices for the grapes they purchased from growers. Thus, from the beginning, there has been an adversarial relationship with the Ontario wine industry, and this continued as the LCBO enforced the policy of granting no new grape winery licenses over the following four decades, until the mid 1970's, and refused to allow the wineries to develop new retail outlets. At the same time, it restricted the marketing and sales of wine through inane advertising regulations and maintained a retail system for decades that was anything but consumer friendly with no liquor in view, only a clerk behind a wire grille to accept your written order (he had the power to cut back or deny a purchase altogether!). It was as if, after Prohibition, consumers of alcoholic beverages just could not be trusted to behave themselves, or at least that was a primary excuse for the 'control'.

In the 1960's the first steps were taken to 'modernize' LCBO retail stores and since then there have been seven reviews conducted to achieve reforms although recommendations have seldom been implemented because of the complexity of dealing with four different beverage alcohol categories while satisfying the needs of government at the same time and working to safeguard public health and welfare against the excessive use of alcohol.

The new millennium has brought with it a new attitude to the sale of alcohol, focused on providing customers safe access to the products they want and considering when and where they want them. Since 2011, Ontario businesses whose primary functions are not the sale of alcohol and food have been eligible for liquor licences to permit on-site consumption, and that includes movie theatres, spas, and small grocers.

In 2019, the Conservatives led by Doug Ford chose Ken Hughes as Ontario's Special Advisor on Beverage Alcohol to create a report as a basis for initiating substantive reforms in the sale and distribution of beverage alcohol, like expanding the sale of beer and wine into grocery and convenience stores, as well as several other liquor reforms. While this stepped on the toes of social responsibility, it was a move that was welcomed by the industry and most Ontarians.

To-day, the LCBO is still the sole custodian of wine retailing in the province, a monopoly acting as a funnel for the sale of all wine, no matter the sales channel. These include some 663 LCBO stores, 209 privately-run smaller Agency Stores, another 200 new "LCBO Convenience Outlets" in underserved communities, a potential 450 grocery stores which will sell wine and cider as well as beer, 292 off-site winery stores owned by six 'grand-fathered' wineries, over 200 on-site retail outlets owned by wineries, and 15 privately-owned, duty-free stores at airports and border crossings that sell alcohol.

As of April 2020, with the arrival of the pandemic, The Alcohol and Gaming Commission (AGCO) introduced a small change in the regulations that would allow all businesses with a liquor licence, like restaurants and bars, to sell wine, beer, and spirits to consumers for take-home use. This sudden liberalization of entrenched liquor laws was intended to help the hospitality sector in Ontario that had been struggling with the impact of COVID, and it appears that the change will be permanent. This adds yet another retail opportunity for the alcohol industry, at least for those consumers who are willing to pay a little more for the convenience!

Obviously, the LCBO will remain the predominant alcohol retailer in the province although the pandemic has opened the door for a long over-due new approach to liquor laws. With its power and authority, it continues to run a tight ship, dealing with both small and large producers of spirits, wines, beers, and ciders from both local and domestic suppliers as well as importers. However, given the very competitive nature of the alcohol business, it is difficult to please all suppliers at the same time and it is no wonder that someone is always raising an issue about the job performed by the LCBO, our arbiter of good taste. This has made complaining about the LCBO almost a provincial sport!

Ontario wineries are continually voicing their unhappiness over what they call an uneven playing field, citing fundamental inequities in the 'system', and it is the LCBO that bears the brunt of the government policies and attitudes which have made life so difficult for many of the players. It may be the product listing process which some find a serious barrier to overcome or the matter of limited shelf space available for VQA products, or one of several other challenges in dealing with the LCBO that upsets some suppliers, but for the wine industry, it is the issue of 'taxation' that causes the most grief, making the LCBO a perennial adversary!

Although the matter is quite complicated, it may be instructive to examine the nature of taxation on Ontario wine in order to understand why wineries are so unhappy with a taxation protocol they find not only burdensome but also unfair to both the consumer and the industry. The LCBO insists that their pricing models are completely transparent, but it is the sheer number of different 'categories' of product types, along with the number and variation in the charges applied to each, that makes the matter so confusing. For wine alone, the taxation structure deals separately with different styles of wine (table, light, dessert), EU wine, NAFTA wine, 'other' wine, and domestic/international blends, involving some 10 different pricing charges. "Ontario" table wines follow their own format, varying in tax structure depending on where the wine is sold, the LCBO, a Winery Retail Store, Wine Boutiques, Licensees, or Duty Free stores, with an even more complex set of charges. Understanding the mass of information is challenging and requires a skilled individual to deal with the recording of sales and necessary payments to government, a task that must be done each month, within 10 business days of the end of the month!

One of the first things to appreciate is the fundamental categorization of "wine" (I will consider only 'table wine') whether imported from outside Ontario, domestic wines blended from imported material and Ontario grape product, and 100% Ontario grape wine. No matter the category, all wine that passes through the hands of the LCBO is described as 'imported', even wines coming from a Canadian province, and the LCBO is the 'importer of record'. This has allowed Ontario and other provincial governments to establish legal and regulatory hurdles that make it difficult for wineries and breweries and spirit makers to get into another province's distribution channels. These trade barriers have proven to be an 'issue' for the free movement of Canadian wine across the country in spite of section 121 of the Constitution that states products should be "admitted free into each of the other provinces". And people who try to 'import' alcohol from one province to another on their own risk significant fines for acting illegally!

There never has been a more opportune time to foster 'internal trade' than now in order to empower the economy and help businesses survive the pandemic. Food distribution rules have changed thanks to on-line ordering and it is simply time to allow direct-to-consumer alcohol programs between provinces as well. There is serious money involved as some industry estimates peg the global on-line alcohol market at $35 billion in 2020 while in Canada last year, over $350 million worth of alcohol was sold on-line, an increase of 75% from 2019. Trade liberalization is in the air and both business and consumers are seeking an end to what are truly absurd restrictions that allow provincial governments to maintain their prohibitive control.

All wine that is sold in Ontario must be considered 'imported' but this does not mean that all imported wine is "Ontario". The use of this term on a wine label, since the passing of the VQAO Act, must be restricted solely to grape wines regulated under this Act and approved by the VQAO.

Of course, the wine industry also encompasses numerous fruit wines, including ciders, other 100% local grape wines that either do not pass the VQA process or are made from non-VQA approved grape varieties or those labelled as International-Canadian blends (ICB wines). All of these have to be considered 'non-Ontario' wine even though our fruit wines and craft ciders must be made entirely from an agricultural product grown in this province and the ICB wines must contain a certain percentage of Ontario grape in their make-up (this percentage has varied over time for different reasons but seems to average about 25% to 40% Ontario product). This distinction ensures the integrity of origin of an "Ontario" product, representing the belief that wine is uniquely defined by the place where the GRAPES were grown.

ICB wines (once described as Cellared in Canada) have been a source of controversy ever since the early 1970's when the government convinced Ontario grape growers to allow wineries to use imported material and they continue to be a dilemma for the industry to-day as they far outsell VQA wines. They are produced by a small number of our larger wineries in significant volumes and sell in the LCBO system, where they enjoy considerable shelf space, in wine boutiques, and in the winery's own retail store network, at very reasonable prices for a loyal following of wine drinkers. They are taxed differently than VQA wines, more as we shall see, and this is a matter of annoyance with their producers. Nevertheless, the perception is that they are not equal in quality with a VQA wine and somehow tarnish the image of local wine.

Over time, some people have complained that they have been marketed as authentic Ontario wine, confusing consumers, and with a sales advantage over VQA wines and this has been a source of competitive friction with most wineries who are not allowed to make them. The reality is that if a wine is not crafted entirely from VQA approved grape varieties, it cannot be considered an 'authentic' reflection of our wine culture, no matter its quality or character. And in the end, it means that what we consider to be our wine industry – from the point of view of reputation – is based on only about 25% of its entire production!

No matter the kind of wine, when it comes to pricing structure, the most important number for any winery is the LCBO payment to supplier, the net dollar figure received by the supplier to which the numerous 'taxes' will be applied in order to achieve the eventual consumer price. In order to compare the various categories of table wine on an equal footing, we will use a base supplier payment of $6.23 per bottle, no matter the wine, from the LCBO pricing example sheets of April 2019.

All wineries selling their wine directly to the LCBO would receive payment based on $6.23 per bottle. Wineries that sell VQA wine in their own retail store, thus avoiding the LCBO and its mark-up, retain $11.22, not $6.23, and that is why on-site sales are so important for local wineries. Wineries retain $10.8628 if they sell the wine in their own off-site boutiques (the reduced price is a trade-off charge for the few large wineries who operate their own off-site boutiques when most wineries are not allowed the same privilege). The same wine delivered directly to a Licensee brings the winery $11.55 since it does not really involve the LCBO, with the extra .33 cents per bottle ($3.96 per case of 12 bottles) provided for delivering the wine. As you can imagine, this princely sum comes no where close to paying for the delivery, and wineries are understandably unhappy. They are not allowed to charge more for delivering the wine.

For most VQA sales channels, the supplier payment is the same as the 'landed cost' (a Licensee pays an extra $.2038 per bottle to the LCBO for freight). For all other kinds of wines, imported and ICB, it is necessary to add in the Federal Excise Tax at $.4898 per bottle (VQA wines do not pay excise currently but due to Australia's recent complaint, the tax appears certain to be reinstated in 2022) and $.2038 freight, except for domestic wineries which do not pay freight, in order to achieve the 'landed cost'. It should be mentioned that the LCBO does pick up domestic wines from the wineries at no charge, a service that is not normally acknowledged by anyone.

To summarize, the following prices would reflect the 'landed cost' for different categories of wine: (a) VQA sold to the LCBO, $6.2336, (b) VQA sold in a WRS, $11.2211, (c) VQA sold in wine boutiques, $10.8628, (d)

VQA delivered directly to a licensee, $11.55, (e) VQA delivered directly to a Duty Free Shop, $6.2336, (f) ICB wine, $6.7234, and (g) all other wine $6.9272. Hopefully, this will make sense as you sharpen your red pencils for the next set of charges, as many as 7 in all, depending on the retailing of the wine.

The first charge to consider is the primary source of revenue for the LCBO, called the 'mark-up', which represents what the LCBO retains for their management services. Currently, the mark-up on all wines whether domestic or imported is 71.5% of the landed cost, except for Duty Free Shops which pay only 10%. Prior to the infamous Free Trade Agreement, the mark-up on imported wines was always considerably higher than the mark-up on Ontario wines and this gave our wineries a competitive advantage in establishing prices. At the same time, this allowed them to retain for their business a healthy percentage of the retail price. When the government agreed to change this historical policy some 30 years ago in order to "level the playing field" among all suppliers, the mark-up became the same for everyone with the only increase happening for Ontario wines.

For a while it seemed that the sky had fallen for our wineries and that their lifeblood was being drained away, leaving the grape and wine industry in dire straits. The cottage wineries were able to handle the change much better than the corporate wineries, rising to the challenge with a defiant spirit. However, this did lead to the demise of several large wineries including Barnes, Jordan's, and London, and the merging of Chateau Gai and Bright's, changing the make-up of the wine industry once and for all.

Referring to our pricing examples, one notices that the mark-up on a VQA wine comes to $4.457, for an ICB wine $4.8072, and $4.9529 for an imported wine (based on the landed prices and thus the differences). The LCBO does not charge their mark-up on wines retailed by the wineries themselves, either in their stores or direct delivered, for which the wineries, who do all the work anyway, are very grateful!

But that is where all gratitude ends.

The wine industry has advocated for years and continues to insist that changes to taxation represent a sustainable solution for two major issues – long-term planning and more revenue to grow their businesses. As an example, reference is often made to the 'three-tiered system' for alcohol distribution in Ontario, that is with the LCBO serving first as an importer, secondly as a distributor, and thirdly as a retailer. In the United States, local wineries are subject to just two tiers of taxation involving a distributor and a retailer mark-up with no need for an importer mark-up. Our wineries argue that they deserve the same tax treatment and advantage that U.S. wineries receive in their own country, a step that would remove approximately 30%-35% of the mark-up on Ontario wines sold in the LCBO. Until governments decide to accept what everyone else knows 'importing' to be, no change is likely to happen concerning these 'mark-ups'.

As well, there is one tax that is applied only on wine sold in winery retail stores and wine boutiques and no where else. It is labelled Ministry of Finance Basic Tax and is applied at 6.1% for VQA wines and 9.6% for non VQA wines on the retail price minus other taxes and deposits. This 'extra' tax on local wines is hardly a crowd pleaser for as winemaker Sue Anne Staff comments... "There isn't any other product in Ontario, there isn't any other commodity in this country, there isn't anything else subjected to that extra tax on wine...it's just ridiculous." It increases the price of our example in a winery store by $.6845 and is seen by wineries as "basically" discriminatory and unjust.

A recent on-line petition held by Change.org addressed these two taxes and demanded a better treatment for local wines. More than 10,000 people signed it in an amazing show of support. Richard Linley, President of Ontario Craft Wineries, was delighted with the response, pointing out that the local economic impact of Ontario wineries "is at least 400% greater than their import competitors" and he asked why government policy continues to subsidize foreign competition. To date, the Ford Government has not responded to what are clearly unfair taxes.

However, the pendulum swings back with the next two charges, the first of which is called the LCBO Wine Levy. Levy is derived from the Latin verb "to raise", as in to raise a tax by authority, while also raising the price of the wine. It concerns all wine sold in the LCBO only and not wine sold at winery stores, boutiques, or VQA wine direct delivered to licensees. The Levy is the same for all wines, imported or domestic, at $1.62 per litre, or $1.2150 per 750 ml. bottle. Added in here as well for all wines, except domestic products, is something called the "Cost of Service" which varies from $.4511 on EU wines to $.02369 for NAFTA wines to $.4872 on 'other' wines, per 750 ml. bottle. Since the price of a bottle includes the LCBO mark-up already, one might legitimately wonder why it is necessary to add two additional fees or at least something called a cost of service when all LCBO stores are truly self-serve (unless you 'consult' with an employee on a given purchase).

The same could be said about the next charge, called the LCBO Volume Levy. This, of course, has nothing to do with 'volume discount', which certainly does not apply in a store that does not encourage the consumption of alcohol, but is simply a per litre fee of $.29. Most wines do not sell in a litre volume, so the fee is only $.2175 per 750 ml. bottle, but the fact that this is the third charge in a row for somewhat nebulous reasons, speaks volumes about government's ability to use wine as a lucrative source of revenue.

To achieve what can be called the "Basic Price" (but not the final price), one more charge is necessary, the LCBO Environmental Levy at $.0893 per container (wine comes mostly in bottles but also in boxes, pouches, and cans), not because drinking wine is bad for the environment but because government has to show some concern or responsibility for the environment and this means consumers have to comply. At the same time there is an actual container deposit of $.20 to add on top, and the icing on the cake, the HST at 13%. Almost out of breath, we have reached the retail or consumer price. Fortunately, consumers see only the price they need to pay and will not lose any sleep considering the myriad of other charges concealed from human awareness, a number so complex that no winery attempts doing the math without a computer.

So, what is the bottom line, the one you see at the bottom of the sales slip?

The consumer price for a bottle of the VQA wine outlined above is $14.00, of which some 45% ($6.2336) is paid to the winery when the bottle is sold in an LCBO store, and 80% ($11.2211) if sold at the winery retail store. It is clear, then, that the winery retail store is a critical component in the potential success of a winery, especially a smaller winery that does not seek LCBO sales. At $6.23 a bottle, there is not much 'profit' in that LCBO sale, given the cost of the grapes and everything related to the production of the wine, and all the other expenses associated with running the business. For a winery to be successful in the end, considering the limitations posed by having only one retail store, it would have to sell a significant volume to the LCBO in order to generate any real value and that is a challenge given the nature of the LCBO 'system", listing requirements, shelf space, location of the wine on the shelf, and marketing costs. Wines that would be priced substantially higher than $14 a bottle have their own issues, with the result that most of these are sold in Vintages where most products are ordered by the LCBO only in limited quantities and just once a year.

Sales to licensees are another matter of concern. Many wineries direct delivery their wine to a licensee and receive $11.55 of the licencee price of $13.74 in our example. One would think that a licensee would pay significantly less for this wine in order to make the price a customer then pays in the restaurant attractive, but this is just not the case. The licensee pays the same price for wine he picks up at the LCBO, but in this case the LCBO keeps much more of the money and not the winery!

Following the same tax structure, a domestic non-VQA wine would end up retailing for $14.95 and an import from the European Union would cost $15.85. The government of Ontario retains just over 50% of the price and the supplier just under 40% (the Federal Government takes about 8% as well). When the LCBO retails the wine, Government is the big winner, although wineries benefit by province-wide exposure. Yet, it is no wonder that wineries complain about the 'small margins' involved, when they are also expected to pay marketing 'fees' charged by the LCBO, like shelf extenders and end aisle displays, and ads in LCBO magazines to help the LCBO sell their wine. It is a 'system' designed for corporations and the larger wineries of the world, not Ontario's craft wineries.

The wonderful thing about the taxes applied to wine, as any government bureaucrat will tell you, is that there is then no need to tax something else, like milk! However, they are applied in such a way, with so many different layers and exceptions to rules, that all suppliers find some fault with the set-up….and complain.

Of course, that is the nature of taxation which most of us regard as a necessary evil. However, the Ontario wine industry has identified the issue of tight margins on sales through the LCBO (a direct result of taxation) as their top-ranked business challenge, and the major reason why our local wines at times appear to be more expensive than they might be.

While it can be said that anyone entering the wine industry should be aware of the impact of these taxes on their business, it seems that the topic will always be a bone of contention for those who wish to pursue winemaking as a career, given the attitude to taxes that government maintains.

APPENDIX B

Ontario Winemaker of the Year

In the mid-1990's, coinciding with the burgeoning interest in Ontario wines, esteemed wine writer Tony Aspler and the Ontario Wine Society came up with the idea to celebrate the 'Best' of Ontario wines in an annual competition that would also select a winemaker who had made a significant contribution to the industry as "Winemaker of the Year". The event continues to this day and is considered the Oscars of our wine industry, providing an opportunity to celebrate high-quality Ontario wines and the people who make them.

1996 – Herbert Konzelmann: Konzelmann Winery

1997 – Jim Warren: Stoney Ridge Cellars

1998 - Ron Giesbrecht: Henry of Pelham Winery

1999 - Angelo Pavan: Cave Springs Winery

2000 - J-L Groulx: Hillebrand Winery

2001 - John Marynissen: Marynissen Winery

2002 - Sue Ann Staff: Pillitteri Estate Winery

2003 - Eddy Gurinskas: Lakeview Cellars

2004 - Ann Sperling: Malivoire Wine Company

2005 - Carlo Negri: Colio Estates Wines

2006 - Jean Pierre Colas: Peninsula Ridge Estate

2007 - Paul M. Bosc: Chateau des Charmes

2008 - Craig Macdonald/Rob Power: Creekside Winery

2009 - Thomas Bachelder: Le Clos Jordanne

2010 - Darryl Brooker: Hillebrand Winery

2011 - Paul Pender: Tawse Winery

2012 - Andrzej Lipinski: Colaneri Winery

2013 - Marlize Beyers: Hidden Bench Winery

2014 - Brian Schmidt: Vineland Estates

2015 - Emma Garner: Thirty Bench

2016 - Craig Macdonald: Trius Winery

2017 - Shiraz Mottiar: Malivoire Winery

2018 - (rescinded)

2019 - Dave Johnson: Featherstone Winery

2020 - Philip Dowell: Angels Gate Estate Winery

2021 - David Sheppard: Flat Rock Cellars

APPENDIX C

Ontario's 'ghost' wineries: 1980 - 2020

Perhaps overlooked in the recent success of the Ontario Wine Industry, with the opening of so many new wineries, are those grape wineries which have come and gone during the last forty years, selling their licence or changing ownership along with the winery name, or simply closing their doors. The following is a list of these 'ghost' wineries, now disappeared in time but not completely forgotten as many will be fondly remembered by wine enthusiasts.

1. Aure Winery – Beamsville...name changed to London Born Winery
2. Barnes Wines – St. Catharines...sold to Chateau Gai Wines and closed
3. Birchwood Estate – Vineland...sold to Diamond Estates and closed
4. Bright's Wines – Niagara Falls...renamed Vincor and now Arterra Wines
5. Cilento Winery – Vaughn...closed
6. Chesslawn Vineyards – Caledon...closed
7. Coyote's Run – Niagara-on-the-Lake...sold/resold, now closed
8. Chateau Gai/Cartier – Niagara Falls...merged with Bright's Wines
9. Charal Winery – Blenheim...licence sold to Magnotta and closed
10. Crown Bench Estates Winery – Beamsville - closed
11. Culotta Wines – Oakville...licence sold to Kittling Ridge and closed
12. Daniel Lenko Winery – Beamsville...closed
13. Domaine Wagners – Niagara-on-the-Lake... retired

14. Domaine Equifer… St. Catharines, closed
15. De Sousa – Beamsville… sold to Diamond Estates and closed
16. Eastdell Winery – Beamsville…sold. Site became Mike Weir Winery
17. Eagle Point Winery – Mallorytown… closed
18. Erie Shore Vineyard – Harrow…closed
19. Florence Estates – Langton… became Golden Leaf winery –
20. Grape Tree Estate Winery – Leamington…closed
21. Jordan Wines – St. Catharines…sold to Bright's Wines and closed
22. Kittling Ridge Winery – Grimsby…licence sold to Magnotta
23. Lakeview Cellars – Vineland…sold to Diamond Estates & now in NOL
24. Lauro & Burden – Toronto…closed
25. Leblanc Estate Winery – Harrow…closed
26. London Wines – London…sold to Bright's Wines and closed
27. Maleta & St. Henry Estate Winery - Niagara-on-the-Lake…closed
28. Mike Weir Winery – Beamsville…sold - now Locust Lane Estate Winery
29. Milan Winery – Toronto…closed
30. Montravin Winery – Beamsville…sold to Magnotta Winery
31. Nesher Winery – Toronto…closed
32. Newark Winery – Niagara-on-the-Lake…became Hillebrand/ Trius Winery
33. Paul Masson Winery – Beamsville…closed
34. Podamer Champagne – Beamsville…became Montravin
35. Rancourt Winery – Niagara-on-the-Lake…now Ferox Winery
36. Smith & Wilson – Blenheim…closed
37. Solo per amici – Beamsville…closed
38. Thomas & Vaughn – Beamsville…closed
39. Trillium Hill – St. Catharines…closed
40. Twenty Bees – Niagara-on-the-Lake – sold, now Lakeview
41. VP Cellars – Jordan…sold and became Creekside Winery
42. Walker Hall Winery – Beamsville…closed
43. Walters' Winery – Beamsville…sold and became Eastdell Winery
44. Willowbank Winery – Niagara-on-the-Lake…closed
45. Willow Heights – Vineland…sold and became Green Lane Winery

APPENDIX D

The VQA Ontario: Two Decades of Progress

The Vintners' Quality Alliance began life at the end of the 1980's as a voluntary association of wineries dedicated to creating an 'Appellation of Origin' system for Ontario with Peter Gamble as Director. It became incorporated on November 26, 1998, with the VQA Act gaining Royal assent on May 4 the following year. On June 29, 2000, the Act was proclaimed into law and VQAO was designated as Ontario's wine authority with responsibility for administering the VQA Act and its regulations.

These regulations concern only 100% Ontario wine, the origin of the grapes used, specific production methods, and other standards, all part of an Appellation system which guarantees authenticity and basic quality for consumers. Wines are submitted for approval to independent panels and laboratory analysis and if they 'pass', are entitled to use descriptors regulated under the Act for labelling and marketing purposes.

VQAO is governed by a Board of Directors with day-to-day operations run by an administrative staff headed by an Executive Director.

While its primary job is to administer and enforce VQAO standards, the authority is committed to work with the grape and wine industry, governments, and the public to promote an understanding of the appellation system and to participate in national and international activities related to wine standards and trade.

When consumers buy VQA wines, they can be assured that they have passed a process that verifies the information on the wine label and establishes the wine as a quality product which is free from 'faults' and made by rules enforced by law.

Executive Director: Laurie Macdonald (since inception)

President/Chairperson:	2000 – Len Pennachetti, Cave Springs Winery
	2020 – Brian Schmidt, Vineland Estates Winery
Members:	2000 – 51 members
	2020 – 183 members
Membership:	2000 – 3 large wineries, sales over 750,000 litres
	11 mid-size, sales 100,000 to 750,000 l.
	37 small wineries, sales under 100,000 l.
	2020 - 6 large wineries, sales over 750,000 l.
	22 mid size, sales 100,000 to 750,000 l.
	155 small wineries, sales under 100,000 l.

April 1, 2020 – March 31, 2021

Over the 20 years the nature of the appellation system has changed to include 11 sub-appellations, smaller regions within an appellation, while recognizing several new, emerging regions that are growing grapes but not yet in enough volume to qualify for VQAO. A wine with an appellation declaration (e.g. Niagara Peninsula) must contain 85% of its content from the appellation while a sub-appellation must contain 100%.

Label declarations for this year:

1. Niagara Peninsula 51%
2. Prince Edward County 1%
3. Lake Erie North Shore 1%
4. Sub-appellations 10%
5. Ontario 38%

48 different grape varieties were used in VQA winemaking:

1. Riesling 15%
2. Chardonnay 14%
3. Cabernet Franc 11%
4. Merlot 11%
5. Pinot Gris 9%
6. Baco Noir 8%
7. Vidal 7%
8. Cabernet Sauvignon 6%
9. Pinot Noir 6%
10. Sauvignon Blanc 4%
11. Gamay Noir 3%
12. Gewurztraminer 3%
13. Syrah (Shiraz) 2%
14. Other 2%

Sales of VQA wines since 2000:

	Year end March 31, 2001	Year end March 31, 2021
Winery Retail	2,591,260 litres	7,900,545 litres
Licensees	986,191	1,888,709
LCBO	3,454,158	10,683,750
Farmers' Markets	n.a.	38,384
Other (export and	891,480	608,504
Other provinces)		907,784
TOTAL:	7,921,092	21,327,676
Retail Value:	$144,755,723	$412,123,446

In 2000, members submitted 445 wines for VQA approval, an average of 8.7 wines per winery. Twenty years later, applications increased to 2260 and 12.3 wines per winery. The progress and prosperity of the VQA system has been amazing, the more so considering sales for the March, 2021 year end were severely impacted by the pandemic.

CPSIA information can be obtained
at www.ICGtesting.com
Printed in the USA
BVHW051148261122
652785BV00003B/13

9 780228 885436